Public Sector Accounting and Budgeting for Non-Specialists

Public Sector Accounting and Budgeting for Non-Specialists

Jan van Helden
University of Groningen, the Netherlands

and

Ron Hodges
University of Birmingham, UK

 palgrave

First published 2015 by
PALGRAVE

Palgrave in the UK is an imprint of Macmillan Publishers Limited, registered in England, company number 785998, of 4 Crinan Street, London N1 9XW.

Palgrave Macmillan in the US is a division of St Martin's Press LLC, 175 Fifth Avenue, New York, NY 10010.

Palgrave is a global imprint of the above companies and is represented throughout the world.

Palgrave® and Macmillan® are registered trademarks in the United States, the United Kingdom, Europe and other countries.

ISBN 978–1–137–37698–5

This book is printed on paper suitable for recycling and made from fully managed and sustained forest sources. Logging, pulping and manufacturing processes are expected to conform to the environmental regulations of the country of origin.

A catalogue record for this book is available from the British Library.

A catalog record for this book is available from the Library of Congress.

Printed in China

Contents

List of figures and tables

Figures

Tables

Preface

Aim and scope

Managers and other employees who work in public sector organizations are regularly confronted with financial documents. Some of these documents are part of the yearly planning and control cycle, such as budgets, interim reports, a balance sheet, an income statement and a cash flow statement. Other documents are drafted for occasional decisions, such as an investment or a make-or-buy decision. Although financial specialists often prepare these documents, managers and other employees are the main users of these documents. A basic understanding of the principles and rules which underlie such financial documents is then required. However, most of the users of financial information do not have a financial background. This book aims to introduce some basics of public sector accounting and budgeting. This enables non-financial managers and staff members to get a better understanding of the purposes, structures and limitations of financial statements, so that they become more effective users of these documents. It will also help them to be able to be on speaking terms with the financial people in their organization.

In order to achieve this aim of writing a book on public sector accounting and budgeting for non-specialists, our writing was inspired by three principles. First, how to use financial information has to be at the core, not what technical accounting activities are needed to prepare this information. Second, illustrations of various types of financial documents will contribute to gaining an understanding of their value for decision-making and control. Last, but not least, a concise text is required, because the primary tasks and responsibilities of non-financial managers and staff members lie outside the financial domain.

Target group

Our book is of importance to managers and staff members of public sector organizations, who have little or no accounting knowledge. Public sector organizations are taken not only to include governmental authorities (at central, municipal and intermediate levels), but also service bodies in branches such as education and health, which rely significantly on governmental funding and policy making. Managers in such organizations may not have an economic or business administration background and their accounting and financial knowledge may be limited. These professionals have, for example, an educational background in law, public policy or applied sciences, such as engineering. It is our experience from teaching to such professionals that they sometimes show some resistance to accounting procedures and documents. This suggests the need for a type of textbook that acknowledges this feature of the target group, i.e. by focusing on providing an understanding of accounting documents by making use of accessible public sector illustrations. Many of these professionals are encouraged to take executive management training programmes, in which accounting and budgeting play a major role, for example in executive masters programmes in the management of public or non-profit organizations. Larger public sector organizations also have in-house training programmes for their management and staff, in which accounting and budgeting almost always have a high priority. So, our book can be useful in all these training settings, for self-education and more traditional university-based programmes.

Public sector accounting and budgeting is an inherently practice-oriented domain. However, a text book on public sector accounting and budgeting with a practical focus can still have an academic character and be suitable for courses in higher education. The content of this book is embedded in the academic literature, by making use of the findings of academic research as published in international journals. Our book is intended to contribute to the usefulness of public sector budgeting and accounting knowledge in practice through its focus on non-accounting specialists. Managers and staff members in public and non-profit organizations can use this book to improve their understanding by combining its academic foundations and its practical focus.

Outline of the book

Chapter 1: Introduction to public sector budgeting and accounting

This first chapter introduces readers to financial management in a public sector context. It analyses the broad differences between public and private sector accounting and budgeting. It illustrates the importance of high-quality financial information for decision-making and control through two real-life examples of the use of financial documents in public sector organizations. This chapter also introduces New Public Management (NPM), as an influential philosophy underlying many innovations in public sector budgeting and accounting during the last three decades.

Chapter 2: Introducing accounting basics

This chapter introduces the main accounting documents, which are the balance sheet, the income statement and the cash flow statement. The main objective in this chapter is to show what type of information is included in these important financial documents, in the context of a simple household and business organization. This gives a basic knowledge of accounting, which is extended in Chapters 3, 4 and 5, dealing with public sector accounting.

Chapter 3: The income statement, the balance sheet and the cash flow statement of public sector organizations

This chapter illustrates the financial documents of public sector organizations. Different categorizations of costs and revenues within the income statement are given and the basic structure of the balance sheet is explained. The concept of deficit/surplus is introduced. How the surplus/deficit in the income statement increases/decreases equity in the balance sheet is explained. How and why the income statement and the cash flow statement differ, is illustrated. The chapter compares cash-based and accrual-based accounting. The chapter provides an appendix with some notes and illustrations of the principles of bookkeeping.

Chapter 4: Assessing the financial health of an organization through ratio analysis

A financial ratio is the quotient of two figures on an organization's balance sheet, income statement or cash flow statement. The purpose of a financial ratio is to help the user to form a judgment about the financial strengths and weaknesses of an organization. These ratios provide an indication of the organization's financial health in matters such as solvency (Is the organization capable of meeting its long-term obligations?); profitability (To what extent are its costs covered by its income?); and liquidity (Is the organization capable of meeting its obligations in the short term?). The chapter also provides an analysis of the benefits and limitations of ratio analysis.

Chapter 5: Financial accounting conventions and practices

Financial accounting is underpinned by a set of conventions drawn from theory, regulation and practice. This chapter discusses the objectives and the needs of users of financial statements. The main features of financial statements, such as comparability and neutrality, are presented. The so-called 'elements' of financial statements, such as assets, liabilities, revenues and expenses, are defined and discussed. Finally, some issues about the measurement or valuation of these elements are addressed. This chapter also discusses some accounting issues of core governmental organizations, such as expenditure variance analyses and the valuation of community assets.

Chapter 6: Budgeting: principles, functions, types and processes

This chapter considers the functions of a budget, including planning, allocation, authorization and control. The budget process is described. This chapter considers various types of budgets, such as incremental versus zero-base budgets, top-down versus bottom-up budgets and the distinctions between input, activity, output and outcome budgets. The control side of budgeting is discussed by considering the role and structure of interim reports during the execution of the budget. The political context of the budgetary process is highlighted, pointing to aspects of power and coalition-forming in realizing political or managerial priorities. Aspects of budgeting are illustrated with examples from the German city of Oldenburg.

Chapter 7: Cost allocation, costing and cost management

Cost accounting complements budgetary and accounting information. Costs can be recorded to represent different types of expenditure, such as salaries and material costs. Cost allocation deals with procedures for allocating costs to responsibility centres, such as divisions or departments within an organization. The intention is that such information helps managers to control the costs for which they bear responsibility. This chapter introduces various methods for cost allocation and shows how the resulting information might be used. The chapter also discusses the use of cost information for the planning of projects and how public sector organizations can use costing information for managerial purposes.

Chapter 8: Capital investment, outsourcing and partnerships

In addition to supporting the planning and control cycle, accounting information can also support occasional financial decisions. Two of these types of decisions are discussed in this chapter. First, a section on capital investment decisions considers the costs and benefits of investments with a long-term impact, such as infrastructure investment in roads and waterways, or medical equipment in a hospital. Various tools for supporting the financial decisions within these projects, such as the payback period and net present value are introduced and illustrated. Second, public sector organizations often have to consider whether they should produce certain services themselves or procure services from other organizations, including partnerships with other organizations. Cost–benefit considerations may determine the decision of whether to outsource or produce internally particular services. In addition to purely financial assessment criteria, this chapter also introduces other methods for assessing capital investment or outsourcing decisions, especially multi-criteria analysis and cost–benefit analysis. Capital investment and outsourcing decisions are illustrated with real-life cases.

Chapter 9: Public sector auditing

This chapter examines the importance of auditing in the public sector. It considers different meanings of the word 'audit' and gives examples of different systems in use. It analyses the importance of auditor independence and the difficulties in achieving this independence. Different types of audits, such as financial, compliance and performance auditing, are distinguished, and the separate roles of internal and external auditors are considered. The chapter draws on research evidence of the benefits and limitations of audit activities in public sector contexts. Case studies of financial audit and performance audit are included to illustrate the wide application of auditing in the public sector.

Chapter 10: Public sector financial management reforms

Public sector budgeting and accounting have been the subject of ongoing reform during the last three decades or so, as a consequence of accusations that the public sector performs ineffectively and inefficiently, and due to problems of fiscal stress. Some of these reforms revolve around purely accounting issues, such as the transfer from cash to accrual accounting and the introduction of performance budgeting, while others relate to more general managerial issues, such as decentralization of managerial responsibilities and the adoption of private sector styles, especially pay-for-performance systems. This chapter reviews such public sector financial management reforms, including some good practice examples from recent reforms in Australia and Austria.

Throughout Chapters 2, 3, 4 and 5 there is some repetition of key accounting issues, especially concerning the differences between cash-based and accrual-based accounting, as well as the structuring of the various financial documents. This gives the reader the opportunity to build up his/her knowledge and understanding of all of these accounting issues.

Acknowledgements

We wish to thank the following rights holders for permission to reproduce copyright material:

Gemeente Zoetermeer for Tables 1.2 and 1.3; Hansestadt Bremen, Germany, for Table 1.4; Klaus Lüder for Table 2.1 and Figure 10.2; Stadt Oldenburg, Germany, for Tables 6.1, 6.2, 6.3 and 6.5; the OECD for Table 6.4; INTOSAI for extracts from various INTOSAI Standards and Recommendations in Chapter 9 (INTOSAI Professional Standards Committee, PSC-Secretariat, Rigsrevisionen, Landgreven 4, P.O. Box 9009, 1022 Copenhagen K, Denmark, web: http://www.issai.org and INTOSAI General Secretariat – Rechnungshof (Austrian Court of Audit), Dampfschiffstraße 2, 1033 Vienna, Austria web: http://www.intosai.org); the National Audit Office for extracts from the *Report of the Comptroller and Auditor General: Whole of Government Accounts 2012–13*, in Chapter 9; Oxford University Press for Figure 10.1; Springer Verlag/Kluwer for Figure 10.2; Johann Seiwald and Patrícia Gomes, the editor of *Tekhné: Review of Applied Management Studies*, for Figure 10.3 and Table 10.1 from 'Performance framework in Austria: opportunities and challenges' by J. Seiwald and M. Gepple in *Tekhné*, Vol. 11, no.1: 2013; Wiley for extracts from Guthrie, J., O. Olson and C. Humphrey (1999), 'Debating Developments in New Public Financial Management: The Limits of Global Theorizing and Some New Ways Forward', *Financial Accountability & Management*, Vol. 15, no.2–3, pp. 209–28; the International Public Sector Accounting Standards Board (IPSASB) and the International Federation of Accountants (IFAC) for extracts from *Conceptual Framework for General Purpose Financial Reporting by Public Sector Entities: Measurement of Assets and Liabilities in Financial Statements*, October 2014.

Tables 5.2, 5.3 and 5.4, adapted from the Department of Health's *Annual Report and Accounts 2012–13*, are reprinted under Open Government Licence v2.0 © Crown copyright.

We acknowledge the valuable comments and suggestions by Professor Dick Feenstra (University of Groningen, the Netherlands), Professor Howard Mellet (University of Cardiff, United Kingdom) and Professor Christoph Reichard (University of Potsdam, Germany) on an earlier draft of this book. We would appreciate further feedback on this book. Readers are kindly invited to approach us via our email addresses.

JAN VAN HELDEN (g.j.van.helden@rug.nl)
RON HODGES (r.hodges@bham.ac.uk)

About the authors

Jan van Helden is Emeritus Professor of Management Accounting at the Faculty of Economics and Business, University of Groningen, the Netherlands. In recent years his research has focused on management and accounting changes in public sector organizations, with special attention to performance measurement, benchmarking, performance budgeting, and the role of consultants and researchers in public sector innovations. He was a member of the Executive for Financial and Personnel Affairs of the province of Groningen, the Netherlands, in the 1980s.

Ron Hodges is Emeritus Professor of Accounting in the Birmingham Business School at the University of Birmingham in the UK. His research is focused on the financial reporting of public service activities including the regulation of public sector accounting, audit and inspection in local government, and accounting for public–private partnerships and the private finance initiative in sectors such as health and social housing. He is a member of the UK Financial Reporting Advisory Board.

List of abbreviations

ABC	Activity-Based Costing
APB	Auditing Practices Board
ASB	Accounting Standards Board
AME	Annually Managed Expenditure
AVL	Automatic Vehicle Location
CAG	Comptroller and Auditor General
CB	Cost–Benefit
CCS	Communication and Control System
CIGAR	Comparative International Governmental Accounting Research
CP	Conventional Procurement
CVP	Cost–Volume–Profit
DCF	Discounted Cash Flow
DELs	Departmental Expenditure Limits
ECA	European Court of Auditors
EPSAS	European Public Sector Accounting Standards
EU	European Union
FMR	Financial Management Reform Process
GAAP	Generally Accepted Accounting Practices
GPFRs	General Purpose Financial Reports
IAASB	International Auditing and Assurance Standards Board
IASB	International Accounting Standards Board
IFAC	International Federation of Accountants
IFRS	International Financial Reporting Standards
IIA	Institute of Internal Auditors
IMF	International Monetary Fund
INTOSAI	International Organization of Supreme Audit Institutions
IPSAS	International Public Sector Accounting Standards
IPSASB	International Public Sector Accounting Standards Board
IR	Inflation Rate
ISSAI	International Standards for Supreme Audit Institutions
MBT	Mobile Data Transmission
MPs	Members of Parliament
MTEF	Medium-Term Expenditure Framework
NAO	National Audit Office
NDPBs	Non-Departmental Public Bodies
NHS	National Health Service

NPC   Net Present Cost
NPFM   New Public Financial Management
NPG   New Public Governance
NPM   New Public Management
NPV   Net Present Value
NR   Nominal Rate
NWS   Neo-Weberian State
OPA   Old Public Administration
PFI   Private Finance Initiative
PPP   Public–Private Partnership
PV   Present Value
RAB   Resource Accounting and Budgeting
RR   Real Rate
SAI   Supreme Audit Institutions
UK   United Kingdom
US   United States
VfM   Value-for-Money
WAO   Wales Audit Office
WGA   Whole of Government Accounting

1

Introduction to public sector budgeting and accounting

Learning objectives

- Being able to position public sector financial management in the public sector context
- Understand the distinctive character of public sector accounting and budgeting
- Understand the importance of financial documents for decision-making and control
- Being able to give examples of the types of decisions in a public sector organization for which high-quality financial documents are crucial
- Being familiar with principles and tools of innovations in public management labelled as New Public Management (NPM) and New Public Financial Management (NPFM)

1.1 Introduction

Politicians as well as managers and other employees working in public sector organizations are regularly confronted with the need to use financial documents to aid decision-making. The most important financial documents are part of the yearly planning and control cycle, such as a budget, a progress report about the execution of the budget, a balance sheet, an income statement and a cash flow statement. Other documents are drafted for occasional financial decisions, such as an investment in a long-life asset such as buildings or equipment, or a decision on whether to buy in services from external suppliers rather than provide them directly using own resources and employees. Although financial specialists may prepare these documents, both political officials and managers and other employees, such as internal advisers, are the main users of these documents. This first chapter introduces financial management in a public sector context and illustrates the importance of high-quality financial information for decision making and control through two real-life examples of the use of financial documents in public sector organizations.

This chapter introduces financial management in Section 1.2 and discusses it in a public sector context in Section 1.3. Then, Section 1.4 considers the distinctive character of public sector accounting and budgeting including some comparisons with the private sector. The chapter illustrates the relevance of high-quality financial information. Two real-life-cases provide illustrations of decisions as part of the planning and control cycle (Section 1.5) and the preparation of measures for coping with an expected deficit (Section 1.6). This chapter also gives a brief description and analysis of New Public Management (NPM) as an influential philosophy underlying many innovations in public sector budgeting and accounting during the last three decades (Section 1.7). The chapter ends with some concluding remarks (Section 1.8).

1.2   Financial management

Organizations in both the private and public sector have an interest in a properly designed and functioning financial management system. Financial management concerns the planning and control of the financial aspects of an organization. It includes the planning and budgeting of the activities of the organization over a future period, often a year, and, in addition, giving an account of the execution of these plans and budgets. A planning and control cycle includes different types of feedback. This feedback can take place during the year in order to give pointers for the execution of the plans if accomplishments are lagging behind expectations. Another type of feedback occurs when the annual financial statements give rise to an adaption of plans for future periods, for example when the organization needs to adjust its ambitions in a downward direction because they turned out to be insufficiently realistic. Figure 1.1 gives a presentation of the planning and control cycle. In addition to planning and control, financial management also concerns the financial support of 'one-off' decisions, for instance about investments of resources in a new project, as well as decisions about the sources of finance to be used for obtaining those resources. For example, a public sector organization may be able to borrow money from capital markets or public funds, it may use leasing facilities to pay for assets over a number of years, or it may have existing cash resources which it can use to purchase assets or invest in new projects or services.

Given the above explanations, *financial management* can be defined as the planning and control of an organization's financial affairs, giving an account of these affairs, and providing the financial support of investment and financing decisions. The objectives will involve seeking to secure the efficient and effective use of resources to achieve the goals of the organization.

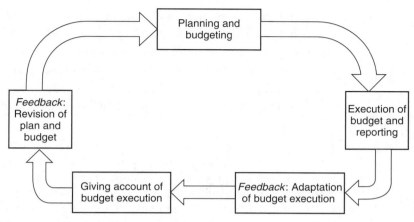

Figure 1.1 The planning and control cycle

1.3   The public sector context of financial management

The public sector context gives a distinctive meaning to financial management.[1] Public sector financial management is specific due to the particularities of the public sector. A key characteristic of the public sector is that top level decision-making is the domain of politicians, e.g. ministers and members of parliament at the central government level and executives and councillors at the provincial or municipal level. In democratic societies members of parliament and councillors are elected by the citizens of their jurisdictions for a certain term, typically from three to six years. They are supposed to represent the interests of these citizens as their voters. In turn, members of parliament elect and appoint the ministers, while the councillors elect and appoint the members of the executive of their province or municipality. Given that top level decision-making is the domain of politicians, the first main function of financial management is *to provide information to support policy and decision-making by politicians*. The second main function of financial management is *to support managers* in public sector organizations to enable them to provide advice on financial affairs and to manage the financial consequences arising from the implementation of policy decisions.

Financial management varies according to the differences in tasks and services of public sector organizations (see also Anthony and Young, 2002, chapter 3). The operations of a governmental organization, such as the state, a province or municipality, concern *a diversity of tasks and services*, including:

---

1 Our definition of financial management, with its emphasis on the planning and control cycle, differs from the definitions found in public finance, which often focus on expenditure management in the context of public budgeting (Allen et al., 2013, p. 2).

a. Conducting activities for the public as a whole, for example in the areas of defence, justice, regional planning, infrastructure and flood control.

b. Providing free and often mandatory public services due to certain legislations (such as primary education and social benefits).

c. Providing services which are fully or partly covered by fees (e.g. issuing driving licences, offering sporting facilities or theatre events).

The *role of taxes as a source of income* is different for each of these tasks and services. Taxes are raised without a direct relationship with the services or tasks for which they can be a source of income. How tax revenue – such as property tax, income tax or value added tax – is allocated to the various tasks and services is a matter of political priority. In contrast, when fees are used as a source of income for certain services, there is a direct link between resource income and resources use, while taxes are a relatively less important source of income.

This also influences *the decision-making role of politicians*. This role is primarily related to the question of how much money will be spent for each of the activities with a collective character and each of the mandatory and free-of-charge services. That is, budgeting and ensuring that budgets and related plans are executed, according to laws and political priorities are crucial. However, for fee-covering services, budgeting by politicians is relatively less important. Politicians mostly can confine themselves to formulating certain boundaries, in both financial terms (What fee levels are acceptable? What maximum amount of deficit will be covered by tax resources?), and quality terms or service standards (e.g. opening hours or professional qualifications of employees).

A related issue concerns *the organizational positioning of the different types of public sector tasks and services*. Those tasks which concern activities for the public as a whole require intensive political interventions and are often organizationally positioned close to the political domain, i.e. for central government in the core ministries. If political interventions can be restricted to the annual budgetary cycle and they are confined to specific issues, such as tariff levels and deficit coverage, a more remote positioning to the political domain can be expected. For example, the establishment of agencies (which have some operational independence from their sponsoring governmental departments) or autonomous public bodies are appropriate organizational options for these types of tasks or services.

Table 1.1 summarizes the implications of the various public sector tasks and services for *financial management*.

Table 1.1 shows that, at one extreme, those activities with a collective character are sourced by taxes, require intensive political interventions for which the budget is an important steering mechanism, and are positioned close to the political domain. Given these characteristics, financial management primarily supports political decision-making through budgeting, including feedback and giving account of budget execution. At the other extreme, services which are partly or fully covered by fees require fewer political interventions and are

Table 1.1 Financial management for a variety of public sector tasks and services

Tasks and services	Relevance of taxes as source of income	Intensity and character of political intervention	Positioning in governmental organization	Implications for financial management
Activities with a collective character	Important	Large, prioritizing spending opportunities, ensuring proper budget execution	Close to the centre of the organization (e.g. core ministries)	Primarily directed to support political decisions
Services for free and often mandatory	Important	Moderate, prioritizing spending opportunities, ensuring proper budget execution and quality standards	Autonomous (e.g. agencies, autonomous bodies)	Primarily directed to support managerial decisions restricted by political constraints
Services with fully or partly cost-covering fees	Minor or absent	Incidental, setting financial boundaries (fee levels, deficit coverage) and quality standards	Autonomous (e.g. agencies, autonomous bodies)	Primarily directed to support managerial decisions restricted by political constraints

positioned quite independently of the political domain. Under these circumstances financial management mainly serves the needs of managers, who can
run their organization relatively independently within certain boundaries set by
their political stakeholders. The in-between category of free-of-charge and often
mandatory services shares the financial management characteristics of the other
two categories.

1.4   The distinctive character of public sector budgeting and accounting

In this section the distinctive character of public sector accounting and budgeting,
in comparison with the private sector, will be highlighted (see further: Hodges and
Mellett, 2003; Bergmann, 2009, chapters 1 and 2: Jones and Pendlebury, 2010,
chapter 1; Almquist et al., 2013).

A fundamental difference between organizations in the public and private
sectors relates to their respective forms of governance. Private sector organizations have boards of directors as their main steering bodies with accountability
relationships to their owners (their shareholders). Public sector organizations are
part of a *governmental system controlled by politicians.* Politicians are elected by
the population of a specific jurisdiction, i.e. members of parliament for a country
(and a state within a federal system) and members of the council for a municipality or province. A major responsibility of politicians relates to their *authority to
establish a budget,* which is a plan for a particular period (often a year) for executing certain programmes and delivering certain services, including providing
the related resources and financing. This authority is not confined only to the
total amount of resources to be spent and funded in a period; it also concerns
each of the individual programmes or services. The detailed budgetary authority
of politicians in public sector organizations has two main impacts on accounting:
on the one hand, the budget often needs to be *detailed* in terms of its elements
(programmes, services), and on the other hand, *comparisons between the budgeted
and the actual realization* of those elements are crucial.

The budget in a public sector context is not only a financial expression of
planned activities, it is also a legal authorization of any expenditure, which is often
formalized by means of a law. This implies, among other things, that a public
sector budget is accessible to the public (and not confidential, as in many private
sector companies), and that additions to the use of resources during the year may
need to be based on a formal budget revision (see Bergmann, 2009, pp. 8–9).

A second difference between the public and the private sector is that funding
in the public sector comes to a large extent from taxes, which are raised through
the legislative power of the governmental body, such as central government or a
local municipal authority. While private companies have to compete in markets
for their delivery of products and services, public sector organizations do have

a legal right to raise taxes or fees which can be imposed on their citizens. The implication is that politicians have to account for their decisions on taxation and fees, including the ways in which these resources are spent. This reinforces public sector accounting implications regarding *the importance of detailed budgets and comparisons between budgets and actual levels of income and costs.* Taxes are not only a source of income in the public sector for funding programmes or services but also a means for steering the economy as a whole. So, *taxing also has a macro-economic* function, i.e. to guarantee that the governmental deficit – being the gap between the yearly income and costs – will not be above a certain level, or that the total amount of debt is lower than an acceptable upper limit. For example, the European Union requires from its member states that this deficit as a percentage of Gross Domestic Product (GDP) does not exceed 3% and that the debt as a percentage of GDP is lower than 60% (see also Bergmann, 2009, chapter 2). The reasons for these types of requirements are that future generations will not be burdened by too high a level of governmental debt and that the money lent to governments is likely to be paid back. There is an important connection between fiscal policy aiming at achieving an acceptable debt level of the government as a whole, and financial management at the level of individual governmental organizations. Fiscal discipline at the macro level requires affordable spending at the micro level, including the requirement that expected long-term revenues are sufficient to cover expected expenditures and that budgets are executed according to their budgetary limits (Hemming, 2013).

A third difference between private sector and public sector accounting and budgeting is that achieving good financial results in the private sector is considered to be a primary objective, whereas *financial performance is only a secondary objective in the public sector.* Public sector organizations are concerned with providing societally relevant programmes (for example, on crime prevention, poverty reduction and urban planning) or services (such as educational services and services for elderly people). Important goals include the accessibility of programmes or services (Are relevant target groups reached?) and the quality of those programmes and services (Do they accomplish their underlying societal goals? Are users satisfied?). Financial issues also play a role, of course, but that is to support the principal, non-financial objectives. Financial requirements may be viewed as a constraint, particularly when programmes or services have to be produced according to strict budgetary limits. Financial objectives or constraints can also be relevant at the level of the public sector organization as a whole, for instance when an organization needs to assess whether the total of all its revenues (coming from taxes, fees, grants, etc.) is sufficient to cover the total of the resources needed for executing its programmes and delivering its services. The implications are that accountability relates to both *financial and non-financial issues,* and that *financial issues often have the form of constraints on non-financial activities.*

Finally, public sector organizations are faced with *multiple stakeholders with particular and sometimes ambiguous or conflicting interests.* Creditors, who want to be confident that their money will be paid back, or employees who have an interest in sustainable employment and good labour conditions, are important stakeholder groups for both private sector and public sector organizations. Private sector organizations often see their owners (shareholders) and providers of finance (bondholders) as their most important stakeholders, while clients are of growing importance (with user satisfaction and customer value as criteria). In the public sector the politicians who control the organization may be the most powerful stakeholders, although their interests may be diverse, ambiguous and conflicting. In addition to politicians, some other stakeholders can be important in a public sector context, particularly users of services and their representatives (with an interest in accessibility, quality and costs of services), oversight bodies (often with financial interests, but also with policy related interests) and partners in both the private and public sector, who are engaged in collaborative projects (with a diversity of interests). The accounting implications of having multiple stakeholders with diverging and sometimes ambiguous or conflicting interests are on the one hand that *accountability often relates to a diversity of aspects of an organization's operations*, and that an overarching criterion for control is lacking. The latter implies that accounting information not only serves *controlling purposes*, but can also be an input for *dialogue and debate* between different stakeholders with their diverging interests (see Hofstede, 1981; Brignall and Modell, 2000).

The characteristics and background of public sector accounting and budgeting have to be nuanced because trends of convergence between private sector and public sector accounting can be observed. This is especially the case with the adoption of businesslike management and accounting tools in the public sector. Some parts of the governmental sector, especially core governmental domains, such as defence, justice and spatial planning, have the characteristics of public goods, and are more distinct than service-oriented parts of the public sector, such as educational, welfare and health services. This implies that public sector accounting should be distinctive from private sector accounting in the core governmental branches (see Barton, 2004; Christiaens and Rommel, 2008).

To sum up: public sector accounting and budgeting is distinctive from that in the private sector as a consequence of the particularities of the public sector:

- Public sector organizations are controlled by politicians and governments can impose taxes on citizens, so that budgets need to be detailed in terms of their elements (programmes, services), and comparisons between the budgeted and the actual realization of those elements are crucial.
- In addition to its function to raise resources for expenditures, taxing has a macro-economic function, for example to guarantee that the governmental deficit and debt will not be higher than a certain standard.
- Public sector organizations' goals are concerned with providing societally relevant programmes and services, so that non-financial indicators are core,

while financial issues may be forms of constraint, for example by acting within budgetary limits.

– Public sector organizations have multiple stakeholders with diverging and sometimes ambiguous or conflicting interests, so that accountability relates to a diversity of aspects of an organization's operations. Accounting information serves controlling purposes, and can also be an input for dialogue and debate between different stakeholders with their diverging interests.

Notwithstanding the relevance of non-financial information in the public sector, this book will focus mainly on financial issues.

1.5   Case study: programme budgeting in the Dutch municipality of Zoetermeer[2]

Before presenting the case on the budget of the Dutch municipality Zoetermeer, some backgrounds of municipal budgeting in the Netherlands are sketched. Dutch municipalities are supposed to draft a so-called programme budget for their councils. A programme includes a range of interrelated activities aimed at achieving certain outcomes. The programme budget contains an overview of the activities planned, the resources involved and the outcomes to be achieved. The Council authorizes future spendings at the level of programmes. This means that reallocations of resources within a programme are the domain of the managers, while reallocations of resources over different programmes require approval from the Council.

The municipality of Zoetermeer in the Netherlands has 123,000 inhabitants and is located close to the country's capital The Hague. A concise version of Zoetermeer's programme budget and annual account for 2012 is presented in Table 1.2.

Table 1.2 shows the budgeted costs and revenues as well as the actual costs and revenues for each programme. The final column shows the difference between budgeted and actual costs or revenues. There are two versions of the budget; one is the original budget which was drafted in the autumn of 2011 and the other is the revised budget, which is an updated version of the budget which takes account of relevant internal and external contingencies during the year 2012.

Several observations can be made about Zoetermeer's programme budget:

– Some programmes have relatively high own revenues, often specific grants from central government or service fees; these programmes are largely independent of the general revenues coming from central government's grants and

---

2 Case information is based on Gemeente Zoetermeer (2013) and the case analysis is the authors' responsibility. The authors are indebted to Mrs Monica Grims, staff member of the financial department of Zoetermeer, for her feedback on a previous draft of this case.

Table 1.2 Programme budget and accounts in 2012 of Zoetermeer, the Netherlands (in millions of euros)

Programme	Original budget		Revised budget		Annual account		Difference revised budget annual account	
	Costs	Revenues	Costs	Revenues	Costs	Revenues	Costs	Revenues
1. Social benefits	78.3	55.0	81.5	58.2	78.3	58.5	3.2 F	0.3 F
2. Welfare and care	29.2	3.2	29.4	3.2	30.7	3.9	1.3 U	0.7 F
3. Sustainability	21.1	20.1	21.0	20.2	19.3	20.2	1.7 F	0.0
4. Education/Youth	29.1	4.0	31.9	4.0	31.4	4.5	0.5 F	0.5 F
5. Art, culture, libraries	13.5	1.8	13.5	1.8	13.3	1.7	0.2 F	0.1 U
6. Sports and fitness	17.8	6.1	17.9	6.1	15.7	5.6	2.2 F	0.5 U
7. Safety	12.1	0.1	12.2	0.2	12.1	0.4	0.1 F	0.2 F
8. Service and governance	29.2	2.3	29.8	2.3	28.0	3.2	1.8 F	0.9 F
9. City infrastructure	73.2	76.4	72.1	64.1	47.1	45.4	25.0F	18.7 U
10. Economic affairs	2.3	1.4	2.4	1.2	2.4	0.6	0.0	0.6 U
11. Living and building	8.7	2.3	9.5	2.3	8.4	2.6	1.1 F	0.3 F
12. Public area	34.4	3.3	35.0	3.3	32.2	3.5	2.8 F	0.2 F
Tot. specific revenues/costs	348.8	176.0	356.2	166.9	318.9	150.0	37.3F	16.8 U
General revenues	—	167.4	—	169.1	—	172.2	—	3.1 F
Total	348.8	343.4	356.2	336.0	318.9	332.2	37.3F	3.7 U
Deficit (D) / Surplus (S)		5.4 (D)		20.2 (D)	13.3 (S)			

Source: Derived from Zoetermeer, 2013, pp. 115–18 after some simplifications. In the final column, F stands for favourable (lower actual costs than budgeted or higher actual revenues than budgeted), while U stands for unfavourable (then the opposite applies). Small differences between the figures in this column and the previous columns can occur due to rounding-off effects.

municipal taxes; this includes, for example, the city infrastructure programme, which is the largest programme in terms of resources, and is also funded by land purchases for building houses or businesses.

- Many programmes have relatively low own revenues, so that their primary funding comes from the general revenues, for example the Education/Youth and Service and Governance programmes.

- The differences between the revised budget and the annual account are mostly quite small, but the largest programme, i.e. City infrastructure, shows substantial differences, also in relative terms. Zoetermeer provides extensive explanations of these differences, which will not be discussed here (in general, various infrastructure projects were delayed, and resources for these projects were transferred to the following year).

– The municipality expected to incur a deficit in 2012, but the annual account ultimately showed a surplus.[3]

Table 1.2 only gives financial information about each of the programmes, but non-financial information is provided by Zoetermeer, especially about the goals to be accomplished, the underlying activities and goal-related performance indicators. This type of information makes the budget an outcome-oriented programme budget, as Table 1.3 illustrates.

The case presented in this section illustrates several distinctive aspects of public sector budgeting and accounting, as introduced in the Sections 1.3 and 1.4. First, it shows that *budgeting in a public sector context is mainly a reflection of the political priorities*: how much will be spent for each programme is an

Table 1.3 Examples of programme goals and related performance indicators

Programme	Example of goal	Related indicators		
1. Social benefits	Fighting poverty and promoting participation by providing income support facilities	Percentage of low income households: Target: 9.1% Actual: 10.5%	Client appreciation of municipal service: Target: grade 7 Actual: grade 7	Familiarity with low income support facilities Target: rise by 5% Actual: not available
3. Sustainability	Stimulating energy conservation in households	Number of energy conservation subsidies: Target: 300 Actual: 389	Total of sustainable energy capacity: Target: 10 MW Actual: 10 MW	–
4. Education/Youth	Encouraging young people's involvement in their neighbourhood	Appreciation of specific educational activities: Target grade: 7 Actual grade not available	Number of youngsters involved in supporting activities: Target: 28 Actual: 35	Participation rate of youngsters in sports: Target: 89% Actual: 86%
9. City infrastructure	Up to date regional planning of various functions in the city	Appreciation of the city's spatial quality: Target grade: 7.5 Actual grade: 7.6	Number of spatial plans: Target: 9 Actual: 3	–

Source: Derived from Zoetermeer, 2013.

---

3 This municipality also makes certain provisions for expenditures to be expected in later years, which are disregarded here for simplification reasons.

important decision for the Council and the Executive of a municipality. Second, the politicians have a strong interest in scrutinizing that the *budget is properly executed*: hence, actual and budgeted costs and revenues are compared and explanations are provided when differences between actual and budgeted figures are substantial. Finally, in addition to financial information, *non-financial information is crucial*, especially on the underlying activities and goals. Chapter 6 further discusses these various budgeting issues.

1.6   Case study: a multi-year deficit reduction programme by Hansestadt Bremen, Germany[4]

In Germany, measures have been taken to prevent future deficits at both the federal and state level. States with a deficit are obliged to reduce their deficit gradually so that they will reach a break-even situation by 2020, in the sense that the yearly costs are no longer higher than the yearly revenues, which is also called a 'balanced budget requirement'. For the federal government a similar deadline is set at 2016. In those years – 2016 for federal government and 2020 for the states – the total debt of these governments is allowed to reach its maximum but a further rise in the years thereafter is prohibited. This is called the *debt brake* policy (in German: *Schuldenbremse*). The main motive for a debt brake policy is that a continuing rise of total debt would lead to an increase of interest costs, which reduces spending opportunities for regular governmental activities. This resonates with the debt criterion of the EU, as discussed in Section 1.4: according to EU criteria, state debt should not rise above 60% of GDP in order to prevent a too high financial burden for future generations.

One of the states with a huge deficit is Hansestadt Bremen, which is both a city and a state, located in the North-Western part of Germany with a population of about 550,000 inhabitants. Bremen built up a total debt of about €20 billion, which amounts to around 500% of its yearly budget. Table 1.4 shows how Bremen plans to reduce its deficit during the years 2012–2016, while a further deficit reduction is foreseen between 2017 and 2020.

The enormous debt also explains why the interest costs are as high as about 15% of the total costs. The severe financial problems of Bremen were a reason for the federal government to support Bremen's deficit reduction programme by a yearly grant of €300 million.

In order to prepare a deficit reduction programme, a public sector organization mostly starts by estimating its future deficits without taking deficit reduction

---

4 The case information is based on Stadtstaat Bremen (2012) and the case analysis is the authors' responsibility.

Table 1.4   Planned revenues and costs in 2012, 2014 and 2016 of
Hansestadt Bremen, Germany (in millions of euros)

Revenue/cost category –Year	2012	2014	2016
Tax-related income	2,953	3,228	3,470
Specific income for operations	548	558	563
Specific income for investments	87	88	88
Total revenues	*3,588*	*3,874*	*4,121*
Personnel costs	1,420	1,445	1,474
Social benefit-related costs	777	803	831
Other operations costs	1,213	1,166	1,152
Investment costs	492	496	448
Interest costs	689	708	807
Total costs	*4,591*	*4,619*	*4,712*
Deficit = total costs less total revenues	*1,004*	*746*	*591*
Federal support for deficit reduction	300	300	300
Net-deficit	*704*	*446*	*291*

Source: Derived from Stadtstaat Bremen, 2012, p. 11 (planning dated
August 2011).

measures. These are so-called policy neutral forecasts. In order to make such forecasts an organization needs to have solid financial information about its own past,
such as its revenues and costs in the most recent years. This is the main input
for a well-informed guess about its future deficits and the extent of its financial problems. After the estimated deficits over a number of years are known, a
target can be set regarding the ultimate deficit reduction, including its pace of
change. In the case of Bremen, the deficit has to be reduced from €1,004 million
in 2012 to zero in 2020. Subsequently, various deficit reduction measures can be
considered, ranging from tax and fee increases to a reduction of subsidies, post-
ponements of planned investments and staff reductions. It is mainly a political
matter to decide which mix of the various types of measures is the most appropriate, but the political debate can benefit from a set of strategies with well-informed
financial consequences.

   Table 1.4 indicates the way in which Bremen plans to reduce its deficit and
we can see that income increasing measures, such as raising taxes, are far more
important than spending cutting measures, such as reducing the organization's
staff. Tax-related incomes rise from €2,953 million in 2012 to €3,470 million
in 2016, that is an increase of approximately 17%, while total costs only rise
from €4,591 million in 2012 to €4,712 million in 2016, which is an increase of
about 2.5 %.

Table 1.4 can be regarded as a *multi-year budget* at a very *aggregate level*. This table shows an expression of the planned revenues and costs over a period of five years, 2012–2016, with figures for three years, i.e. 2012, 2014 and 2016. Moreover, the figures presented in the table show very broad categories of revenues and costs. This is appropriate for getting a global view on financials over a period of five years, which enables the Bremen parliament to monitor the success of the deficit reduction programme. However, for steering and control a more detailed budget – at least yearly but probably also over a number of years – is needed, for example, showing the revenues and costs for the various functions of Hansestadt Bremen (infrastructure, employment programmes, environmental affairs, kindergarten, etc.), as in the Zoetermeer case in Section 1.5, and an overview of the large investment projects and their expected costs. This example also illustrates that the ultimate *financial outcome*, in the form of a deficit or surplus, is a *constraint*, while the goals of the organization include societal activities and services, as explained in Section 1.4.

If an organization looks ahead for many years, as Hansestadt Bremen does, uncertainties about the financial impacts of the various types of measures will increase. This may require *scenario analyses* which encompass an investigation of the financial impacts of different sets of assumptions about important variables, such as population growth or decline, employment developments and the rate of inflation. Subsequently, the desirable or necessary sets of measures belonging to each of these scenarios can be set out and analysed, and policy options may be determined.

1.7   New Public Management and New Public Financial Management

New Public Management (NPM)

New Public Management (NPM) refers to the introduction and application of businesslike tools and styles in public sector management. Pollitt and Bouckaert (2011, chapter 4) argue that NPM reforms have evolved around six dimensions, e.g. privatization, marketization, decentralization, output orientation, quality systems, and intensity of implementation. According to Hood (1995, p. 94) its basic doctrines are a lessening or removing of the differences between the public and the private sector, as well as a move from an emphasis on the control of processes to the control of results and accountability. Table 1.5 shows the striking differences between traditional public administration and NPM.

Accounting plays a pivotal role in NPM, particularly by emphasizing output and results control for which explicit performance targets are important, as well as by a budgeting focus on achieving efficiency. The accounting elements of NPM have been elaborated further in New Public Financial Management (NPFM).

Table 1.5   Differences between traditional public administration and New Public Management

Feature	Traditional Public Administration	New Public Management (NPM)
1. The structure of the organization	Centralized, including uniform control	Divisionalized with units organized around products
2. Relationships between and within units	Unspecified and open-ended agreements	Contract-based
3. Styles and practices	Governmental ethics and styles	Private ethics and styles
4. Budgeting focus	Stable, focused on budgets	Efficiency-oriented, aimed at cutting of resources
5. Management profile	Inactive: policy skills and knowledge of rules are important	Visible hands-on management
6. Performance-oriented	Qualitative and implicit standards	Explicit standards, related to clearly defined targets
7. Focus of control	Focused on rules and procedures	Focused on output and results

Source: This table was drawn up by the authors and only encompasses a simplified picture of the differences in question (see for more details, see Hood, 1991, pp. 4–5; 1995, p. 96).

New Public Financial Management (NPFM)

In their comparative study of the adoption of NPM-related accounting tools across various countries, Guthrie et al. (1999, pp. 209–11) coined the label New Public Financial Management (NPFM) as consisting of five different categories:

1. Accrual-based accounting for financial reporting in combination with standards developed by the accounting profession.
2. Market-oriented management systems for contracting and pricing, both within the organization and in transactions with external parties.
3. Performance measurement, comprising financial and non-financial performance indicators, and including benchmarking and league tables.
4. Devolvement and decentralization of budgets in combination with the linkage of budgeting and reporting information on both financial and non-financial issues.
5. Auditing of efficiency and effectiveness (value-for-money auditing).

This list of NPFM categories reveals various attempts to adopt private sector accounting tools in the public sector. This applies to accrual accounting which has been the dominant accounting system in the business sector for ages, and is now promoted in the public sector to replace cash-based accounting. A recent study shows that the adoption of accrual accounting is widespread among governmental organizations in European countries (Christiaens et al., 2010; see also Groot and Budding, 2008). In addition, performance management can be regarded as the other key theme in NPFM. Devolvement and decentralization of budgets go hand in hand with control and accountability by means of performance information. Moreover, open-ended contracting is replaced by contracting through numbers. The changing focus of control from procedures to results further strengthens a move from relational contracting to more tightly-constructed contracts with quantitative specifications. Performance information becomes a main element of both budgeting (performance budgeting) and auditing innovations, where compliance with rules is complemented by value-for-money auditing.

Controversies around NPM and NPFM

NPM and NPFM have achieved substantial support around the world but controversies about their underlying principles still remain. Diefenbach (2009), for example, argues that NPM (and implicitly NPFM) created new values of quantification and monetization, but it ignored or even destroyed traditional public sector values and public service ethos, commitment to impartiality, social equality, equity and a communitarian focus (see also Broadbent, 2013). Moreover, Diefenbach points to various paradoxes in NPM, such as a decentralization of operational tasks which is often supplemented by a centralization of core strategic tasks, and the move away from traditional bureaucracy which has created a new bureaucracy of accounting by numbers. In addition, NPM seems to place managers in a powerful position, which especially harms the discretionary powers of professionals working in the public sector. While performance-oriented control and accountability have become widespread in the public sector, there is a continuous debate about its negative side-effects, particularly its measurability bias which drives out a focus on what is really important (also called a 'tick-box' mentality; Lapsley, 2009). In addition, there is not always convincing evidence that NPM and NPFM claims live up to their expectations (Guthrie et al., 1999; see also Ter Bogt, 2008). Related to this, public sector organizations seem to be inclined to copy the tools and styles of other organizations, which are regarded as modern or fashionable.

1.8   Concluding remarks

This chapter has defined financial management as decision-making about the planning and control cycle of an organization's financial affairs, as well as about the financial aspects of incidental events such as investments. Financial management in the public sector differs according to the types of tasks and activities. It shows, for example, production-oriented tasks have more similarities with the private sector than purely governmental tasks, such as infrastructure and defence.

This chapter has further clarified the distinctive character of public sector accounting and budgeting in comparison with the private sector as a consequence of the particularities of the public sector. Budgeting is far more important in the public than the private sector. This is due to the fact that public sector organizations are controlled by politicians who can decide to impose taxes on citizens. The implication is that politicians have to show on a detailed level how much money raised by taxes will be spent on each of the programmes and services and whether spending plans are executed accordingly. In addition, whereas financial issues are main goals in the private sector, they are mostly constraints in the public sector. Although acting within budgetary limits is often important, accomplishing societal relevant goals is crucial in the public sector. Two real-life cases have been presented in this chapter to illustrate the particularities of public sector budgeting and accounting.

Finally, this chapter has described and analysed New Public Management (NPM) as a main driving force in public sector financial management reforms over the last decades. NPM has imported ideas from the private sector into the public sector. Important reform aspects of financial management have been the move from cash to accrual accounting and from input to performance budgeting. NPM is, however, not undisputed due to its neglect of the specifics of the public sector.

The next four chapters deal with accounting. Chapter 2 provides some basic accounting knowledge. Subsequently, Chapters 3, 4 and 5 will discuss public sector accounting, and particularly the various types of financial statements including the way they can be used for decision-making and control.

References

Allen, R., R. Hemming and B.H. Potter (2013), Introduction: the meaning, content and objectives of public financial management, in: Allen, R., R. Hemming and B.H. Potter (eds), *The International Handbook of Public Financial Management*, Palgrave Macmillan, Basingstoke, ch. 1.

Almquist, R., G. Grossi, G.J. van Helden and C. Reichard (2013), Public sector governance and accountability, *Critical Perspectives on Accounting*, Vol. 24, no. 7–8, pp. 479–87.

Anthony. R.N. and D.W. Young (2002), *Management Control in Non-Profit Organizations*, 7th edition, Irwin, Boston.

Barton, A. (2004), How to profit from defence: a study in the misapplication of business accounting to the public sector in Australia, *Financial Accountability & Management*, Vol. 20, no.3, pp. 281–304.

Bergmann, A. (2009), *Public Sector Financial Management*, Prentice Hall/Pearson, Harlow.

Brignall, S. and S. Modell (2000), An institutional perspective on performance measurement and management in the 'New Public Sector', *Management Accounting Research*, Vol. 11, no. 3, pp. 282–306.

Broadbent, J. (2013), Editorial: reclaiming the ideal of public service, *Public Money & Management*, Vol. 33, no. 6, pp. 301–94.

Christiaens, J., B. Reyniers and C. Rollé (2010), Impact of IPSAS on Government Financial Information Systems: A Comparative Study, *International Review of Administrative Sciences*, Vol. 76, no. 3, pp. 537–54.

Christiaens, J. and J. Rommel (2008), Accrual accounting reforms: only for businesslike (parts of) government, *Financial Accountability & Management*, Vol. 24, no.1, pp. 59–75.

Diefenbach, T. (2009), New Public Management in Public Sector Organizations: The Dark Sides of Managerialistic 'Enlightenment', *Public Administration*, Vol. 87, no. 4, pp. 892–909.

Gemeente Zoetermeer (2013), *Jaarstukken 2012 (Annual Report over 2012)*, Zoetermeer.

Groot, T.L.C.M. and G. Budding (2008), New Public Management's Current Issues and Future Prospects, *Financial Accountability & Management*, Vol. 24, no.1, pp. 1–14.

Guthrie, J., O. Olson and C. Humphrey (1999), Debating Developments in New Public Financial Management: The Limits of Global Theorizing and Some New Ways forward, *Financial Accountability & Management*, Vol. 15, no. 2–3, pp. 209–28.

Hemming, R. (2013), The macro-economic framework for managing public finances, in: Allen, R., R. Hemming and B.H. Potter (eds), *The International Handbook of Public Financial Management*, Palgrave Macmillan, Basingstoke, chapter 2.

Hofstede, G. (1981), Management control of public and not-for-profit activities, *Accounting, Organizations and Society*, Vol. 6, no. 3, pp. 193–211.

Hodges, R. and H. Mellett (2003), Reporting Public Sector Financial Results, *Public Management Review*, vol. 5, no. 1, pp. 99–114.

Hood, C. (1991), A Public Management for all Seasons, *Public Administration*, Vol. 69, no. 1, pp. 3–19.

Hood, C. (1995), The 'New Public Management' in the 1980s: Variations on a Theme, *Accounting, Organizations and Society*, Vol. 20, no. 1–2, pp. 93–109.

Jones, R. and M. Pendlebury (2010), *Public Sector Accounting*, 6th edition, Prentice Hall/Pearson, Harlow.

Lapsley, I. (2009), New Public Management: The Cruellest Invention of the Human Spirit?, *Abacus*, Vol. 45, no. 1, pp. 1–21.

Pollitt, C. and G. Bouckaert (2011), *Public Management Reform: A Comparative Analysis*, 3rd edition, Oxford, Oxford University Press.

Stadtstaat Bremen (2012), *Finanzplan 2011–2016 (Financial plan 2011–2016)*, Bremen.

Ter Bogt, H.J. (2008), Recent and Future Management Changes in Local Government: Continuing Focus on Rationality and Efficiency?, *Financial Accountability & Management*, Vol. 24, no. 1, pp. 31–57.

2

Introducing accounting basics

Learning objectives

♦ Understand the function of a balance sheet, an income statement and a cash flow statement

♦ Be able to interpret the information included in a balance sheet, an income statement and a cash flow statement of a household and a simple organization

♦ Be able to see the relationships between a balance sheet, an income statement and a cash flow statement

♦ Have a preliminary understanding of the difference between cash-based and accrual accounting

♦ Be familiar with the meaning of some key terms in accounting

2.1 Introduction

This chapter introduces some accounting basics. The main accounting documents considered here are the balance sheet, the income statement and the cash flow statement. These three documents, including their relationships, are illustrated for two simple cases. The first case concerns the finances of a private household over the year 20XX. This household gets an income from salaries and has various costs of living. The household has possessions, such as a house and a car, which have a longer lifetime than a year, so we need to consider what these possessions may be worth and, as a result, which costs to account for over the year 20XX. The second case considers the finances of a simple production company over the year 20XX. While a private household is primarily spending money on its living expenses, the company earns money by producing and selling certain things which (hopefully) have a higher economic value than their costs. These two cases are discussed in Sections 2.2 and 2.3 respectively. The main objective is to show what type of information might be included in important financial documents of simple households and organizations (see also Gowthorpe, 2005, for an introduction to private sector accounting). This provides a basic knowledge of accounting, which is needed in the subsequent Chapters 3 and 4, which deal with public sector accounting. Section 2.4 provides definitions of some key accounting terms and Section 2.5 contains some concluding remarks.

2.2   Accounting documents of the Johnsons, a private household

This section presents and discusses the financial data of the private household of Mr and Mrs Johnson and their two children over the year 20XX. So, information is given on things like the salary income, the cost of living, the part-repayment of a student loan, the replacement of a car, value changes of a house, mortgage changes, the change in the student loan, a gift from the parents, and a bank deposit. These data form the input for the income statement and cash flow statement over the year 20XX, and for the balance sheet at the beginning and the end of the year 20XX. Moreover, relationships between these three documents are explained. Two questions are answered: how did this household perform, in a financial sense, during the year 20XX and how has its state of wealth changed during this year?

The financial figures

– Mr and Mrs Johnson earned together a total gross income of €100,000, from which they have income taxes and social contributions deducted of €35,000, leaving net income paid to them of €65,000.

– In addition, the parents of Mrs Johnson provided them with a gift of €10,000 in cash.

– Their costs of living were €38,000, excluding repayments for mortgage and student loan and interest costs, but including the maintenance costs of the house.

– The Johnsons possess a house, which was bought for €400,000 at the end of the previous year.

– The mortgage loan secured on the house was €300,000 at the beginning of the year. Interest charged by the bank is at 3% per annum on the full €300,000.

– The obligatory repayment of the mortgage in this year was €10,000, in addition to the payment of interest on the mortgage, and this was paid in cash during the year.

– The Johnsons maintain their house properly, so that the house will not lose value due to its use; it can only lose or gain value due to decreases or increases in the market prices of houses. Unfortunately 20XX was a bad year and house prices declined by 3%.

– Mr Johnson had a remaining student loan of €30,000 at the beginning of the year for which an obligatory repayment during 20XX of €5,000 had to be made, in addition to the payment of interest on the loan. Interest on the loan was 4% on the remaining balance of €25,000.

– At the beginning of 20XX the Johnsons replaced their old car for a new one; they received €6,000 for their old car and paid €28,000 for their new car, which has an expected lifetime of 5 years and an expected residual (resale) value of €8,000 at the end of that period.

– Their bank deposit at the beginning of the year was €15,000.

The cash flow statement

This statement can be compiled quite easily. It comprises the cash inflows (what comes in via the cash or bank) at the top of the statement and the cash outflows (what goes out via the cash or bank) at the bottom of the statement. Table 2.1 shows the cash flow statement.

When cash outflows are higher than cash inflows, there is a net cash deficit, which will be subtracted from the bank balance at the start of the year. So, the bank deposit at the beginning of the year will be decreased by the cash deficit over the year, and this results in the lower cash in the bank account at the end of the year. Contrasted to that: if cash outflows are lower than cash inflows, this will result in an increase in the bank balance. As can be seen from Table 2.1, the Johnsons have a cash deficit of €10,000 this year, so the bank deposit, which was €15,000 at the beginning of 20XX, will be reduced to €5,000 (€15,000 less the cash deficit of €10,000) at the year end. Does this imply that the Johnsons have been performing badly in a financial sense during 20XX? Not necessarily; we need to consider their income statement, and their balance sheet at the end of the year, to get a clearer picture.

Table 2.1 Cash flow statement of the Johnson family over 20XX (in euros)

Cash inflows

Gross salaries	100,000
Less: income taxes and social security deducted	35,000
Net salaries received	65,000
Gift from Mrs Johnson's parents	10,000
Sale of old car	6,000
Total cash inflows	81,000

Cash outflows

Cost of living expenses	38,000	
Repayment of mortgage loan	10,000	
Interest paid on mortgage loan (3% of 300,000)	9,000	
Repayment of student loan	5,000	
Interest paid on student load (4% of 25,000)	1,000	
Purchase price of the new car	28,000	
Total cash outflows		91,000
Cash deficit for the year		10,000

The balance sheet at the beginning of the year

The balance sheet at the beginning of 20XX is shown in Table 2.2. The top section shows the possessions of the household; these are called the 'assets', i.e. the house, the car and the bank deposit, in total €421,000. The middle section shows how the possessions are financed, i.e. by a mortgage and a student loan, in total €330,000, which are 'liabilities' of the household as they represent amounts owing to others. This means that the value of the assets is higher than the value of the liabilities; the difference is called equity, being the 'owners' capital' of this household. This is shown in the bottom section of the balance sheet; assets (€421,000) minus liabilities (€330,000) = equity of €91,000. The balance sheet has to show an equilibrium position, meaning that assets are always equal to the sum of the liabilities and equity. So, equity can be seen as the extra value of the assets over the debt. Consider how the equity can be built up by a household. This is done by earning more than is spent in the past, and this surplus can be saved in cash or, for example, by buying a house partly with a mortgage (a liability or debt) and partly with their 'own money', as apparently is the case with the Johnsons.

Table 2.2   Balance sheet of the Johnson family, at 1 January 20XX (in euros)

Assets	
House	400,000
Old car	6,000
Bank deposit	15,000
Total assets	421,000
Liabilities	
Mortgage loan	300,000
Student loan	30,000
Total liabilities	330,000
Equity	91,000

The income statement

In order to get a well-founded answer on the question of how the Johnsons have been performing over the year 20XX, we need to calculate the value of their income over that year and compare it with the costs *which can be attributed to that year*. The result is the income statement. We will see that costs are not always equal to cash outflows. Let's take the house and the car as examples.

First, the Johnsons want to maintain their house in such a way that it will not lose value due to its use, but due to unfavourable price developments in the housing market over 20XX, they lost 3% on their house. Originally, its value was €400,000, but at the end of the year, it will be €388,000 (€400,000 less 3% of €400,000 = €12,000). So, the balance sheet at the end of the year will show a value of the house of €388,000, while the income statement will show a cost in the form of a loss in value of €12,000. However, there was no cash outflow due to this value reduction. On the other hand, there was a part repayment of the mortgage of €10,000, which is a cash outflow but not a cost because it has the effect of reducing the liability for the remaining mortgage loan.

Second, the old car had a value of €6,000 at the beginning of the year 20XX; then it was replaced by a new one, which was bought at a price of €28,000. It would not be fair to see the costs of the use of the car over 20XX as the difference between the selling price of the old car and the purchase price of the new car, i.e. €22,000 = €28,000 less €6,000. Why not? Because this new car will be used for five years and will still have an estimated remaining value of €8,000 when sold. So, over a period of five years the value reduction due to use will be €20,000 (from €28,000 to €8,000). If we assume that the use of the car will be the same during all five years, each year has to bear 20% of €20,000 = €4,000, which is part of the annual cost of the use of the car. This amount of €4,000 is called *depreciation*, being the value reduction in a specific year due to use of an asset with a longer lifetime than one year. Depreciation is a cost on the income statement, and it will lead to a reduction of the value of the new car at the year end of the same amount; so the value of the new car at the end of 20XX will be €28,000 (the purchase price of the car) less €4,000 (the depreciation accumulated to date on the car) = €24,000. This is called the *book value* of an asset with a longer lifetime than one year. So, there is a net cash outflow as a result of the replacement of the car of €22,000, but a cost of only €4,000 during 20XX. After five years of use the book value of the car will be €28,000 less 5 x €4,000 = €8,000, which is exactly the value for which the car is expected to be sold then.

The other cash inflows and cash outflows are equal to the revenues and costs in the income statement respectively. However, the gift from the parents of Mrs Johnson can be regarded as an irregular income (because we do not know whether her parents will also donate in other years). The repayment of the student loan of Mr Johnson is not an expense (or cost) as the repayment will reduce the debt by the same amount. In contrast, the interest paid on the student loan is an expense (or cost) because it uses up cash without reducing the amount of the debt. Table 2.3 gives the income statement over 20XX. The upper section indicates the income (or revenues) of the household while the lower section lists the expenses (or costs). Here, the revenues are higher than the costs, which results in a surplus of €11,000 (€75,000 revenues less €64,000 costs).

Table 2.3   Income statement of the Johnson family over 20XX (in euros)

Revenues

Gross salaries	100,000
Less: income tax and social security deducted	35,000
Net salaries	65,000
Gift from Mrs Johnson's parents	10,000
Total revenues	75,000

Expenses (costs)

Cost of living	38,000
Interest on mortgage loan	9,000
Interest on student loan	1,000
Value reduction of house	12,000
Depreciation of new car	4,000
Total expenses	64,000
Surplus for the year	11,000

The balance sheet at the year-end

Table 2.4 shows the balance sheet at the end of 20XX. All components are already explained above.

Table 2.4   Balance sheet of the Johnson family, at 31 December 20XX (in euros)

Assets

House	388,000
New car	24,000
Bank deposit	5,000
Total assets	417,000

Liabilities

Mortgage loan	290,000
Student loan	25,000
Total liabilities	315,000
Equity	102,000

Assessment of finances

At the beginning of this section two questions were raised: how did this household perform in a financial sense during the year 20XX and how has its state of wealth changed during this year? Given the cash flow statement and the income statement over 20XX, and the balance sheet at both the beginning and the end of 20XX, compiled above, we can now answer these questions.

If we compare the balance sheet at the beginning and the end of the year, equity has been improved by €11,000, i.e. €102,000 at the end of the year compared with €91,000 at the beginning of the year. How can this increase in wealth of the Johnson family be explained? This is because the income statement shows a surplus of €11,000. So, unlike the cash deficit of €10,000, the surplus of €11,000 can be linked directly to the equal improvement in the household's wealth shown in the financial statements. So, in general the Johnsons seem to have performed quite well in 20XX. There are, however, some concerns. If the gift from Mrs Johnson's parents of €10,000 is only applicable to 20XX, and will not be repeated in subsequent years, the surplus will be close to zero in the future years. The other concern regards the market for houses which, if it is expected to remain problematic, implies that further decreases in house values may occur.

The income statement, in combination with the balance sheet changes, gives us a view of the extent to which this household has been performing over the year 20XX. This is mainly because, in addition to cash inflows and cash outflows, the income statement accounts for changes in the value of assets, while it ignores the purchase of assets and the repayment of loans. Note that there are some differences in the treatment of the motor car and the house in this example. The decrease in the value of the new car is because its value has been reduced through its use, in this example one-fifth of its total useful life – this expense is called depreciation. In contrast, the fall in the value of the house has resulted from the use of market values or prices, rather than deterioration in the house itself. The cash flow statement is also important as it gives information about the extent to which a household receives sufficient money for all its payments, and whether its bank deposit is high enough to cover possible cash deficits.

Relationships between the financial documents

The surplus over 20XX can be related to the changes in the balance sheet items at the end of the year in comparison with those at the beginning of the year.

Changes in assets (U = unfavourable; F = favourable):
- The value of the house decreased from €400,000 to €388,000:   €12,000 U
- The value of the car increased from €6,000 to €24,000:   €18,000 F
- The bank deposit decreased from €15,000 to €5,000:   €10,000 U

Total of changes in assets   €4,000 U

Changes in liabilities (U = unfavourable; F = favourable):
- The value of the mortgage decreased from €300,000 to €290,000:   €10,000 F
- The student loan value decreased from €30,000 to €25,000:   €5,000 F

Total of changes in liabilities: €15,000 F

Changes in equity (U = unfavourable; F = favourable):

Asset value changes (€4,000 U) and liability value changes (€15,000 F) =   €11,000 F

Note that the purchases of assets and the repayments of liabilities do not influence the surplus or deficit in the income statement. Only balance sheet items will change. Suppose, for example, that an obligation for a part-repayment of the mortgage over 20XX did not exist, then the mortgage would remain at €300,000, which is €10,000 higher than the balance sheet at the end of the year in Table 2.4. However, the bank deposit would also be €10,000 higher than in the year-end balance sheet in Table 2.4. So, both sides of the balance sheet would be €10,000 higher, and equity would be the same as in Table 2.4. A similar analysis can be made for the purchase of assets: if the replacement of the car did not take place, the book value of the car would be €20,000 lower than in the year-end balance sheet in Table 2.4, but the bank deposit would be €20,000 higher.

We can also relate the income statement and the cash flow statement and explain why a cash deficit of €10,000 was registered in the cash flow statement, while the income statement shows a surplus of € 11,000.

The cash flow statement does not contain non-cash changes which are part of the income statement, i.e.:

– Reduction in the value of the house:	€12,000
– Depreciation of the car:	€ 4,000
– Total costs:	€16,000

On the other hand, the cash flow statement includes purchases of assets and repayments of loans, which are not part of the income statement, i.e.:

– Replacement of car: net cash outflow of €28,000 less €6,000 =	€22,000
– Part repayment of mortgage:	€10,000
– Part repayment of student loan:	€ 5,000
– Total cash outflows:	€37,000

We observe that cash outflows amounting to €37,000 were not seen as costs in the income statement, while €16,000 of the costs were not seen as cash outflows in the cash flow statement, which results in a difference of €21,000, which equals the difference between the cash deficit of €10,000 and the surplus of €11,000.

This completes our analysis of the finances of a private household. The next section expands this analysis by introducing some additional complications, based upon the accounts of a small production company.

2.3   Accounting documents of Baker and Baker, a small production company

Richard and June Baker are running a small catering company. They own this company together with their father, who primarily holds a background position since his retirement a couple of years ago. Father, brother and sister are the three directors of the company and they each own one-third of the shares in the company, which further employs three people on full-time contracts. The Baker and Baker Company prepares and delivers meals on demand, for example for wedding parties and staff parties and also for elderly people who can afford a meals-on-demand subscription.

Contrasted to the private household in the previous section, a production or manufacturing company earns money by producing and selling goods. This implies that we are dealing with similar accounting issues as in the previous section, such as depreciation of fixed assets, but now also other elements of the financial statement are discussed, especially accounts receivable, accounts payable and inventory, as well as provisions and the so-called costs of goods sold.

The current section on accounting for production and sales can be relevant for understanding public sector accounting because some public sector organizations also produce and sell services, for instance a museum, a municipal swimming pool or public transport company. Many governmental activities, however, do not lead to the production and sales of services, because they are fully funded by tax income, such as regional planning, social services and prisons. In these cases accounting for expenditure becomes the main issue.

The financial figures for 20XX

- The Baker and Baker Company is located in its own building with a market value of €750,000, which remains unchanged over the year; no depreciation is needed due to a solid maintenance practice.
- Kitchen equipment has an original purchase price of €150,000, with an expected lifetime of 5 years and 2 years to go (with no residual value).
- The company has a van for delivering meals, with an original purchase price of €50,000 and an expected lifetime of 3 years, 2 years to go and a residual value of €20,000.
- The bank deposit is €25,000 at the beginning of the year.
- Inventories of materials are €22,000 at the beginning of the year and €18,000 at the end of the year.
- Accounts receivable, related to sales which have not been paid for by customers, are €25,000 at the beginning of the year and €50,000 at the end of the year.
- Accounts payable, related to material costs purchased from suppliers, are €10,000 at the beginning of the year and €22,000 at the end of the year.
- The mortgage loan on the building is €400,000, without repayments during the year.
- There is other long-term debt of €280,000, of which €180,000 is a bank loan with a repayment obligation of €30,000 during 20XX, and €100,000 is a loan from Mr Baker senior with no repayment obligations during the year.
- Cash received from customers for sales during the year amounts to €700,000.

- Cash outflows to employees for salaries are €195,000 (including salaries for Richard and June Baker), to suppliers for materials €250,000, for interest €33,000, for distribution costs (van running expenses and deliveries) €55,000 and for others (administration, marketing, energy, etc.) €58,000.
- The company incurs maintenance costs on its building of €20,000 at the end of 20XX which has not yet been invoiced to the company for payment.
- For simplicity, taxes are ignored in this example.

The cash flow statement

Table 2.5 shows the cash flow statement: a cash surplus of €79,000 is realized over the year 20XX. So, the bank balance at the beginning of the year of €25,000 will be increased by €79,000 to be €104,000 at the year-end.

Table 2.5 Cash flow statement of the Baker and Baker Company over 20XX (in euros)

Cash inflows	
Received from customers	700,000
Cash outflows	
Salaries paid to employees	195,000
Material payments to suppliers	250,000
Interest paid	33,000
Distribution costs paid	55,000
Other payments	58,000
Repayment of bank loan	30,000
Total cash outflows	621,000
Cash surplus for the year (700,000 – 621,000)	79,000

The balance sheet at the beginning of the year

The balance sheet at the beginning of 20XX is shown in Table 2.6. Most of the assets can be straightforwardly derived from the data (building, stock, accounts receivable and bank balance). The book value of the kitchen equipment and the van deserve some explanation.

- Kitchen equipment has an original purchase price of €150,000, with an expected lifetime of 5 years and 2 years to go and no residual value; so, depreciation per year is €30,000 (20% of €150,000), and the book value at the beginning of the year is €60,000 (= €150,000 – 3 × €30,000) and €30,000 at the year-end (= €150,000 – 4 × €30,000).
- The company has a van for delivering meals, with an original purchase price of €50,000 and an expected lifetime of 3 years, 2 years to go and a residual value of €20,000; so, depreciation per year is €10,000 (33% of €50,000 less €20,000), and the book value at the beginning of the year is €40,000 (= €50,000 – 1 × €10,000) and €30,000 at the year-end (= €50,000 – 2 × €10,000).

All liabilities can be straightforwardly derived from the data (accounts payable and loans from the bank and Mr Baker senior). The value of the assets is higher than the value of the liabilities; the difference is called equity (owners' capital), which is €232,000.

Table 2.6 Balance sheet of the Baker and Baker Company at 1 January 20XX (in euros)

Assets

Building: at cost		750,000
Kitchen equipment:	Cost 150,000 – Accumulated Depreciation 90,000	60,000
Motor van:	Cost 50,000 – Accumulated Depreciation 10,000	40,000
Inventory		22,000
Accounts receivable		25,000
Bank account		25,000
Total assets		922,000

Liabilities

Accounts payable	10,000
Mortgage loan	400,000
Bank loan	180,000
Loan: Mr Baker senior	100,000
Total liabilities	690,000
Equity	232,000

The income statement

The income statement in Table 2.7 compares the income over 20XX with the costs *which can be attributed to that year*. The objective is to match the revenues earned in 20XX with the costs incurred in generating that income. In this simple example, many cash outflows are equal to the costs. This applies to salaries, interest, distribution costs and other costs. The depreciation of the kitchen equipment and the van has been explained above. Three other items require further explanation:

– Material costs: Cash outflows for materials amount to €250,000. However, two adjustments have to be made to the amount paid in the year in order to find the material costs incurred in generating the sales income. First, the inventory of materials was €22,000 at the beginning of the year and €18,000 at the end of the year, which means that the stock of materials used during the year was €4,000 higher than the amounts paid for in cash. Second, the accounts payable (related to amounts for material costs owing to suppliers) were €10,000 at the beginning of the year and €22,000 at the end of the year, which means that materials purchased from suppliers during the year are €12,000 higher than the amounts paid for in cash So, material costs used to generate sales during the year are: €250,000 (the cash outflows for materials) + €4,000 (the decrease in the stock of materials over the year) + €12,000 (the increase in the accounts payable to suppliers for materials over the year) = €266,000.

– Provision for maintenance costs: The business has incurred a cost of €20,000 for maintenance of its building towards the end of the year. The work has been completed but Baker and Baker Company has not yet received the invoice for the work done. However, this will be recorded as a cost for 20XX and as a liability at the end of the year because Baker and Baker have a contractual obligation for this payment now that the work on the premises has been done. The obligation in the balance sheet is called a *provision*, which means it is a known obligation where the precise amount (the €20,000 may only be an estimate) and/or the date of the payment for it (this depends on when the invoice is issued) are not known with certainty.

– Sales revenues: Cash sales were €700,000, but at the beginning of the year there were sales from the previous year for which payment was still due from customers (accounts receivable of €25,000 at 1 January 20XX), while at the end of the year sales of €50,000 were still due from customers (accounts receivable of €50,000 at 31 December 20XX); so sales taking place in 20XX were €700,000 – €25,000 + €50,000 = €725,000.

Table 2.7 Income statement of the Baker and Baker Company over 20XX (in euros)

Sales revenues		725,000
Costs of sales		266,000
Gross profit		459,000
Expenses		
Salaries	195,000	
Interest costs	33,000	
Distribution costs	55,000	
Other costs	58,000	
Depreciation of equipment	30,000	
Depreciation of van	10,000	
Maintenance costs	20,000	
Total expenses		401,000
Net profit for the year		58,000

Table 2.7 shows a surplus (called profit) on the income statement of €58,000, which is lower than the cash surplus of €79,000 (compare with Table 2.5). In business accounting a distinction is often made between gross-profit and net-profit. Gross-profit is equal to revenues less the costs of production, so €725,000 – €266,000 = €459,000. Costs of production are sometimes labelled as costs of goods sold. Net-profit is the gross-profit less all other costs, so €459,000 – (€195,000 + €33,000 + €55,000 + €58,000 + €30,000 + €10,000 + €20,000) = €58,000.

The balance sheet at the year-end

Table 2.8 shows the balance sheet at the end of 20XX. All components are explained above.

Table 2.8 Balance sheet of the Baker and Baker Company at 31 December 20XX (in euros)

Assets

Building: at cost		750,000
Kitchen equipment:	Cost 150,000 – Accumulated Depreciation 120,000	30,000
Motor van:	Cost 50,000 – Accumulated Depreciation 20,000	30,000
Inventory		18,000
Accounts receivable		50,000
Bank account		104,000
Total assets		982,000

Liabilities

Accounts payable	22,000
Provision for maintenance costs	20,000
Mortgage loan	400,000
Bank loan	150,000
Loan: Mr Baker senior	100,000
Total liabilities	692,000

Equity   290,000

Assessment of the financial position of Baker and Baker Company

Equity has increased from €232,000 to €290,000 (compare the balance sheets at the beginning and end of the year in Tables 2.6 and 2.8), which equals the surplus (profit) of €58,000 over the year (see the income statement in Table 2.7). We can relate the recorded profit to the equity at the year-end in order to find the return on investment for the owners: €58,000/€290,000 = 20%. This is a good result, at least much better than the return available if the Bakers had put their money in a savings account at their bank. The Bakers could withdraw some or all of the 20XX profit from the company for personal purposes – this will lower the equity remaining in the company – or they can leave it in the company as a buffer, for lowering the company's interest costs or for future investment in assets of the company.

Relationships between the financial documents

The surplus over 20XX can also be reconciled to the balance sheet items at the end of the year in comparison with those at the beginning of the year.

Changes in assets (U = unfavourable; F = favourable):

- Building value remained unchanged at 750,000:   €–
- Book value kitchen equipment decreased from 60,000 to 30,000: €30,000 U
- Book value van decreased from 40,000 to 30,000:   €10,000 U
- Accounts receivable increased from 25,000 to 50,000   €25,000 F
- Stock decreased from 22,000 to 18,000   €4,000 U
- Bank balance increased from 25,000 to 104,000   €79,000 F
- Total of changes in assets   €60,000 F

Changes in liabilities (U = unfavourable; F = favourable):

– Mortgage remained unchanged at 400,000	€–
– Bank loan decreased from 180,000 to 150,000	€30,000 F
– Loan from Mr Barker senior remains unchanged at 100,000	€–
– Maintenance provision increased from 0 to 20,000	€20,000 U
– Accounts payable increased from 10,000 to 22,000	€12,000 U
– Total of changes in liabilities:	€2,000 U

Equity:

Changes in asset values (€60,000 F) combined with changes in liability values (€2,000 U) resulted in an increase of equity (equivalent to the net profit) of   €58,000 F

We can also reconcile the income statement to the cash flow statement and explain why a cash surplus of €79,000 was recorded in the cash flow statement, whereas the income statement shows a surplus or profit of €58,000.

The cash flow statement does not contain non-cash changes which are part of the income statement, i.e.:

– Depreciation of the kitchen equipment		€30,000
– Depreciation of the van		€10,000
– Increase in the maintenance provision		€20,000
– Material use by decreasing stock		€4,000
– Material use by increasing accounts payable		€12,000
– Less increase in accounts receivable	€25,000	
– Total		€51,000

On the other hand, the cash flow statement includes a repayment of a loan of €30,000, which is not part of the income statement. Consequently the cash flow statement shows a €21,000 (= €51,000 – €30,000) higher surplus than the income statement, which is confirmed by the difference between the cash surplus of €79,000 and the profit of €58,000.

This completes our analysis of the finances of a simple production company. In this chapter we have illustrated an accounting system called *accrual accounting* using the two examples of this and the previous section. This gives an appropriate opportunity to define and explain this accounting system more explicitly now.

Accrual accounting

In drafting an income statement of an organization for a particular year in combination with its balance sheets at the beginning and end of the year, we are trying to give a fair view of its financial performance and position over the year. In the income statement, the revenues attributed to that year are matched against the

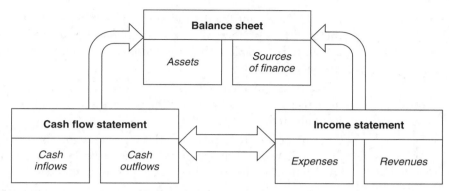

Figure 2.1 The three components of accounting
Source: Adapted from Lüder, 1999.

resources consumed to realize those revenues. For example, we take into account the depreciation of fixed assets as an expense in the income statement, rather than the full purchase price of such a fixed asset, which will instead be recorded in the balance sheet. This also explains why the cash outflows for materials have to be adjusted by the changes in the inventory and changes in the accounts payable to find the real resource consumption for the costs of goods sold. Similarly, the cost of maintenance of the building is treated as a cost for the year, although it will not be paid for in cash until the following year. In all these cases we need the balance sheet to connect changes in cash flows to changes in costs and revenues in the income statement. This applies, for instance, to the book values of fixed assets, the stock, the accounts receivable, the accounts payable and the provisions. This accounting system, which matches the revenues with the related resource consumption, is called accrual accounting. Literally accrual means the accumulation (of financial data concerning relevant economic events) over a certain period.

Accrual accounting is more complex than cash-based accounting, because the latter only registers the cash inflows and cash outflows within a certain year. But we can afford complexity by using accrual accounting because it can give us better information for decision-making and control, particularly regarding the financial surplus or deficit of the activities of an organization, the costs of these activities (for an assessment of efficiency) and the value changes in assets and liabilities.

Figure 2.1 summarizes the relationships between the balance sheet, the income statement and the cash flow statement as explained and illustrated in this chapter. It clarifies that a transaction or an event leads to simultaneous changes in two or all three of these financial documents. A few examples can illustrate this:

– Paying monthly salaries to the employees of an organization leads to a cost on the income statement and a cash outflow on the cash flow statement, as well as a decrease of the bank deposit on the balance sheet.
– A sales transaction at the end of the year for which 50% is paid by the customer in this year and the other 50% in the next year leads to a sales revenue on the

income statement for the full amount, to a cash inflow of half the amount on the cash flow statement and to an increase in both the bank deposit and the accounts receivable of half the amount at the year-end in the assets shown in the balance sheet.

– A depreciation charge leads to an expense in the income statement and a decrease of the book value on the balance sheet, while the cash flow statement is unaffected.

– A contribution to a provision leads to an expense in the income statement and an increase in the liabilities recorded in the balance sheet; it is a non-cash transaction, so the cash flow statement us unaffected.

– Repayment of a loan leads to a decrease in the bank deposit and the loan in the assets and liabilities in the balance sheet respectively, as well as a cash outflow in the cash flow statement, but it leaves the income statement unaffected.

These are examples of bookkeeping which underlie the drafting of the three components of accounting, as shown in Figure 2.1. Appendix A.3.1 (in Chapter 3) contains further notes on the essentials of bookkeeping.

Presentation of the financial statements

The balance sheet, income statement and cash flow statement can be presented in a number of different ways, so do not be surprised if you find different formats of these statements when you look through annual reports and accounts of organizations. This chapter uses the vertical form of presentation of these statements. However, there is a horizontal form of presentation in which, typically, the balance sheet shows the assets on the left-hand side and the liabilities and equity on the right-hand side, and in the income statement expenses are shown on the left-hand side and revenues on the right-hand side. A horizontal method of presenting individual accounts in bookkeeping is called a *T-form of accounts*.

Examining real-life examples of financial statements will often be much more complicated than the simple examples used in this chapter. Do not be put off by this! The principles of the preparation of financial statements still apply as shown in this chapter.

2.4   Key accounting terms

This section lists a number important accounting terms as introduced and illustrated in this chapter.

Financial statements:

– The balance sheet provides an overview of the assets and sources of finance (liabilities and equity) at a certain moment, often the year-end;

– The income statement (or operations statement or profit-and-loss account or income and expenditure account) gives an overview of the expenses/costs and income/revenues during the year;

– The cash flow statement produces an overview of the cash inflows and cash outflows during the year.

Terms in the financial documents:

– Assets are the resources available to the organization for performing its activities; they are often classified in a balance sheet into:

  ○ Fixed assets which are those held for continued use by the organization and which have a useful lifetime of more than one year (such as buildings, machines and equipment); and

  ○ Current assets which are not held for continued use by the organization and which usually have a lifetime of less than one year and are easily transferable into cash (such as inventories, accounts receivable and bank deposits).

– Liabilities are the sources of financing the assets with obligations to others outside the organization; they are often classified into:

  ○ Long-term liabilities with a repayment obligation beyond one year from the date of the balance sheet (such as a mortgage, a long-term loan from a bank and some long-term provisions); and

  ○ Current liabilities with a repayment obligation within one year of the balance sheet date (such as accounts payable and a bank overdraft and short-term provisions).

– Equity is the owners' own capital in the organization as part of the total sources of financing the assets (calculated as assets less liabilities).

– Provision is an accumulation of costs over more than one year which will lead to a cash outflow in the future, such a maintenance provision or a pension provision; a provision is an obligation for payments in the future, while the exact value or timing of this obligation is uncertain and has to be estimated (a provision is a liability).

– Revenues are the amounts recorded in the income statement as a source of funding for the activities of the organization attributed to a year, such as revenues from sales, subsidies or taxes.

– Costs are the amounts recorded in the income statement to reflect the resources consumed in generating the revenues, such as salary costs, material cost and depreciation.

– Expenses are equivalent to costs.

– Cash inflows are the flows of cash coming into the organization, also called cash receipts.

– Cash outflows are the flows of cash going out of the organization, also called cash payments.
– Depreciation is the value reduction of a fixed asset due to a reduction in its economic use to the organization, e.g. as a result of its use during a year.
– Book value is the net value of a fixed asset in the balance sheet; typically this is the purchase price of the fixed asset less the cumulative depreciation during its lifetime to date.

Accounting systems:

– Cash accounting is based on the recording of cash inflows and cash outflows during the accounting period.
– Accrual accounting is based on the recording of the revenues attributed to the accounting period and the recording of the cost of the resources consumed to realize those revenues.

2.5   Concluding remarks

This chapter has introduced some basic accounting knowledge. The main accounting documents considered here were the balance sheet, the income statement and the cash flow statement. These three documents, including their relationships, were illustrated for two simple cases.

This chapter has shown that a cash flow statement, which contains an overview of the incoming and outgoing cash flows over a year, mostly does not provide a true view of the financial performance of an organization. It was argued that an income statement for a particular year in combination with its balance sheets at the beginning and end of the year gives a fair view of the organization's financial performance and position over the year. In the income statement, the revenues attributed to that year are matched against the resources consumed to realize those revenues. For example, the depreciation of fixed assets is taken as an expense in the income statement, rather than the full purchase price of such a fixed asset, which will instead be recorded in the balance sheet.

The chapter has also discussed the distinction between accrual-based and cash-based accounting. An interrelated use of an income statement and a balance sheet refers to a so-called accrual-based accounting system, whereas the exclusive use of a cash flow statement for indicating the organization's financial performance is related to a cash-based accounting system. Finally, this chapter has defined some key accounting terms, especially the different types of financial statement including their main elements.

The following three chapters, which deal with public sector accounting, build on the basic accounting knowledge provided in the current chapter.

References

Gowthorpe, C. (2005), *Business Accounting and Finance for Non-specialists*, 2nd edition, South-Western-Cengage Reading, London.

Lüder, K. (1999), *Konzeptionelle Grundlagen des neuen kommunalen Rechnungswesens*, Speyerer Verfahren (Springer).

3

Financial statements of public sector organizations

Learning objectives

◆ To understand the nature of income and expenses of public sector organizations

◆ To understand the ways in which income and costs may be classified

◆ To be aware of the structure of and common items included within a balance sheet, an income statement and a cash flow statement of public sector organisations

◆ For those who are interested in some accounting procedures, to familiarize themselves with some bookkeeping knowledge

3.1 Introduction

This chapter builds upon the accounting basics of Chapter 2 by extending our knowledge and understanding of the income statement, the balance sheet and the cash flow statement in the context of public sector organizations. Section 3.2 introduces an example concerning the finances of a housing authority. This section considers the nature of income and costs of this public sector organization and shows how these can be classified in a number of different ways in the financial statements, using cash-based accounting to illustrate some of these methods. Section 3.3 considers further the distinction between cash-based and accrual-based accounting in public sector organizations. Section 3.4 outlines the structure of each of the main financial statements (income statement, balance sheet and cash flow statement) under accrual-based accounting using the earlier introduced example of the housing authority. In Section 3.5, we provide a brief review of the financial performance of this example and link the three financial statements to see the relationships between them. This enables us to relate the example of the current chapter to those of a household or a simple business organization that were described in Chapter 2. Section 3.6 is a short concluding section of the chapter. Appendix A.3.1 contains some notes and examples of the recording of transactions in the accounting records.

3.2   The nature of income and costs of a public sector organization

Public sector organizations, irrespective of their size and purpose, can be expected to receive income from a variety of sources and are faced with different types of costs in carrying out their activities. Public sector organizations may use different ways to categorize their income (or revenues), dependent upon the types of activities they perform or the information needs of their stakeholders. For example, the nature of the income of different public sector bodies will obviously vary considerably according to the nature of their activities. Central governments will typically rely on their tax collecting powers to obtain much of their income, local government authorities may obtain income from local tax collecting powers and also rely upon grants from central or regional government authorities. So, one feature of public sector accounting is that some public bodies are able to derive resources from transactions which do not involve a direct exchange of value with the other party; such arrangements are referred to as 'non-exchange transactions' (for example IPSASB, 2006). The most significant type of non-exchange transaction is the ability of governments to raise revenue from taxes. There may also be other non-exchange transfers of value, such as grants, fines and gifts for which public bodies receive value as revenue or give value as expenditure.

Some public sector bodies will obtain large proportions of their income from various forms of 'user charges'. For example, a housing authority will collect rents from its tenants while a public sector railway board or a motorway authority might collect fares or tolls from its passengers or road users. These may be referred to as 'exchange transactions' (IPSASB, 2001). The users get some direct benefit or service in exchange for the charges that they pay. Some public bodies may be required to raise revenue through user charges to cover all of their costs; others may use a combination of exchange transactions, such as user charges, and non-exchange transaction, such as grants or subsidies from public sources, to meet their operational and financial objectives.

In a similar way, while the incurring of costs is ubiquitous, the nature of such costs will vary from one type of public sector entity to another. Some public bodies will incur significant non-exchange transaction costs; for example the costs of national or regional social security payments and publicly funded health systems will often represent large expenditures of central and local government.

A common feature in the public sector is that the costs of staff employment, such as wages and salaries, pension contributions, employment taxes, training and staff development, form a high proportion of the total costs of the organization, because so many public sector organizations provide people-based services to individuals or groups of service users. Some public sector organizations will need to expend considerable resources on property, plant, equipment and materials to carry out their activities. For example, the armed services will need to equip their forces with weapons and defence systems, while healthcare bodies require medical facilities, premises and equipment to support some health interventions. Some public sector organizations may carry out their activities by contracting for services using intermediaries, such as private firms or voluntary sector bodies, so that much of their costs represent the procurement of external services rather than producing services directly to end users. These differences in operating methods may result in different structures of costs and, in some cases, lead to different ways of structuring the financial statements.

The different types of income and costs of public sector organizations are complicated further by the possibility that their financial statements might *classify* the items of income and costs in different ways. For example, items of income might be classified by the type of income that has been received, or by the source of such income, or by the particular programme for which income has been received. Similarly, the costs of items might also be classified by the type of costs incurred, by the function of each particular cost or by the programme to which it relates. In practice the allocation of income and costs into each category may be both complex and subjective, leading to some public sector organizations using the simplest available approach unless they are convinced that there are particular benefits, perhaps in terms of accountability to their stakeholders, in adopting a more complex allocation method.

There are, potentially, many different groups of stakeholders of public sector organizations. They may have different interests in the organization and their accountability needs may differ, so that it is unlikely that any set of financial documents can meet the needs of all stakeholders (see also Section 1.4 about multiple stakeholders in public sector accounting). For example, tax payers may have an interest in obtaining evidence that a public sector organization has used its resources effectively in achieving its objectives (value-for-money) or, more narrowly, that resources to it have been kept to a minimum to keep tax levels low. A user of public services may be interested in ensuring that a public sector organization is funded sufficiently to ensure that public services of an appropriate quantity and quality are available. Regulatory or oversight bodies may need to ensure that statutory duties have been achieved and that resources have been applied consistently with legal requirements. We conclude that these varied responsibilities to stakeholders may require public sector bodies to use multiple forms of communication with stakeholders. From a financial perspective, it is likely that information about the availability and use of resources is needed to provide an indication of how the organization has performed recently and the risks that it faces to remain sustainable in the future.

An example of financial statement preparation using cash-based accounting

An example below illustrates the main principles involved in using a cash-based accounting system. For simplicity, in this example, we will assume that all income is received and all costs are paid up in the year and that no assets or liabilities are to be recognized in the financial statements other than the bank balance. Payments for costs are also called expenditures. The statement of financial performance is represented by the cash flow statement.

The Acme County Housing Authority manages the rent collection and maintenance of three publicly owned housing estates (areas A, B and C). It collects rents and service charges from tenants. It also receives housing benefit (a form of social security) directly from the government and also grants and loans from a government-backed housing development fund as part of a housing capital subsidy scheme.

- At the start of the year its only asset is its working bank account balance of €200K.
- During the year it receives the following items of income:
  o Rents from tenants – A €1,200K; B €2,400K; C €3,000K
  o Housing benefit receipts – A €800K; B €1,600K; C€ 2,000K
  o Service charges – A €600K; B €1,000K; C €1,500K
  o Grants and loans received – A €1,200K; B €900K; C €NIL
- During the year it pays the following costs or expenditures:
  o Staff employment costs – A €400K; B €800K, C €1,300K; head office unallocated €300K.
  o Sub-contracting costs – A €1,500K; B €900K; C €1,400K.
  o Other costs – A €600K; B €1,100K; C €1,700K; head office unallocated €5,800.

From this we can calculate a cash surplus or deficit for the year and calculate the balance in the bank account at the end of the year. The individual figures can be calculated in different ways according to how the income and costs are classified. However the balance in the bank account at the end of the year, which would appear in the Authority's balance sheet, should be the same, irrespective of how the income and costs are classified.

Classification by type of income or expenditure

This statement can be compiled quite easily from the data provided and the result is shown in Table 3.1. As all transactions are cash or bank transactions, we can show this as a simple cash flow statement, similar to those shown in Chapter 2.

Table 3.1 Cash flow statement of the Acme County Housing Authority (in thousands of euros) classified by type of income and expenditure

Cash inflows

Rents (1,200 + 2,400 + 3,000)		6,600
Housing benefits (800 + 1,600 + 2,000)		4,400
Service charges (600 + 1,000 + 1,500)		3,100
Grants and loans received (1,200 + 900)		2,100
Total cash inflows		16,200

Cash outflows

Staff costs (400 + 800 + 1,300 + 300)	2,800	
Sub-contracting (1,500 + 900 +1,400)	3,800	
Other costs (600 + 1,100 + 1,700 + 5,800)	9,200	
Total cash outflows		15,800
Net cash surplus for the year		400

The inflows and outflows are combined line-by-line based upon the type of income and expenditure. In this example, the income flows equate to the cash inflows of €16.2 million, while the costs equate to the cash outflows of €15.8 million, leaving a surplus for the year of €0.4 million. The allocation of income and costs in this way has the advantage of simplicity in that it involves merely combining similar types of transactions to arrive at the figures shown in the cash flow statement. One limitation of this approach is that it does not identify the financial impact of individual programmes or activities; in this case no analysis is provided of the separate financial impact of each of the three housing estates and the cost of the head office function.

Classification by activity or programme

An alternative to the 'line item' approach is to seek to classify income and costs according to separate activities or programmes. This can help to provide more useful information to inform decision-making and promote accountability for particular activities or programmes within an organization. Tenants in each of the areas or their representatives might, for instance, show a primary interest in the financial figures for their own area rather than the authority as a whole, raising questions such as: are sufficient resources available for maintenance and renovation; are housing rents not too high given the cost level?

We can adopt this approach in this example by restating the cash flow statement between the three housing estates and the head office function; this is shown in Table 3.2.

Table 3.2 Cash flow statement of the Acme County Housing Authority (in thousands of euros) classified by activity or programmes

Cash inflows

Area A (1,200 + 800 + 600 + 1,200)	3,800
Area B (2,400 + 1,600 + 1,000 + 900)	5,900
Area C (3,000 + 2,000 + 1,500 + 0)	6,500
Total cash inflows	16,200

Cash outflows

Area A (400 + 1,500 + 600)	2,500	
Area B (800 + 900 + 1,100)	2,800	
Area C (1,300 + 1,400 + 1,700)	4,400	
Head office (300 + 0 + 5,800)	6,100	
Total cash outflows		15,800
Net cash surplus for the year		400

This type of classification may draw out some interesting issues. In this example, it is not clear why the head office costs form such a large proportion of the total costs of the organization; this might because there could be a further allocation of some of these costs to each housing area or because the head office provides essential support such as legal, financial and administrative services that are not recharged to the individual housing areas. Alternatively, perhaps the head office is unnecessarily draining some of the resources of Acme! All three housing areas make a financial surplus. This might reasonably be expected as each makes a financial contribution to head office unallocated costs and to the surplus for the year of the organization. The following calculations provide a further insight into the cash surplus or deficit of each of the areas.

First, a comparison can be made between the cash inflows and 'own' cash outflows, without taking notice of the head office outflows, for each the areas:

– Area A: €3.8 less €2.5 = €1.3 and, as a percentage of the cash outflow, this gives a surplus of: €1.3/€2.5 = 52%.

– Area B: €5.9 less €2.8 = €3.1 and, as a percentage of the cash outflow, this gives a surplus of: €3.1/€2.8 = 111%.

– Area C: €6.5 less €4.4 = €2.1 and, as a percentage of the cash outflow, this gives a surplus of: €2.1/€4.4 = 48%.

So, it appears that area B is far more beneficial to the organization, at least in a financial sense, than the other two areas.

Second, as a further refinement, we could attribute the head office cash outflows to the areas proportionally to their own cash and then again calculate the net-cash result of each. Total head office cash outflows are 6.1, which is 62.9% of the total of the own cash outflows of the areas: 6.1 / (2.5 + 2.8 + 4.4) = 6.1 / 9.7 = 62.9%.

- Area A: €3.8 less €2.5 less 1.6 (= 62.9% of 2.5) = −€0.3 and as a percentage of the cash outflow: − €0.3/€4.1 = −7%.
- Area B: €5.9 less €2.8 less 1.8 (= 62.9% of 2.8) = €1.3 and as a percentage of the cash outflow: €1.3/€4.6 = 28%.
- Area C: €6.5 less €4.4 less 2.8 (= 62.9% of 4.4) = − €0.7 and as a percentage of the cash outflow: −€0.7/€7.2 = −10%.

So, we can conclude that, on a cash basis, area A breaks even, area B is very beneficial in a financial sense, while area C shows a loss. However, extreme care must be taken with the interpretation of these results. First, the income generated and expenses incurred during the year are not identified here because the cash basis of accounting has been used. The accruals basis, which takes into account uncollected income and expenses incurred but not paid, might result in a different set of conclusions. Second, it is not apparent whether the allocation of the head office costs by this simple percentage method is necessarily appropriate. Further information about the support services provided by the head office would provide a stronger basis of allocation of costs aligned to the services which each area receives from the head office.

The balance sheet

How does all this affect the organization's balance sheet? One option for cash-based accounting systems is to ignore the balance sheet altogether, as the organization's financial position is reflected solely by its cash and bank account balance in hand (asset) or overdraft (liability). We can, however, construct a simple balance sheet from this example. We saw in Chapter 2 that a surplus in the year results in an increase in the *equity* of the organization in its balance sheet and will be represented by an increase in the *net assets* (assets minus liabilities). In this very simple example we are assuming that all transactions are in cash and that the organization's only asset is the balance in its bank account. The surplus for the year in the cash flow statement results in the bank account balance increasing from €0.2 million by €0.4 million to €0.6 million by the end of the year. Table 3.3 shows the closing balance sheet.

Table 3.3 Balance sheet of the Acme County Housing Authority at 31 December (in thousands of euros)

Assets
Bank account   600

Sources of finance
Equity (opening 200 + surplus 400)   600

3.3   Comparing cash-based accounting with accrual-based accounting

The example used in Section 3.2 provided an illustration of accounting based entirely upon cash transactions.[1] The resulting financial statements represent a type of accounting known as *cash-based accounting*. The cash basis will be considered here before comparing it, later in this section, with a more comprehensive system called *accrual-based accounting*.

Cash-based accounting

Cash-based accounting is 'a basis of accounting that recognizes transactions and other events only when cash is received or paid' (IPSASB, 2010, p. 1397, *Financial Reporting under the Cash Basis of Accounting*, par. 1.2.1).

The cash basis of accounting results in the surplus or deficit for the year representing the change in cash and cash equivalents during the period. The income statement becomes essentially the same as the cash flow statement. There may be no balance sheet constructed or, if there is one, it indicates only the assets and liabilities within the definition of cash (i.e. under assets there may cash in hand, cash in bank accounts and short-term cash-like investments; under liabilities there is likely only to be bank overdrafts or other short-term obligations in bank accounts). In the example in Section 3.2, the accounts recognized a surplus of €0.4 million which resulted in the closing balance sheet showing a bank account balance and equity of €0.6 million.

The cash basis of accounting provides relatively little information to the users of financial statements because of its restricted scope; by definition any income, expense, asset or liability that is not represented by a cash receipt or payment will not be recognized in cash-based financial statements. Nevertheless, the cash basis of accounting is adopted by public sector organizations in many parts of the world and is accepted by the International Public Sector Accounting Standards Board (IPSASB) as a basis for the presentation of financial statements of public sector bodies. However, IPSASB encourages governments to progress to the accrual basis of accounting and to harmonize national requirements in line with IPSASB's accrual-based standards (IPSASB, 2010, p. 1388).

Accrual-based accounting

Accrual-based accounting is 'A basis of accounting under which transactions and other events are recognized when they occur (and not only when cash or its equivalent is received or paid). Therefore, the transactions and events are recorded in

---

[1]   In this context cash transactions include cash (notes and coins), receipts and payments made through working bank (current) accounts, together with bank deposits which are accessible on demand and 'cash equivalents' which are short-term, highly liquid investments that are readily convertible into known amounts of cash.

the accounting records and recognized in the financial statements of the periods to which they relate. The elements recognized under accrual accounting are assets, liabilities, net assets/equity, revenue and expenses' (IPSASB, 2010, p. 1513, *Glossary of Defined Terms*).

The accrual basis of accounting was used in the examples in Chapter 2. Accrual-based accounting has a number of significant features which distinguishes it from cash-based accounting:

1. Revenue (or income) and expenses (or costs) in the income statement will not consist entirely of cash transactions. As illustrated in the previous chapter, depreciation is, for example, a cost in the income statement but not a cash outflow. As a result the surplus or deficit in the income statement will differ from that in the cash flow statement.

2. A greater variety of assets will be present in the balance sheet. There will be fixed or non-current assets, which may be used in the organization for a number of years, such as buildings and equipment. There will be other current assets (in addition to cash and bank balances) such as inventories and receivables.

3. A greater variety of liabilities will be present in the balance sheet. There will often be long-term liabilities, such as loans or debt, which are due to be repaid in more than one year from the date of the balance sheet. There will often be short-term or current liabilities (in addition to bank overdrafts) which are payable within one year of the balance sheet date, such as short-term debt and amounts payable to suppliers.

4. The change in total equity in the balance sheet is related to changes in all balance sheet items, not just the cash position. Often the total equity in the balance sheet of a public sector organization will be sub-divided into different categories (known as reserves or funds) to reflect the different uses to which the resources of the organization may be put in the future.

3.4   An example of financial statement preparation using accrual-based accounting

We will use the same example of the Acme County Housing Authority but with additional information provided to enable us to use an accrual basis of accounting. Here is the financial information for this example:

The Acme County Housing Authority manages the rent collection and maintenance of three publicly owned housing estates (areas A, B and C). We will now assume that the Authority owns the properties on the estates and that these are mainly financed by long-term debt.

– At the start of the year it had the following assets: housing properties valued at €110.0 million; house property internal fittings of €10.0 million; machinery and equipment with a cost of €2.0 million minus accumulated depreciation of €0.8 million; rents due from tenants from the previous year of €0.3 million; and a bank account of €0.2 million. Liabilities of the Authority consist of long-term debt of €80.0 million; and amounts owing to sub-contractors of €1.0 million.

- During the year it receives in cash the following items of income;
  o Rents from tenants – A €1.2 million; B €2.4 million; C €3.0 million; (total €6.6 million)
  o Housing benefit: – A €0.8 million; B €1.6 million; C €2 million; (total €4.4 million)
  o Service charges – A€ 0.6 million; B €1 million; C €1.5 million; (total €3.1 million)
  o Grants and loans – A €1.2 million; B €0.9 million; C €NIL; (total €2.1 million)
  o The €1.2 million for area A is a long-term loan repayable over 20 years towards the cost of constructing additional properties. The €0.9 million for area B is a grant received for a community safety project completed during the year.

- Rents owing from tenants at the end of the year are: A €0.2 million; B €0.1 million; C €0.2 million; (total €0.5 million). Housing benefit receipts are up to date.

- During the year it pays in cash the following costs:
  o Staff employment costs – A €0.4 million; B €0.8 million, C €1.3 million; head office unallocated €0.3 million; (total €2.8 million).
  o Sub-contracting costs – A €1.5 million; B €0.9 million; C €1.4 million; (total €3.8 million).
  o The sub-contracting costs are all for routine repairs and maintenance of properties except for a scheme of internal refurbishment in area A costing €1.1 million.
  o Other costs – A €0.6 million; B €1.1 million; C €1.7 million; head office unallocated €5.8 million; (total €9.2 million).
  o The head office unallocated costs of €5.8 million include €1.8 million for the construction of additional housing stock in area A; €1.0 million towards the community safety project in area B; €2.7 million interest paid on long-term debt and €0.3 million capital repayment of long-term debt.

- Amounts owing to sub-contractors at the end of the year, for maintenance costs, were €1.2 million.

- The properties are maintained in good condition and are expected to be usable for about 50 years, so they are depreciated at 2% per annum based upon their value at the start of the year. Some of the internal fittings are renewed every ten years and a depreciation charge of €1.0 million is to be allowed for this.

- Depreciation on machinery and equipment of €0.4 million is to be provided.

– The housing stock is valued at the end of the year at €109.4 million with an additional €10.1 million for internal fittings, giving a total valuation of €119.5 million.

Balance sheet at the start of the year

The opening balance sheet, shown in Table 3.4, can be constructed from the information given at the beginning of the question.

Table 3.4 Balance sheet the Acme County Housing Authority at 1 January (in millions of euros)

Non-current assets	
House properties (110.0 + 10.0)	120.0
Machinery and equipment (2.0 − 0.8)	1.2
Current assets	
Receivables (rent)	0.3
Bank account	0.2
Total assets	121.7
Sources of finance	
Current liabilities	
Payables (sub-contractors)	1.0
Non-current liabilities	
Long-term	80.0
Total liabilities	81.0
Equity	40.7

The housing properties, including internal fittings, are given at a valuation. The other fixed assets of machinery and equipment are presented at cost (i.e. the purchase price paid in the past) minus its accumulated depreciation; you may recall that the resulting figure is called the net book value. The other two items are current assets – they are the amounts due from tenants for rent (receivables) at this date and the bank balance. The liabilities in the balance sheet consist of the long-term debt and the short-term or current liability (payables) due to sub-contractors. The difference between the total assets (€121.7 million) and the total liabilities (€81.0 million) is the equity figure (€40.7 million) needed to complete the balance sheet.

Cash flow statement

Drafting the cash inflows and cash outflows may appear to be much more complicated than the previous example. However, we can see that the total of receipts and payments are the same in both examples. So, we can construct the cash flow statement from the previous example, although there are some differences in analysis of individual items (see Table 3.5).

Table 3.5 Cash flow statement of the Acme County Housing Authority
(in millions of euros) classified by type of expenditure

Cash inflows

Rents (1.2 + 2.4 + 3.0	6.6
Housing benefits (0.8 + 1.6 + 2.0	4.4
Service charges (0.6 + 1.0 + 1.5	3.1
Loan received	1.2
Grant received	0.9
Total cash inflows	16.2

Cash outflows

Staff costs (0.4 + 0.8 + 1.3 + 0.3)	2.8	
Maintenance (0.4 + 0.9 + 1.4)	2.7	
Refurbishment (1.1 + 0.0 + 0.0)	1.1	
Construction of additional housing stock	1.8	
Community project costs	1.0	
Interest paid	2.7	
Repayment of debt	0.3	
Other costs (0.6 + 1.1 + 1.7)	3.4	
Total cash outflows		15.8
Net cash surplus for the year		0.4

Income statement

The calculations to determine the income statement will be considerably more complex than under the cash basis of accounting.

Receipts which represent amounts to be repaid will not appear as revenue in the income statement, but instead will be reported as liabilities in the balance sheet; the new loan received of €1.2 million is an example of this. The revenues reported in the income statement should represent the amount due in the year, not necessarily the amount of cash received; the calculation of rental income (below) is an example of this.

Payments for acquiring additional fixed assets will be recognized in the balance sheet rather than being treated as expenses in the income statement; the amounts paid for new housing stock, for community facilities and for refurbishment are examples of this. Expenses for the year should reflect those amounts due over the year, not necessarily the amounts paid; the calculation of sub-contracting costs (below) is an example of this. Amounts paid during the year that reduce liabilities affect the balance sheet and not the income statement; the part-repayment of long-term debt is an example of this.

On the other hand there will be expenses to recognize in the income statement that do not result from cash transactions in the year; depreciation of fittings and machinery and equipment are examples of this together with the loss on the value of the housing stock as a result of market price changes. Table 3.6 shows the income statement of the Authority for the year, followed by an explanation of the calculation of each figure within the income statement.

Table 3.6   Income statement of the Acme County Housing Authority (in millions of euros)

Revenues (income)

Rents (note a)		6.8
Housing benefits (note b1)		4.4
Service charges (note b2)		3.1
Grant received (note c)		0.9
Total income		15.2

Expenses (costs)

Staff costs (note d)	2.8	
Sub-contract maintenance (note e)	2.9	
Other costs (note f)	3.4	
Community safety project (note g)	1.0	
Interest on debt (note h)	2.7	
Depreciation of housing (note i)	2.2	
Depreciation of machinery (note j)	0.4	
Depreciation of fittings (note k)	1.0	
Fall in value of properties (note l)	0.2	
Total expenses		16.6
Deficit for the year		1.4

a. Income for rents is based upon the total rents received and receivable for the year, rather than the amounts received. It is computed from the cash received (€6.6) minus the amount owing for last year's rents (€0.3) plus the rent still owing from tenants at the end of the year (€0.5).

b. (1) The housing benefits income here is the amount received (€4.4) because the benefits received are up to date. (2) The service charge income here is the amount received (€3.1) because there is no mention of service charges due at the start or end of the year.

c. The grant income is the amount received during the year (€0.9). Note that the loan received (€1.2) is not recorded as income because, unlike the grant, it is repayable in the future and so is recognized, instead, in the balance sheet as a liability.

d. Staff costs recognized in the income statement are equal to the amount paid in the year (€2.8) because there are no amounts owing to employees at the start or end of the year.

e. Sub-contracting costs are calculated as the amount paid (€2.7) minus the amount that was owing at the start of the year which relates to last year's costs (€1.0) plus the amount still owing to sub-contractors for maintenance costs at the end of the current year (€1.2).

f. Other costs are the amounts paid during the year but excluding the community project costs and interest on loans (which are listed further down in the income statement) and excluding the capital expenditure on new housing (€1.8) which is added to the value of the housing stock in the balance sheet.

g. The costs of the community safety project are treated as an expense here, on the assumption that it is not capital expenditure that directly increases the value of the housing stock.

h. Interest on the long-term debt was paid during the year. The repayment element (€0.3) of long-term debt is not shown here because it reduces the liability owing in the balance sheet.

i. The assumption being made here is that the houses have a useful economic life of fifty years so that they are being depreciated at 2% per annum. An important principle of depreciation is that it should be accounted for as an expense when fixed assets have a limited useful life, even if the market value of the asset temporarily increases during that lifetime period. The expense is therefore 2% of €110 million = €2.2 million.

j. This depreciation charge must be included as an expense as it reduces the net book value of the machinery and equipment in the balance sheet.

k. This depreciation charge must be included as an expense as it reduces the net book value of the house fittings in the balance sheet.

l. The market value of the properties appears to have fallen during the year and this reduction is recognized in the income statement and matches the fall in the value of the housing stock in the balance sheet. The calculation is as follows:

The houses and fittings at the start of the year (€110.0 + €10.0)	€120.0
Add the additional capital expenditure (€1.8 + €1.1)	€ 2.9
Deduct the depreciation of the houses and fittings (€2.2 + €1.0)	−€ 3.2
Ignoring changes in market value, this gives:	€119.7
The value at the end of the year of (€109.4 + €10.1)	€119.5
Giving a loss in market value during the year of	€ 0.2

The balance sheet at the year-end

Table 3.7 shows the balance sheet at the end of the year.

Table 3.7   Balance sheet the Acme County Housing Authority at 31 December (in millions of euros)

Non-current assets	
House properties (note m)	119.5
Machinery and equipment (note n)	0.8
Current assets	
Receivables (note o)	0.5
Bank account (note p)	0.6
Total assets	121.4
Sources of finance	
Current liabilities	
Payables (note q)	1.2
Non-current liabilities	
Long-term debt (note r)	80.9
Total liabilities	82.1
Equity (note s)	39.3

m. The book value of the properties at the start of the year of €120.0 is increased by the additional capital expenditure in the year of €2.9 and is reduced by the depreciation expense for the year of €3.2 and the fall in market value of €0.2. See note l to Table 3.6 above.

n. The book value at the start of the year of €1.2 is reduced by the depreciation expense of €0.4.

o. The receivables relate to rent owed by tenants referred to in note a to Table 3.6 above.

p. The bank account at the start of the year of €0.2 in increased by the cash surplus over the year of €0.4.

q. The payables relate to sub-contracting costs; see note e to Table 3.6.

r. The long-term debt at the start of the year of €80.0 is increased by the new loans received of €1.2 and decreased by the capital repayment of €0.3; see note h to Table 3.6.

s. Note that if the income statement accounts for all income, expenses, gains and losses during the year then the net result in the income statement added, if a surplus, or deducted, if a deficit, from the equity at the start of the year, should produce an equilibrium in which *assets = liabilities + equity*. We can see that equity decreased during the year from €40.7 (balance sheet at the start of the year in Table 3.4) to €39.3 (balance sheet at the end of the year in Table 3.7), which is equivalent to the deficit of €1.4 shown on the income statement (see Table 3.6).

3.5   Assessment of finances and the linkages between the financial statements

So how did the Acme County Housing Authority perform, in a financial sense, during the year and how has its state of wealth changed during this year?

The cash flow statement reports a small surplus of €0.4 million, increasing the bank balance to €0.6 million by the end of the year. In contrast, the income statement reported a deficit of €1.4 million which is reflected by the fall in the net assets during the year. As in Chapter 2, we can explain these differences by understanding that the income statement reflects a wider range of value changes during the year than does the cash flow statement. The differences between the income statement and the cash flow statement are caused by income or costs which have not affected the cash position during the year.

A reconciliation between the reported loss in the income statement and the changes in the bank balance during the year is given below. This type of reconciliation is typical of what might be expected to be given as a note to the cash flow statement in a published set of accounts.

The deficit recognized in the income statement for the year was €1.4 million

We need to allow for changes in short-term assets and liabilities which have changed in the balance sheet over the year because cash has not been paid or received. These are quite small items here and, by coincidence, they happen to cancel each other out:

Receivables for rent have increased from €0.3 to €0.5 million	€0.2 million
Payables to sub-contractors have increased from €1.0 to €1.2 million	€0.2 million
Net total	€0.0 million

To calculate cash flow we need to add back those costs or expenses which do not represent cash payments in the year. These are:

The depreciation charge on the housing stock	€2.2 million
The depreciation charge on machinery and equipment	€0.4 million
The depreciation charge on fittings	€1.0 million
The fall in the market value of the property	€0.2 million
Net total	€3.8 million

We need to allow for the cash paid or received for items which affect the balance sheet rather than the income statement – mainly payments to buy fixed assets or to repay long-term loans and receipts from the sale of fixed assets or obtaining new long-term loans. These are:

Payment to purchase additional house properties	€1.8 million
Payment for internal refurbishment	€1.1 million
Payment to repay part of the long-term debt	€0.3 million
Less: receipt from new long-term loan	€1.2 million
Net total	€2.0 million

So the overall increase in cash is $(-€1.4 + €3.8 - €2.0)$ million $= €0.4$ million

The organization has managed to produce a small cash surplus, but its wider measure of income, using accrual-based accounting, shows a deficit for the year. The fall in value of the housing may only be a temporary setback caused by falling market prices. The Authority is likely to take a long-term view about its property portfolio, so that only continuing losses on property value would cause concern. Its repayment of long-term debt is low at only €0.3 million, but this may reflect a planned schedule of repayments over a long period. We do not know how successful the Authority has been in achieving its non-financial objectives (or indeed even what those objectives are) so it is difficult to draw clear conclusions from the limited information supplied. There is no immediate reason to believe that the organization is in financial difficulty as its level of debt appears to be well below the value of its property portfolio.

It is useful to remind ourselves here that the resources available to public sector organizations are often restricted by annual budgets set by central, regional or local governments. The budget of public sector bodies assumes an importance that may be greater than in the private sector. This is because the level and type of activity of public sector bodies is often driven by the budget (resources) made available to it from higher authorities. In contrast, the budgets of private sector businesses are more likely to be determined by expected or actual levels of sales revenues from customers. So, in the example of the Acme Housing Authority described above it would helpful to have knowledge of the expected (budgeted) performance for the year as well as the actual (out-turn) results given above. Furthermore, we might expect the budgets to include longer-term financial projections, e.g. the expected levels of borrowing and repayments of such borrowings, so that the current year position could be compared with those longer-term plans. The comparison of budgeting (plans) and financial reporting (out-turn) is an important part of the financial management of all public sector organizations (see also Section 1.4).

3.6   Concluding remarks

This chapter has outlined the principles of cash-based and accrual-based accounting in the context of public sector entities. In some countries, accrual-based accounting is used for both budgeting and financial reporting; in other countries cash-based accounting is used extensively, either for budgeting or financial reporting or for both. There are a number of reasons why different jurisdictions take alternative approaches to their accounting procedures.

First, we have seen in this chapter, even with the use of highly simplified examples, that the accrual basis of accounting is much more complex to apply than cash-based accounting, requiring more sophisticated information systems and involving much more judgment in its application of techniques to particular economic events. Public sector bodies, ranging from governments to individual entities, may not consider that they have the skills or resources to adopt accrual-based accounting or may be unconvinced by the benefits of accrual accounting when compared with the additional costs incurred by its implementation.

Second, the cash-basis of accounting may be considered to be more relevant to short-term decision making, when the availability of cash to meet current obligations is of paramount importance. For example, short-term budgeting decisions are often about how to use the limited cash which is available to meet short-term operational objectives. In these types of decisions the treatment of the event for accrual-based financial reporting may be of little concern. A possible outcome of this perspective is that budgets continue to be constructed and used on a cash basis even if annual financial reporting is switched to an accrual-based approach. However, the absence, in cash accounting, of records of longer-term assets and liabilities remains a fundamental weakness of cash-based accounting. Governments may consider it appropriate to develop accrual-based accounting systems while continuing to regard, and to measure, the cash position of public sector organizations; for example, accrual accounting can still be adopted alongside a strong position on cash control using the cash flow statement, cash-based budgets and applying strict borrowing limits to departments and agencies.

Third, it might be considered by public authorities that a cash perspective on public spending is more appropriate for its link to fiscal policy (such as rates of taxation) than accrual-based accounting. For example, a local government authority may wish, or be required, to limit its tax collection to meet its spending obligations over a relatively short period rather than to build up large cash reserves for future projects. These circumstances may imply that cash-based financial reporting and budgeting is much more relevant to its decision about local taxation levels than an accrual-based reporting system that incorporates many non-cash transactions and events. Once again, a longer-term perspective may be encouraged through the use of accrual-based accounting and budgeting.

A number of broad concepts underlie accrual-based accounting. In order to limit the length of this chapter, these are included in Chapter 5, together with brief descriptions of how these concepts influence the financial statements of public sector entities. However, before these concepts are discussed, Chapter 4 is dedicated to a practice-oriented use of financial statements through so-called ratio analysis.

References

International Public Sector Accounting Standards Board (2001), *IPSAS 9 - Revenue from Exchange Transactions*, IFAC, New York.

International Public Sector Accounting Standards Board (2006), *IPSAS 23 - Revenue from Non-Exchange Transactions (Taxes and Transfers)*, IFAC, New York.

International Public Sector Accounting Standards Board (2010), *Handbook of International Public Sector Accounting Pronouncements*, IFAC, New York.

Appendix A.3.1 Notes on bookkeeping

What is bookkeeping?

Bookkeeping is the recording of the financial impacts of economic events of importance to an organization. A transaction implies a transfer of goods or services between two parties, e.g. between a seller and a buyer or between a landlord and a tenant. So, transactions include, for example, the sales of goods or services, the purchase of materials or the renting of a building. In some cases an event is not a transaction but an event or action with financial impacts, for instance, the depreciation of fixed assets, such as equipment or machines, or the contribution to a provision for future pensions payable to employees. Transactions or events are recorded one by one, but at the end of a certain period similar transactions and events can be totalled. This leads to, for example, totals of sales, depreciation costs and salary costs. These totals over a year are the inputs for an income statement and balance sheet as introduced in Chapter 2. Bookkeeping thus concerns necessary recordings for drafting the financial documents of an organization.

It goes beyond the scope of this book to provide a full description of systems of bookkeeping. It is only feasible to highlight some basic principles and to give some examples of bookkeeping entries.

Single-entry and double-entry bookkeeping

Two basic systems of bookkeeping can be distinguished. *Single-entry bookkeeping* only records each transaction once, for example, a receipt of money for sales in the sales account and a payment of salaries in the salary expenditure account. This is quite similar to making entries in the cash book of a private household or a simple organization, like an owners' union of an apartment building. Larger and more complex organizations in the public sector mostly make use of *double-entry bookkeeping*. This bookkeeping system is based on the premise that each transaction (or event) requires a *debit* entry on one account and an equal *credit* entry on another account. So, this system requires two related recordings for each transaction (or event), which explains the label 'double entry-bookkeeping'. Contrasted to single-entry bookkeeping, double-entry bookkeeping enables us to accomplish coherence and comprehensiveness in recording the financial impacts of transactions and events, and to follow the results through to create an income statement and a balance sheet.

Principles of double-entry bookkeeping

The fundamental rule in double-entry bookkeeping is for every *debit* entry in the accounts there is an equal value *credit* entry. This creates a logical connection between the income statement and the balance sheet. The surplus in the income statement, which is the result of higher revenues than costs over a certain year, equals the increase in equity over that year. And this increase in equity is the result of a positive difference between the value increase of the assets and liabilities over that year.

The total of debit and credit entries over a certain period (e.g. a year) has to be the same in double-entry bookkeeping. This is achieved by requiring that the debit and credit entries for each transaction or event are the same. How different types of accounts can be debited or credited will now be explained.

There are five types of accounts: assets, capital (equity), liabilities, revenues (income) and expenses.

1. Assets accounts: debit entries increase assets and credit entries decrease assets.
2. Liabilities accounts: credit entries increase liabilities and debit entries decrease liabilities.
3. Revenues or income accounts: credit entries increase revenues and debit entries decrease revenues.
4. Expenses or costs: debit entries increase expenses and credit entries decrease expenses.
5. Capital (or equity) accounts: credit entries increase capital and debit entries decrease capital.

Table A.3.1 summarizes these debit and credit rules.

There are logical relationships between these debit and credit rules, for example:

– Earning income by realizing revenues will have a two-sided impact: revenues will go up (credit) and bank deposit or a receivable (an asset) will go up (debit).
– Incurring costs for production resources (salary costs or material costs) will also have a two-sided effect: an increase in expenses or costs (debit) and an increase in a bank overdraft or an account payable, a liability (credit) or a decrease in cash at the bank (decrease in an asset).

This still looks quite abstract, but taking notice of the following examples will contribute to an understanding of double-entry bookkeeping.

Table A.3.1 Summary of debit and credit rules of the various types of accounts

Types of accounts	Debit entries in the account	Credit entries in the account
Assets accounts	Increase	Decrease
Liability accounts	Decrease	Increase
Revenues accounts	Decrease	Increase
Expenses accounts	Increase	Decrease
Capital or equity accounts	Decrease	Increase

Examples of recordings in double-entry bookkeeping

Seven examples of double-entry bookkeeping are given below. The examples are designed to show the effect on the income statement and balance sheet of an organization, rather than representing the format of any particular bookkeeping system. The first five examples were already introduced at the end of Chapter 2 and the sixth example comes from Chapter 3; the final example is public sector specific and concerns a tax transaction.

Example 1: A sales transaction

An organization completed a sales transaction at the end of the year 2012 of €500,000; 50% was paid in 2012 and the other 50% will be paid in the next year 2013. This leads to sales revenue on the income statement of €500,000, and to an increase in both the bank deposit and the accounts receivable at the year-end of Ăy250,000 each. Because the bank deposit and the accounts receivable, being assets, are increased by €250,000 each, these are debit bookings; the related credit booking is an increase of the sales revenues of €500,000. So, an increase on the left-hand side of the balance sheet (a debit entry) goes hand in hand with an increase on the right-hand side of one of these statements (a credit entry). The bookkeeping entries are:

Debit bank deposit	€250,000
Debit accounts receivable	€250,000
Credit sales revenues	€500,000

Tables A.3.2 and A.3.3 show these entries.[2]

Table A.3.2 The effect of the sales transaction in the income statement) (in euros)

Expenses (costs)	Revenues	
	Revenues from sales	500,000

Table A.3.3 The effect of the sales transaction in the balance sheet (in euros)

Assets		Sources of Finance
Bank deposit	250,000	
Accounts receivable	250,000	

---

2 Keep in mind that only this sales transaction is shown, while other bookings to make the balance sheet and income statement complete are disregarded; this remark also applies to the following examples.

Example 2: A payment transaction

An organization makes monthly payments for the salaries of its employees of €380,000. This leads to a cost on the income statement and a decrease of the bank deposit on the balance sheet. So, the bank deposit, being an asset on the left-hand side of the balance sheet, is decreased, which is a credit booking, while the salary cost, being an expense on the left-hand side of the income statement, is increased, which is a debit booking. The booking is thus:

Debit salary costs   €380,000
Credit bank deposit   €380,000

We assume in Tables A.3.4 and A.3.5 below that the bank deposit at the beginning of the month was €550,000, so this is reduced by €380,000 to €170,000. If there was no money in the bank account, the organization would need to arrange an overdraft facility and would have an overdraft of €380,000 after the transaction.

Example 3: A repayment of a loan

If an organization has to repay a loan amounting to €75,000 before the end of the year, this will lead to a decrease in the bank deposit on the asset side (a credit booking) and an equal decrease in the loan on the liability side (a debit booking) of the balance sheet. Note that the income statement remains unaffected. The booking is:

Debit loan   €75,000
Credit bank deposit   €75,000

The booking is shown in Table A.3.6, assuming that the available bank deposit before the repayment of the loan is €170,000 and that the loan is completely repaid after this transaction.

Table A.3.4 The effect of the payment transaction in the income statement) (in euros)

Expenses (costs)		Revenues
Salary costs	380,0000	

Table A.3.5 The effect of the payment transaction in the balance sheet (in euros)

Assets		Sources of finance
Bank deposit decrease from 550,000 by 380,000 to	170,000	

Table A.3.6 Effect of a loan repayment in the balance sheet at the year-end, 31 December 2012 (in euros)

Assets		Sources of finance	
Bank deposit decrease from 170,000 by 75,000 to	95,000	Loan decrease from 75,000 by 75,000 to	0

Example 4: Depreciation

An organization uses a van for transporting its products to its clients. The van was purchased at the beginning of 2010 at a price of €50,000; it will be used by the organization for three years and then be sold at a residual value of €20,000. So the yearly depreciation is €10,000 (€50,000 less €20,000 spread over three years). The book value of the van at the beginning of 2012 is then €30,000 (€50,000 less €20,000, i.e. two years of depreciation), while the depreciation cost is €10,000 in 2012. The recording of the depreciation expense for 2012 contains a depreciation cost (expense) on the left-hand side of the income statement, which is a debit entry, and a reduction of the book value of the van on the left-hand side of the balance sheet, which is a credit entry (i.e. an asset being reduced in value). So, the booking is:

Debit depreciation expense van   €10,000
Credit book value van   €10,000

Tables A.3.7 and A.3.8 show this booking.

Table A.3.7 Effect of the depreciation expense in the income statement (in euros)

Expenses (costs)		Revenues
Depreciation expense van	10,000	

Table A.3.8 Effect of depreciation in the balance sheet (in euros)

Assets		Sources of finance
Book value van decreases from 30,000 by 10,000 to	20,000	

Example 5: Provision

A public sector organization expects to incur legal obligations towards employees who are expected to be made redundant as a result of public expenditure cutbacks. It is uncertain how high the expenses will be, but a yearly obligation of €150,000

Table A.3.9 Redundancy costs in the income statements and the provision in the balance sheets from 2014 to 2017

2014	2015	2016	2017
Income statement	*Income statement*	*Income statement*	*Income statement*
Expense for the year = €150,000	Expense for the year = €160,000	Expense for the year= €175,000	Expense for the year = €6,000
Balance Sheet	*Balance Sheet*	*Balance Sheet*	*Balance Sheet*
Provision at year end = €150,000	Provision at year end = €310,000	Provision at year end = €175,000	Provision at year end = €0

in each of the years 2014, 2015 and 2016 is seen as the best guess, as around one-third of the total number of redundancies will occur in each year. Payments to these former employees are expected to be made in two stages; two thirds early in 2016 and the remaining amount in 2017. This means that each year, spread over the years 2014 up to and including 2016, an expense towards the redundancy provision has to be made of €150,000. By the end of 2015 the provision will be €300,000 (= 2 years x €150,000 each year). A payment of €300,000 is expected to be paid in 2016. A further expense of €150,000 will be charged to the provision in 2016 and then this provision covers the final bank payment expected in 2017.

Provisions are estimates of costs that have been incurred but where the precise amount and timing of the payment is uncertain. The uncertainty around the amount and timing of provisions means that they need to be estimated in each financial period, so the amount of the provision is adjusted to the best estimate that is available at the end of each financial period. In this example, let us suppose that the amount paid early in 2016 turns out to be €310,000 (rather than the €300,000 originally estimated) so that the provision at the end of 2015 is adjusted to reflect this new expectation. We will also assume that the provision required at the end of 2016 is reassessed to be €175,000, but that the final amount of redundancy payment in 2017 is €181,000.

The transactions in the accounting records are listed below and summarized in Table A.3.9.

Year 2014

Debit redundancy costs   €150,000
Credit provision for redundancy costs   €150,000
Explanation: this is the original estimate of €150,000 for the first year cost.

Year 2015

Debit redundancy costs	€160,000
Credit provision for redundancy costs	€160,000

Explanation: this consists of the original estimated costs of €150,000 plus the addition €10,000 needed to increase the provision to a total of €310,000, which will be paid early in the next accounting period.

Year 2016

Debit provision for redundancy costs	€310,000
Credit bank account	€310,000

Explanation: this is the payment made early in 2016.

Debit redundancy costs	€175,000
Credit provision for redundancy costs	€175,000

Explanation: this is the expected cost of the final redundancy payment that will be made in 2017.

Year 2017

Debit redundancy costs	€6,000
Credit provision for redundancy costs	€6,000

Explanation: there needs to be recorded a cost of €6,000 in 2017 because the provision created at the end of 2016 of €175,000 is too small to cover the final payment of €181,000.

Debit provision for redundancy costs	€181,000
Credit bank account	€181,000

Explanation: the final payment is made from the bank account and this clears the provision account.

This example shows that, as provisions are estimates of liabilities where the amount and timing of the payments are not known with certainty, the expense of the provision each year is likely to vary as estimates are adjusted over time based upon the most recent reliable information.

Example 6: Different steps in purchase of course material

A public sector agency is seeking to purchase a set of books about public sector accounting and budgeting for use on its staff training courses. Some time is spent investigating an appropriate text. After two weeks a decision is made and an order is placed with a publisher. Three weeks later, the books are received from the publisher, together with an invoice for the cost of the books (160 copies at €50 each, so €8,000 in total). The books are put into store in readiness for the course. Two weeks later the course is run and each participant is provided with a free copy of the book. A week after this the publisher's invoice is paid. The table below shows when entries might be made in the agency's accounting records.

	Cash-based accounting	Accrual-based accounting
Week 0: Investigation of an appropriate text book.	No entry because no cash has been paid.	No entry because no asset has been purchased and there is no obligation to pay.
Week 2: An order is placed with the publisher.	No entry because no cash has been paid.	No entry because the books have not yet been received and there is no obligation to pay until the supplier has met this contractual requirement.
Week 5: The books are received together with an invoice for the cost.	No entry because no cash has been paid.	AN ENTRY IS RECORDED as an asset (the cost of the books is included in the inventory of the agency) and as a liability (an obligation to pay the amount shown on the invoice to the publisher).
Week 7: The training course is held and the books are given out to course participants.	No entry because no cash has been paid.	AN ENTRY IS RECORDED as the inventory is reduced by the cost of the books used on the training course and these costs are added to cost of staff training.
Week 8: Payment is made to the publisher.	AN ENTRY IS RECORDED as the bank account balance is reduced and the amount paid is recorded as part of staff training costs.	AN ENTRY IS RECORDED as the bank balance is reduced and the liability to the publisher is eliminated.

What are the bookings under accrual accounting?
Books received (week 5)
Debit stock of books   €8,000
Credit accounts payable   €8,000
(balance sheet recordings)

Books provided to course participants (week 7)
Debit costs of courses   €8,000
Credit stock of books   €8,000
(income statement and balance sheet recordings respectively)

Payments of books (week 8)
Debit accounts payable   €8,000
Credit bank deposit   €8,000
(balance sheet recordings)

The income statement and balance sheet implications are obvious and not further shown.

Example 7: A tax transaction

A municipality raises property tax of €15.5 million in total in a certain year. In an accrual-based accounting system there would be at least two sets of transactions to record. The first is when the taxes are imposed and an estimate can be made of the expected tax revenue that will eventually be received. The second is when the taxes are paid to the municipality by the taxpayers. If we assume that all taxes are correctly assessed and are duly paid then the entries to record are as follows:

Taxes imposed:
Debit tax to be paid   €15,500,000
Credit tax revenues   €15,500,000
(balance sheet and income statement recordings respectively)

Taxes paid to the municipality:
Debit bank deposit   €15,500,000
Credit taxes to be paid   €15,500,000
(balance sheet recordings)

The income statement and balance sheet implications are obvious and not further shown.

4

Assessing the financial health of a public sector organization through ratio analysis

---

Learning objectives

- ◆ Understand what is meant by a financial ratio
- ◆ Being able to calculate and interpret financial ratios about solvency, liquidity and financial result
- ◆ Being able to suggest other types of ratios
- ◆ Understand how ratio analysis has to be conducted and used in a public sector context

---

4.1   Introduction

A financial ratio is the quotient of two figures on an organization's balance sheet, cash flow statement or income statement. The purpose of a financial ratio is to help the user to form a judgment about an organization's 'functioning' in the context of its use of resources (cash flow statement or income statement), or its financial position (balance sheet). A financial ratio provides a snapshot of an aspect of the organization's financial health. This is meaningful because the financial statements often contain too much information to make a relevant and quick judgment. Ratios may enable easier comparisons, than using absolute figures, between organizations of different size. This chapter conceptualizes ratio analysis as a financial management tool of an organization (see Gowthorpe, 2005, Chapter 13) for an introduction to ratio analysis in private sector companies). In addition, ratio analysis can be used by oversight bodies to detect current or future financial problems of the organizations that are subject to oversight (see Kloha et al., 2005).

This chapter introduces a specific public sector organization with its income statement, cash flow statement and balance sheet (Section 4.2). Important financial ratios can be calculated and interpreted on the basis of these documents (Section 4.3). After an overview of a variety of ratios (Section 4.4), the chapter discusses the way in which ratios can be used (Section 4.5). The chapter ends with some concluding remarks (Section 4.6).

4.2   An introduction to the financial statements of the municipality of Bergstadt

Public sector organizations have to account for their actions to relevant stakeholders. The yearly published financial statements are often the most important documents in this respect.

The financial figures

We will now present an example of the financial statements of a municipality called Bergstadt, which are based on accrual accounting. This means that expenses (or costs) and revenues are recognized when they are earned and incurred respectively, not when cash is received or paid. Moreover, costs and benefits of activities are matched (Chapter 3 discussed the distinction between accrual and cash accounting). In Tables 4.1, 4.2 and 4.3 the income statement, the cash flow statement and the balance sheet of Bergstadt are presented. Items in the financial statements are given a reference here to assist in the explanation of the ratios used later in the chapter. Such references would not usually be found in published financial statements.

Public sector organizations often present their income statement over a certain year in comparison with the budget over that year and the income statement over the previous year. Comparing budgeted and actual figures over a certain year is important for assessing the extent to which the plans of an organization are accomplished (see Chapter 1, Section 1.4, for the importance of this analysis of variances in a public sector context). The inclusion of actual figures over the previous year enables the user to assess the changes in the actual figures in the course of time. A closer look at Table 4.1 reveals that the accounts for 2013 show a deficit (expenses are larger than revenues), which obviously has stimulated the Bergstadt Legislative (i.e. the Council) to present a budget for 2014 which aims to show a surplus (with higher revenues than expenses). However, this policy has not been successful, because the accounts for the year 2014 also show a deficit.

Table 4.1 Income statement of Bergstadt for 2014 (in millions of euros)

		Accounts 2013	*Budget 2014*	*Accounts 2014*
Revenues				
R1	Taxes	12	13	12
R2	General (unrestricted) grants	8	8	8
R3	Specific (restricted) grants	11	12	11
R4	Fees and tariffs	6	8	7
R5	Total revenue	37	41	38
O	Deficit on operations	3	–	2
Expenses (costs)				
E1	Salary costs	25	22	24
E2	Depreciation	9	9	9
E3	Interest on debt liabilities	3	3	3
E4	Other expenses	3	4	4
E5	Total expenses	40	38	40
O	Surplus on operations	–	3	–

The cash flow statement (Table 4.2) includes actual cash flow figures over the current and the previous year, without giving budgetary cash flow figures over the current year. A cash flow statement can give a detailed overview of many different types of incoming and outgoing cash flows, but Table 4.2 is an example of a condensed type of cash flow statement. Only the net-cash flows are shown, being the differences between cash inflows and cash outflows. In addition, there are only two components: first, the operational cash flows which concern the operations of the municipality (taxes, fees and grants as revenues as well as operational expenditures), and second, the cash flows for investments and the way these investments are financed. Investments result in cash outflows and disinvestments in cash inflows. New loans for investments result in cash inflows and the repayment of existing loans leads to cash outflows.

Table 4.2 Cash flow statement of Bergstadt for 2014, condensed version (in millions of euros)

	2013	2014
Operational cash flows	7	6
Cash flows for investments and financing	−3	−8
Total net cash flow (= change in bank deposit)	4	−2

The balance sheet of a public sector organization presents an overview of assets and sources of finance at the end of the current year, and – for comparative reasons – at the end of the previous year, as Table 4.3 illustrates.

Table 4.3   Balance sheet of Bergstadt at 31–12–2013 and 31–12–2014 (in millions of euros)

		31–12–2013	31–12–2014
Fixed assets			
A11	Tangible assets	50	44
A12	Intangible assets	6	6
A1	Total fixed assets	56	50
Current assets			
A21	Bank and cash	12	10
A22	Accounts receivable	13	12
A23	Inventory	2	3
A2	Total current assets	27	25
A3 Total assets		83	75
Liabilities			
L11	Long-term liabilities	40	35
L12	Short-term liabilities	21	20
L1	Total liabilities	61	55
Equity			
L21	Unrestricted equity	10	8
L22	Restricted or Designated equity	12	12
L2	Total equity	22	20
L3	Total sources of finance	83	75

Further explanations of the figures in the income statement and balance sheet

The income statement

– The top section of this statement shows revenues and the lower section shows the expenses or costs of the organization.[1] This format is commonly used in public sector financial statements when the organization seeks to cover its costs through taxation and grants rather than directly selling services to its users.

– In the top section of the income statement, we see various types of revenues which are specific for municipalities: local taxes (for instance, property tax), general grants (revenues coming from central government without an obligation for a specific spending direction), block grants (revenues from central government with an obligation for a specific spending direction, for example for infrastructure or environmental affairs), fees and tariffs (related to prices of particular services, for example, for using the swimming pool or the library).

– In public sector organizations salary costs are often by far the most important, because these organizations are labour-intensive service providers. Costs of investment in assets are relatively less important for many public services,

---

1   However, in some countries, such as the UK, an opposite presentation is used, i.e., costs at the top and revenues in the lower section.

although for some services, for example infrastructure (roads, railways and canals), sewerage and garbage collection, and defence costs, the costs relating to the use of assets may be much higher than the salary costs.

- The use of accrual accounting is especially observable from the fact that this municipality does not account for new capital expenditure as an expense but charges depreciation of assets as an expense, being the estimated value of the use of fixed assets for service delivery. In Table 4.1, we see that depreciation is 9 in 2014, while the value of the fixed assets, in Table 4.3, is 50. Does this mean that on average depreciation is 18% (9/50)? No, because the original purchase price of the assets may be much higher than its current book value; if all assets are on average halfway through their lifetime, the original purchase value has been 100 (2 × 50), so depreciation is then only 9% of this purchase value (9/100).

- The debt interest costs are 3, which is about 5.5% of the total debt of 55 (see the liabilities section of the balance sheet).

- Other costs can include costs for material, energy and consultancy services.

- As with the balance sheet, the income statement has to show an equilibrium position: if revenues are higher than expenses, there is a surplus, and, if revenues are lower than expenses, there is a deficit (as in Table 4.1 – a deficit of 2 over 2014).

- How is the deficit financed? Answer: the equity at the beginning of the next year will be decreased by the value of the deficit; contrasted to that, a surplus will increase equity (in Table 4.3 equity decreases in the course of 2014 from 22 to 20).

The balance sheet

- Consists of assets in the top section (what the municipality possesses) and sources of finance in the lower sections (how the assets are financed).

- Fixed assets are assets with a long lifetime; they are mostly tangible, such as buildings and equipment (e.g. IT equipment and motor vehicles); some fixed assets may be intangible, such as patents (for unique processes) or goodwill (due to the market position of certain services); intangible assets are normally absent or unimportant in the public sector. Public sector organizations' tangible fixed assets may be classified between community assets, which do not have revenue earning power (for example parks and monuments) and economic assets (from which revenues are earned, such as garbage collection vans or public transport vehicles).

- Current assets are characterized by a short lifetime; these assets can be converted into money at short notice: for example, cash or bank deposits, accounts receivable (sales for which cash not has yet been received) and inventory which are converted into cash after payment by debtors.

- On the sources of finance side, we see liabilities or debts with a short and a long payback period, for example, payments due to be made to suppliers for goods or services already delivered to the organization (called accounts payable) and money borrowed from the bank as overdrafts or short-term debt, as well as mortgages on buildings or long-term debt.

- If we take the balance sheet at the end of 2014 and subtract the value of the liabilities (55) from the value of the assets (75), this results in equity (20), being the value of the assets not financed by debt, so to be considered as what the organization contributes to the financing of its own assets, i.e. 'its own wealth'. Equity may be divided into general equity (without any spending restriction) and restricted or designated equity (which has a specific direction for its future use, e.g. for a new swimming pool or theatre).

- Also note that the value of the assets has to be equal to the value of the sources of finance; this is the equilibrium requirement of the balance sheet.

How can the operating net cash flow in the cash flow statement be derived from the incomes statement and balance sheet?

Starting with the surplus or deficit from operations, there are a number of adjustments needed to move from the accruals basis to the cash basis to arrive at the net cash flow:

First, because *depreciation* is a non-cash item, the surplus or deficit in the income statement has to be corrected by adding back the depreciation to calculate the cash flow from operations (positive effect on cash flow).

Second, because *accounts receivable decrease* in the current year, this decrease is an additional cash inflow (think of this as if the organization has received additional cash from its customers regarding the previous year).

Third, because *stock increases* in the current year, this results in additional cash outflow (think of this as if the organization has spent some cash to buy extra stock).

Fourth, because *current liabilities decrease* in the current year, this results in a cash outflow (think of this as if the organization has spent cash to pay off some of the amount owing to suppliers from the previous year).

The calculations for 2014 are:

The surplus or deficit in the income statement (here deficit)	−2
Plus the depreciation expenses	9
	7
Plus the decrease in accounts receivable	1
	8
Less the increase in stock	1
	7
Less the decrease in current liabilities	1
End-result (net cash inflow)	6

How can the investment-financing net cash flow in the cash flow statement be derived from the income statement and balance sheet?

The fixed assets at the year-start are 56; depreciation during the year is 9.

So, without additional investments, the fixed assets at the year-end would be $56 - 9 = 47$.

However at the year-end fixed assets are 50, so additional investment must have been $50 - 47 = 3$ (cash outflow).

Long-term liabilities decreased from 40 at the year-start to 35 at the year-end, which is equivalent to a repayment of loans of 5 (cash outflow).

So, net cash outflow = 3 + 5 = 8.

The net cash inflow from operations of 6 plus the net cash outflow of investments/financing of 8 results in *a total net cash outflow of 2 (= 8 - 6)*; see Table 4.2.

This is confirmed by the decrease in the bank and cash account from 12 at the year-start to 10 at the year-end (see Table 4.3).

This explanation about the relationship between the cash flow statement and the income statement can also inform a more detailed version of the cash flow statement over 2014 than the condensed version of Table 4.2; see Table 4.4 (IS = Income Statement).

Table 4.4   Cash flow statement of Bergstadt for 2014, extended version (in millions of euros)

	Accounts 2014 (operations)
Revenues	
Taxes	12 (IS)
General (unrestricted) grants	8 (IS)
Specific (restricted) grants	11 (IS)
Fees and tariffs	<u>8</u> (= 7 from IS + 1 from decrease in Acc. Rec)
Total revenue	<u>39</u>
Expenditures	
Salary costs	24 (IS)
Interest on debt liabilities	3 (IS)
Other expenses	<u>6</u> (= 4 from IS + 1 decrease Stock +1 decrease Acc. Pay)
Total expenditures form operations	<u>33</u>
Cash surplus on operations	6
	Accounts 2014 (investments and financing)
Outflows	
Investments	3 (change in fixed assets over the year plus depreciation)
Loan repayment	<u>5</u> (change in long-term liabilities over the year)
Total cash deficit on inv./finan.	8
Total cash deficit	2 (= 6 - 8)

4.3   What about the financial health of Bergstadt? Ratio analysis

Now we will assess the Bergstadt financial statements by making use of *ratios*. A ratio expresses a relationship between two variables by taking the value of the first variable and dividing it by the value of the second variable. Just as an example, the effectiveness of a programme for drug rehab could be measured by taking the number of participants in the programme that leave this programme successfully over the total number of participants. The higher this ratio (70%, 80%, 90%) is, the more effective the programme might be judged to be. Ratios are often of modest value, but a comparison of ratio estimates with relevant standards can contribute to a well-justified assessment of the financial health of an organization.

Basic financial ratios

What ratios can be used for financial analysis of a public sector organization? Ratios on the following aspects of financial health can be calculated:

1. *Solvency*: refers to the extent to which an organization is able to pay off its liabilities in the long run to avoid bankruptcy or significantly curtailing its activities. For example, an organization with high equity compared with its debt may be in a stronger position to avoid financial difficulties, so the ratio between equity and debt, known as *gearing*, implies that the higher this ratio, the stronger the solvency of the organization.

2. *Liquidity*: refers to the extent to which an organization can pay its short-term debts by means of its current assets, for example the measure of the ratio between current assets and short-term liabilities, known as the *current ratio*, is seen to be stronger if it is above 1.

3. *Financial performance*: refers to the extent to which an organization can cover its costs by means of its revenues, for example by taking revenues over costs (this ratio is preferably above 1). This is also denoted as a cost *coverage ratio*.

Given these definitions and the information in Tables 4.1 and 4.3, we can answer the following questions:

a. Which ratios about financial health aspects 1, 2 and 3 can be calculated?
b. Given the results under a, is Bergstadt doing well?
c. Which alternative ratios can be suggested for each of these financial health aspects?
d. Going back to answers a and b: are there acceptable ranges of values for each of these ratios (taking into consideration the public sector context)?

e. Given the answers a and b: is there a trade-off between the three aspects of financial health, so being better on one aspect can be at the expense of another aspect?

f. Are there other types of ratios; what calculations and interpretations are needed?

The answers below give the combinations of letters and numbers referring to the categories in the balance sheet or income statement, as presented in Tables 4.1 and 4.3 (we will illustrate cash flow statement ratios later on). Calculations are made for 2014 (income statement) and 31–12–2014 (balance sheet), and subsequently comparative figures are given: the budget over 2014 and actuals over 2013 of the income statement and balance sheet at 31–12–2013.

Calculation and assessment of the ratios

1. Solvency: Equity over total sources of finance, L2/L3 = 20/75 = 0.27 or 27%. Or equity over debt, L2/L1 = 20/55 = 0.36. Or debt over total of sources of finance, L1/L3 = 55/75 = 0.73 or 73%.

This is quite a good solvency position for a public sector organization with a low risk profile. Public sector organizations can often finance themselves largely by debt because they have the backing of central government with its tax raising powers. The ratio value of 0.27 indicates that equity covers 27% of the total of the sources of finance. So, the organization knows that even if the value of the assets were to drop by 27%, all debtors could be paid. It also knows that future losses can be covered by equity up to €20 million (this is the total amount of equity). The latter refers to the so-called *buffer function of equity*. This function can be explained as follows. Suppose an organization is faced with serious cuts in its revenues, then it has to adapt the scale of its activities to this lower income level, meaning it has to cut costs. The existence of equity enables the organization to adapt to this lower level of activity more easily than an organization with little or no equity. In other words, equity gives 'breathing space' in a cost cutting operation.

The comparative figures of the solvency ratio equity over total sources of finance are shown below; these figures do not indicate substantial changes over the year 2014. Although equity decreased from 22 to 20, the total sources of finance also decreased from 83 to 75.

Ratio——Year-end——→ ↓	31–1–2013	31–12–2014
Equity over total sources of finance	0.27	0.27

2. Liquidity: Current assets divided by short-term liabilities, A2/L12 = 25/20 = 1.25.

This is good, because short-term assets are 25% higher than short-term liabilities. So, the organization has some room in its current assets for paying its creditors in the short term. However, the cash/bank part of the current assets is rather low, and this is the most liquid part of the current assets. So, if we calculate bank and cash balances (A21) over current liabilities (L12), the result is 10/20 = 50%, indicating that our available cash and bank balances only cover half of the short-term debts. So, liquidity is good when we accept a broad definition of current assets, but adopting a narrow definition of current assets makes liquidity problematic. The implication is that Bergstadt has to be confident that it can collect its accounts receivable (A22) quickly if it is to have enough cash to pay off all its short-term liabilities.

The comparative figures of the two liquidity ratios are shown below; these figures indicate some decline in the liquidity over the year 2014.

Ratio——Year-end——→ ↓	31–12–2013	31–12–2014
Current assets over short-term liabilities	1.29	1.25
Bank/cash over short-term liabilities	0.57	0.50

3. *Financial performance*: Total of revenues over total of costs (R1 + R2 + R3 +R4) / E5 = 38/40 = 0.95 (this is called the cost coverage ratio, which indicates a deficit over total of operations), or alternatively operations result over total of costs, O1/E5 = −2/40 = −5%.

This is poor, pointing to a failure to cover the cost of its total expenses. Such a loss is not insurmountable, as profits and losses may alternate over time, and then the equity value can be quite stable. However, when deficits come year after year, the organization can be in trouble. In this example, equity is 20 and the loss in 2014 is 2, so if similar losses are incurred in the coming years, equity will become zero after about ten years (10 × 2 = 20). Of course, a public sector organization may not go bankrupt, but it can be faced with a loss of autonomy (because oversight bodies do not accept a situation of continuous losses and a lack of equity), and banks will require higher interest rates or more restrictive borrowing conditions if they believe that their loans are subject to higher risks. So, we can conclude that a one year loss of this extent is not a serious problem, but a continuing situation of making losses would be highly problematic.

The comparative figures of the cost coverage ratio as an example of the financial performance ratio are shown below; these figures indicate that cost coverage remains problematic with values below 1, and the obviously too ambitious target in the budget over 2014 has not been reached.

Ratio——Year-end——→ ↓	Accounts 2013	Budget 2014	Accounts 2014
Cost coverage ratio	0.93	1.08	0.95

Are there acceptable ranges of values for each of these ratios taking into consideration a public context?

This is an important issue. Being very profitable is desirable for a private sector organization, but it is very questionable in a public sector context. In order to be profitable, costs have to be much lower than revenues, but this would imply serious cuts to programmes and activities or much higher user charges, which may be inconsistent with the wider, non-financial objectives of a public sector organization. So, profit (it may be better to speak about a surplus) refers to a condition of a public sector organization rather than its primary objective.

Ranges of appropriate values for solvency and cost coverage will depend on the risk profile of the organization. The higher the risk, the more equity may be needed. So, if an organization is largely dependent upon (what it believes to be) a stable income from a higher government layer, it is faced with a limited extent of risk, and it can hence afford to have a low level of equity. However, an organization would have to bear a much higher risk if it has to compete in the market for the sale of services; and then a relatively higher level of equity as a buffer is needed (see Feenstra and van Helden, 2003 on the equity positions of academic hospitals). Organizations in the same part of the public sector and characterized by a similar risk profile are often compared with each other through a process called *benchmarking*.

Other ratios

Here calculations are restricted to the year 2014 (income statement and cash flow statement) or the end of this year (balance sheet).

The simplest ratios are the shares of certain components over a total, for example: salary cost (E1) as percentage of total costs (E5): $24/40 = 0.6 = 60\%$; or intangible assets as a percentage of total assets ($A12/A3 = 5/75 = 0.07 = 7\%$).

A balance sheet item can also be related to an income statement item, for example by taking depreciation costs as a percentage of tangible assets or fixed assets ($E2/A11 = 9/40 = 0.23 = 23\%$; $E2/A1 = 9/50 = 0.18 = 18\%$).

Another interesting ratio can be: collection cost ratio of taxes; suppose these collection costs of taxes are half of the other costs, so 2 (50% of 4), then the ratio is $2/R1 = 2/12 = 0.17$. This means that collecting 100 euros of taxes requires collection costs (especially related to the tax office) of 17 euros. This is quite high, because only 83% (or 83 from 100 euros) is then available for spending opportunities concerning governmental programmes.

An often used ratio relates the long-term sources of finance (equity plus long-term debts) to the fixed assets: $(L2 + L11)/A1 = (20 + 35)/50 = 1.1$. This is quite good because it shows that the assets with a long lifetime are financed by long-term sources of finance. It is a general principle of financing that long-term assets should be financed by long-term sources of finance (the so-called golden balance sheet rule), which appears to apply in this case. It could be risky if a part of the fixed assets were to be financed by short-term liabilities, such as short-term bank loans. These bank loans may have to be paid on a shorter notice than the lifetime of the assets and probably also with poorer conditions such as higher interest rates, which makes the financing of these fixed assets less solid.

Finally, some *cash flow ratios* are defined and illustrated.

Operating cash flow ratio = net cash flows from operations divided by current liabilities.

This ratio measures the extent to which cash flows from operations are sufficient for meeting short-term obligations. According to Table 4.4 the net cash flow from operations is 6 in 2014, while the current liabilities at the year-end are 20 (see Table 4.3). This results in a ratio value of 0.33 (6/20), which is of course below the standard of 1.0, and thus suggests a problematic situation. The ratio is, however, contestable because it compares the net cash flow over a period with the short-term obligations at a moment. A better option for assessing the degree to which an organization can meet its short-term obligations is to use the liquidity ratios as introduced above; these ratios compare current assets or a part of these current assets with short-term obligations, which are both measured at the same moment, i.e. the year-end.

Interest coverage ratio = financial performance plus interest payments plus depreciation divided by interest payments plus repayment obligations of long-term loans.

The calculation of this ratio over 2014 is as follows: -2 (financial performance) $+ 3$ (interest payments) $+ 9$ (depreciation) divided by 3 (interest payments) $+$ repayment of long-term debts (40 − 35 on BS) = 10/8 = 1.2. This ratio shows whether the organization can fulfil its obligations towards providers of long-term loans, which is the case because it has 20% more cash available than these obligations.

4.4   Overview of ratios

Table 4.5 shows an overview of possibly relevant ratios (see also Finkler, 2010). Many of these rations have been introduced and illustrated above, but some are new, just to indicate that there is a large variety of ratios.

Many ratios can be applied to both public and private sector organizations, while others are particular to the public sector, such as cost coverage ratios or programme orientation ratios.

4.5   How to analyse ratios

It is not easy to interpret the result of a ratio. In principle, a point of reference is required with which the organization can compare the value of a ratio. Suppose, for example, that our organization's solvency ratio is calculated as its equity

Table 4.5 An overview of ratios

Ratio	Definition	Aspect of the annual account to be assessed
Relative amount	Balance sheet item or item of the income statement as percentage of the total	Indicates the relative amount of a balance sheet item (for example, accounts receivable as percentage of assets), or an item on the income statement (for example, personnel costs as percentage of total costs)
Liquidity: current ratio	Current assets divided by short-term debts	Indicates whether the organization has sufficient current assets to meet its short-term obligations
Liquidity: quick ratio (or: acid test)	Cash/Bank deposits plus accounts receivable divided by short-term debts	Indicates whether the organization has sufficient liquid assets to meet its short-term obligations
Efficiency: accounts receivable	Receipts from accounts receivable divided by accounts receivable	Indicates how quickly an organization has collected money from its customers
Coverage rate, general	Turnover divided by costs	Indicates to what extent the total costs are covered by the organization's turnover, i.e. its income (a kind of financial result ratio)
Coverage rate, specific	Turnover divided by the costs of a specific part of the operations	Indicates to what extent the costs of a particular task component of an organization are covered by the turnover (income) of that task component
Return on investment	The margin of a task (revenues minus specific costs associated with this task) related to the capital invested for this task	Indicates how much is earned per euro investment, which is a popular profit measure in the private sector (it is unusual in the public sector because earning more than the market interest on investment is mostly not seen as a public sector goal)
Programme orientation	Programme costs divided by total costs	Indicates which part of the total costs an organization incurs to perform the tasks for which it has been set up (the other costs are costs of the organization as a whole)
Solvency	Equity divided by debt, or equity divided by total sources of finance	Indicates whether the organization has sufficient equity relative to its debt to counterbalance financial setbacks or deficits
Golden balance sheet rule	Equity plus long-term debts divided by fixed assets	Indicates whether fixed assets (with a long lifetime) are sufficiently financed by long-term sources of finance and equity
Operating cash flow ratio	Net cash flows from operations divided by current liabilities	Indicates the extent to which cash flows from operations are sufficient for meeting short-term obligations
Interest coverage ratio	Financial performance plus interest payments plus depreciation divided by interests payments plus repayment of long-term loans	Indicates whether the organization is able to fulfil its obligations towards providers of long-term loans

divided by its total sources of finance, and that this is 10%. Now, what is the position of our organization? We would need to try to compare it with results from similar organizations. Suppose that we carry out such a benchmarking exercise and we find that three-quarters of the other organizations from the same sector have a solvency ratio of between 8% and 15%, with an average of 12%. The 10% result of our own organization in question may be regarded as neither bad nor good. This is, however, only a superficial assessment, because it depends on whether this organization's risk profile is strictly comparable to that of its peer-organizations in the sector. If the level of risk of our organization is considerably higher, for example because it also executes activities for the external market, an equity buffer larger than the sector average may be desirable.

Another complication in the assessment of ratios is that a value which is too high is often not desirable, while a value which is too low is also problematic. Let us take a liquidity ratio as an example. This ratio can be defined as cash and bank and accounts receivable divided by short-term liabilities. It is normally considered to be a healthy position when the value of the numerator (current assets) exceeds the value of the denominator (short-term liabilities). So, a liquidity ratio which is smaller than 1 may signify that the organization has too few current assets to meet its short-term obligations so that, in an extreme case, the organization is at risk of financial failure. However, if the value of this liquidity ratio is very high, this could be a sign of having a surplus of liquid assets and, in an extreme case, that it is failing to utilize its resources adequately to meet its non-financial objectives. This is why ratios are often best confined to a particular range, for example, a band width for the liquidity ratio between 1 and 1.5 could be used. A benchmarking process across a sector may assist us in deciding what band widths to use in our assessment.

Another example may help to clarify this. A solvency ratio which is too low indicates that an organization has too little equity at its disposal to counterbalance setbacks, especially operations deficits (this refers to the earlier introduced buffer function of equity). However, a solvency ratio which is too high can also be problematic: perhaps the organization has withdrawn too many resources from its regular operations and used them to build up equity. Moreover, there is a risk that organizations with excess resources become less efficient because they can easily meet required financial targets.

Another complication is that the quality of the calculated ratios is dependent on the quality of the underlying financial information. If this quality is low, a calculated ratio may give a misleading signal. If organizations within a particular sector apply different rules in drawing up their balance sheets and income statements, the ratio analysis may also lead to invalid interpretations. The reference points are not unambiguous and this may make the comparison of financial ratios between different sectors particularly difficult.

All in all, ratios are useful tools in the assessment of an organization's finances. However, they should be applied and interpreted with some caution.

4.6   Concluding remarks

This chapter has discussed ratio analysis for assessing the financial health of a public sector organization. A financial ratio is the quotient of two figures on an organization's balance sheet, cash flow statement or income statement. The purpose of a financial ratio is to help the user to form a judgment about an organization's 'functioning' in the context of its use of resources (cash flow statement or income statement), or its financial position (balance sheet). A financial ratio provides, so to speak, a snapshot of an aspect of the organization's financial health. Although a broad variety of financial ratios is available, the most often used ratios concern three aspects of the organization's financial health: *Solvency*, which refers to the extent to which an organization is able to pay off its liabilities in the long run to avoid bankruptcy or significantly curtailing its activities, for example measured by equity over total sources of finance; *Liquidity*, which refers to the extent to which an organization can pay its short-term debts by means of its current assets, for example measured by current assets over short-term liabilities; and *Financial performance*, which refers to the extent to which an organization can cover its costs by means of its revenues, for example by taking revenues over costs.

Financial ratios have the advantage of providing a single number for an aspect of the financial health of an organization. This contributes to a user-friendly way of interpreting often complex financial statements of an organization. However, numbers from ratios should be interpreted with caution. Often appropriate benchmarks and contextual information about the organization (such as its risk profile) are needed in order to establish whether a certain ratio number is good or bad.

References

Feenstra, D.W. and G.J. van Helden (2003), Policymaking on Reserves of Dutch University Hospitals: A Case Study, *Financial Accountability and Management*, Vol. 19, no. 1, 2003, pp. 1–20.

Finkler, S. (2010), *Financial Management for Public, Health, and Not-for-profit Organizations* (3rd International Edition), Upper Saddle River, New Jersey: Pearson Education, pp. 553–606.

Gowthorpe, C. (2005), *Business Accounting and Finance for Non-specialists*, 2nd edition, South-Western-Cengage Reading, London, chapter 13.

Kloha, P., S. Weissert and R. Kleine (2005), Someone to Watch Over Me: State Monitoring of Local Fiscal Conditions, *American Review of Public Administration*, Vol. 35, no. 4, pp. 236–55.

5

Financial accounting conventions and practices

Learning objectives

◆ Being able to list the objectives of financial statements in the public sector and relate these objectives to the groups of relevant users of these statements

◆ Understand what qualitative characteristics financial statements need to have in order to meet the objectives and user needs

◆ Being familiar with the content of the main elements of financial statements, such as revenues and expenses in the income statement and assets and liabilities in the balance sheet

◆ Being able to understand accounting issues that are specific for core governmental organizations, such as variance analyses of expenditures as well as the recognition and valuation of community assets

◆ Understand how certain elements in the financial statements, such as fixed assets, can be measured

5.1 Introduction

Financial accounting in the public sector is underpinned by a set of theories, concepts and approaches that, in this chapter, we refer to as conventions. Such conventions are drawn from a combination of theory, regulation and practice that is sometimes labelled 'Generally Accepted Accounting Practices' (GAAP). Regulation based upon International Accounting Standards may be labelled as *International GAAP* although this term may hide differences in the detail of how international accounting standards are applied from one country to another.

In order to restrain the length and complexity of this chapter, it is not the intention here to describe detailed differences in national approaches to accounting. However, it is useful to be aware that public sector accounting practices vary considerably between countries and even between different layers of government within an individual country. For example, a recent study of public sector accounting practices in the European Union (Ernst & Young, 2012) reports great heterogeneity amongst EU member states.

In this chapter we will describe those broad conventions adopted under conceptual framework documents published by the International Accounting Standards Board (IASB) and the International Public Sector Accounting Standards Board (IPSASB).

The IASB has developed a set of accounting standards for the private sector called International Financial Reporting Standards (IFRS). The IASB is overseen by a private sector, non-profit organization known as the IFRS Foundation. The IPSASB is part of the International Federation of Accountants (IFAC), a non-profit organization representing professional accounting bodies around the world. The IPSASB seeks to develop a set of global accounting standards for use by public sector organizations. These International Public Sector Accounting Standards (IPSAS) are adapted from IASB standards where available, or else are developed by IPSASB specifically for the public sector.

Information on IASB projects are available from its website www.ifrs.org and information on IPSASB can be found at www.ifac.org/public-sector. Many countries base their public sector accounting on IASB or IPSASB standards. Be aware that such conventions and standards are the subject of continuing debates. For example, governments in the European Union are discussing proposals to develop European Public Sector Accounting Standards (EPSAS) based upon IPSASB standards.[1]

We refer to accounting here in the particular context of general purpose financial reports (GPFRs), such as the income statement, the statement of financial position (or balance sheet) and the cash flow statement. It does not cover the production of special purpose statements or reports, such as those resulting from a special inquiry or investigation into fraud or financial mismanagement. For reasons of brevity, we do not seek to discuss all the complexities and perspectives of each of these conventions. However, further reading and references are provided for those who wish to study some of the issues in greater depth. Each section in this chapter will provide some illustrations of the challenges of applying these conventions in the particular context of accounting in the public sector.

The remainder of this chapter proceeds as follows: Section 5.2 considers the objectives of financial statements and who might be the users of these statements. Section 5.3 discusses the desirable qualitative characteristics of financial statements in meeting their objectives and satisfying the needs of their users. Section 5.4 addresses the 'elements' of financial statements, such as assets, liabilities, revenues and expenses. This section provides examples of how they are applied in the context of public sector accounting. Sections 5.5 and 5.6 discusses issues around

---

1   For further information see www.epsas.eu.

the measurement of the elements in the financial statements. The following questions are answered: What valuation methods should be used to measure the elements in the accounts and what particular challenges do these measurement systems bring to the preparation of public sector financial statements? Section 5.7 provides some concluding remarks.

5.2   The objectives and users of financial statements

Conceptual frameworks, such as those being developed by the IASB and the IPSASB, see the objectives of financial statements as being the provision of information to users according to their needs. The IASB framework, for private sector accounting, sees this information as being related primarily to providers of finance, such as shareholders, banks or bond holders. *The Conceptual Framework for General Purpose Financial Reporting by Public Sector Entities* (IPSASB, 2014) identifies broader objectives which reflect the wider use of financial statements to assist accountability for public money.

> *The objectives of financial reporting by public sector entities are to provide information about the entity that is useful to users of GPFRs for accountability purposes and for decision-making purposes . . . (par. 2.1).*[2]

There may be a large number of different users of public sector GPFRs, including those providing resources for the public sector, such as taxpayers, donors and lenders; those who receive or expect to receive the services which are funded from public expenditure, which may include citizens. Information is also needed for those making policy or financial decisions about the resources and uses of resources, including elected officials, managers of services, audit and supervisory bodies.

It is unrealistic to believe that many individual taxpayers and citizens will routinely use GPFRs. The time and effort required to understand the complexity of financial statements, for most people, outweighs the benefits of a detailed understanding of the financial performance and position of a public sector organization. Instead, taxpayers, citizens and service users rely upon representatives or other indirect methods rather than seeking to access public sector financial statements directly. *Politicians* who are members of a legislature (such as the council in a municipality or the parliament at the central governmental level, including politicians belonging to opposition parties) are particularly regarded as the *primary users* of public sector GPFRs. Similarly, the representatives of users of services and providers of resources may find GPFRs useful; these may include statisticians, analysts, the media, financial advisers, together with public interest and lobbying groups.

---

2 Paragraph references in this chapter all relate to IPSASB (2014).

The IPSASB concludes that 'the primary users of GPFR are service recipients and their representatives and resource providers and their representatives' (par. 2.4). The information needs of users are likely to be related to, firstly, an assessment of whether the reporting entity *is using its resources economically, efficiently and effectively* and, secondly, an assessment of *whether resources have been used for the purposes in which they were authorized* by legislative bodies and in compliance with legal authorities.

The first of these assessments relates to the range, volume and costs of services, the ways in which costs are recovered and whether current levels of taxes or user charges are sufficient to maintain the volume and quality of services. Users may also require information about the entity's future service delivery and activities and sources of finance to support those activities (par. 2.8). The second of these assessments relates to accountability for budget execution, that is, whether expenditure is in line with the authorized budget for the period and that the expenditure is consistent with the purpose for which it was authorized. This is a distinctive characteristic of public sector financial statements, which typically results in the disclosure of actual results (sometimes called 'outturn') for the financial year being compared with the budget allocated in the same period. An illustration of this type of presentation is given towards the end of this section (see also Section 1.4 about the particularities of financial statements in public sector organizations). A specific objective regards the *financial health* of the organization as a whole, as reflected by its solvency or financial surplus (as discussed in Chapter 4 about ratio analysis). Creditors and lenders may be especially interested in the achievement of this goal, because they want to be sure that they 'receive their money back'. Oversight bodies will also have an interest in the financial sustainability of the organizations which are subject to their oversight.

Table 5.1 summarizes the objectives of financial statements of public sector organizations and user groups interested in those objectives.

It was mentioned earlier in this section that these objectives sometimes lead to public sector financial statements taking a distinctive form. The example is based upon the accounts of the United Kingdom Department of Health, which is the central government department that oversees the funding and performance of

Table 5.1 Objectives of financial statements and the related user groups

Financial statement objective	Direct user groups	Sometimes represented by
An effective and efficient use of resources	Tax payers and users of public sector services	The legislative, the media
An execution of the budget according to the political priorities	The legislative of the political body (often the council or parliament)	–
Financial health of the organization as a whole	The legislative, oversight bodies, donors, creditors and lenders	Statistical bodies, the media

the UK National Health Service (NHS). One of the financial statements required from all central government departments in the UK is the *Statement of Parliamentary Supply*. This compares the resources estimated and authorized ('voted') by Parliament in the financial year with the actual amount ('outturn') drawn down by that department. Extracts from this statement are shown in Table 5.2 below.[3]

The Statement of Parliamentary Supply is analysed between Departmental Expenditure Limits (DELs) and Annually Management Expenditure (AME). DELs are agreed with HM Treasury as part of four-year spending plans. AME income and expenditure is generally demand-led or exceptionally volatile in a way that could not be controlled by a department or for other reasons the programmes are not suitable for inclusion in four-year spending plans set during Spending Reviews (Department of Health, 2013, p. 91). The UK public sector uses a form of accrual-based accounting known as Resource Accounting and Budgeting (RAB). The net cash requirement is also shown and it is reconciled to the RAB figures elsewhere in the accounts (not shown in Table 5.2).

In summary, this statement indicates that actual voted expenditure for the year is about £2.33 billion lower than budgeted, in resource terms, or £2.25 billion lower in cash terms.

For many government departments, their only or main income comes from taxation rather than the direct sale of goods or services. This may be reflected in the format of their accounts. Rather than showing revenue compared with costs (as shown in Chapters 2, 3 and 4) the accounts indicate some measure of expenditure during the year. An example of this type of format is given in Table 5.3, which

Table 5.2 Extracts from the Department of Health Statement of Parliamentary Supply for the year ended 31 March 2013 (all figures in £000)

	Estimate of Voted Expenditure	Outturn of Voted Expenditure	Outturn compared with Estimate Savings/(excess)
Departmental Expenditure Limit			
– Resource	87,394,720	85,863,608	1,531,112
– Capital	4,495,434	3,782,882	712,552
Annually Managed Expenditure			
– Resource	5,868,302	5,775,114	93,188
– Capital			
Total	97,758,456	95,421,604	2,336,852
Net cash requirement	89,521,476	87,268,029	2,253,447

Source: Adapted from Department of Health, 2013, p. 79.

---

3 To avoid excessive detail and complexity here, and later in the chapter, only extracts from the financial statements are provided; for example comparative figures for the previous year are excluded and some data is excluded or combined within information in the tables. Readers wanting an understanding of the full extent of disclosures should refer to the Department of Health website at www.gov.uk/dh.

Table 5.3 Extracts from the Department of Health Consolidated Statement of Comprehensive Net Expenditure for the year ended 31 March 2013 (all figures in £000)

	Core Department	Departmental Group
Administrative Costs		
– Staff costs	251,079	1,983,107
– Other administrative costs	192,619	1,739,250
– Operating income	(25,210)	(222,776)
– Grant in aid to NDPBs	227,053	–
– Funding to Group Bodies	2,801,544	–
Programme Costs		
– Staff costs	1,290	44,929,955
– Programme costs	5,679,118	68,329,344
– Income	(1,106,623)	(6,406,439)
– Grant in aid to NDPBs	103,776	–
– Funding to Group Bodies	96,984,770	–
– Resources expended by NHS Charities	–	203,815
– Income received by NHS Charities	–	(304,595)
Net Operating Costs for the year	105,109,416	110,251,661
Net (gain)/loss on transfers by absorption	13,349	9
Total Net Expenditure for the year	105,122,765	110,251,670
Other Comprehensive Net Expenditure	16,359	153,296
Total Comprehensive Expenditure for the year	105,139,124	110,404,966

Source: Adapted from Department of Health, 2013, p. 80.

shows extracts from the Consolidated Statement of Comprehensive Net Expenditure of the UK Department of Health. Two columns are used, one based upon the 'Core Department' itself and the other which is a consolidated statement that includes other bodies, including the NHS, some non-departmental public bodies (NDPBs) and NHS charities.

The statement lists out the categories of expenditure, split between administration costs and programme costs, which make up operating costs for the year. There is then an additional item 'net (gain)/loss on transfers by absorption' which is related to the reorganization of the NHS during the year. 'Other comprehensive net expenditure' (analysed in the full accounts) represents gains or losses arising from the revaluation of assets and liabilities during the year.

The figures under 'Departmental Group' provide an indication of the nature and cost of running public health services in the UK. The costs are considerable; over £110 billion in the year, of which nearly £47 billion is related to staff costs. The total comprehensive expenditure is the cost falling on the taxpayer as there is some income recognized in the statement, for example from private patients and health-based charities. The accounts here are accruals-based; for example depreciation charges are included in other administrative and programme costs. The department uses a fair value or replacement cost basis for measuring some of its fixed assets and this gives rise to differences arising from the revaluation each year included in 'other comprehensive net expenditure' (valuation of fixed assets is discussed in Section 5.5).

5.3   Qualitative characteristics of financial statements

How do we define what information should be included in a set of accounts and how the information should be presented? What is required to make a good set of accounts? It is difficult to be precise and specific in answering these questions; after all users may have different decisions to make and therefore need different information. A list of 'qualitative characteristics' below is taken from the IPSASB conceptual framework for public sector accounting (IPSASB, 2014, pp. 28–35) and each is briefly described and put into context with an example in this section.

Relevance

The information provided in financial statements is meant to be relevant for decision-making or accountability. Suppose a municipality wants to raise income by charging fees for certain services, which were provided for free in the past; for example to support library services or theatre events for young people. Accurate calculations about the full costs of these services are important if the municipal council wishes to ensure that a certain proportion of those costs are to be covered through these fees (decision-making) and to seek to gain the understanding of its citizens that the charges are reasonable (accountability). Clearly, other non-financial information is also needed, such as a measure of the use of such facilities by young people and some measure of the desired level of service usage after the changes have been made to determine whether service objectives have been achieved. Both financial and non-financial information is relevant if it makes a difference in achieving the objectives, for the purposes of either accountability or decision-making.

Faithful representation

The basic idea is that financial information provided in GPFRs is free from bias and error. However, providing faithful financial information is not always straightforward. For example, politicians or managers can have an interest in giving a positive impression of a proposal; for example a plan to establish a new arts centre in a city. In order to promote this proposal, they may be inclined to underestimate the total investment required and to overestimate the likely future revenues. Such information could therefore be biased and not provide faithful representation.

Of course, predicting future events is always likely to involve *risk* (where the probabilities of outcomes can be estimated and measured in some way) and *uncertainty* (where outcomes are so much in doubt that such measures cannot be determined). There should be lower levels of uncertainty for events which have already occurred, but that does not mean that all uncertainty has been removed. Suppose, for example, that the arts centre has already been built and paid for, but that revenue from events in the first year has been much lower than originally expected and budgeted. Does this mean that the current value of the arts centre in the financial statements (balance sheet) should be reduced and the budgets for future years should assume lower revenues from ticket sales?

Faithful representation implies that information should be complete, neutral and free from error. It may not be possible for a user to know whether information always meets this strong requirement. A number of general guidelines may help:

– Information should depict the underlying (economic) *substance* of transactions, events and activities, which is not necessarily the same as its legal form (this principle is called substance over form'). For example, a state educational authority arranges a transaction to lease some buses to transport children to school and to educational events. The buses might need to be included as fixed assets of the authority if they are leased for all or nearly all of their useful lives, even though the lease may not lead to legal ownership by the authority.

– Depiction of information as *complete* will normally imply a description of the item (e.g. Land and Buildings), a numerical representation of the aggregate amount of the item (e.g. €5,000,000) and further narrative information (e.g. the method of valuation, including rates of depreciation; a breakdown of the total item into more detailed classes; significant changes in the item during the accounting period as a result of additions, disposals and valuation adjustments).

– *Neutrality* implies that information is presented without an intention to obtain a particular predetermined result or to induce particular behaviour of users. There should be no systematic bias, either by artificially increasing the value of net assets to record surpluses or reduce losses, or by artificially reducing net asset values to reduce reported surpluses or to report losses.

– *Free from error* does not necessarily mean that all items can be assessed with complete accuracy. For example, the amount to record as a provision for a future liability may have to be estimated under conditions of uncertainty. However, the item may be seen to be 'free from material error' if it is estimated within a neutral process (see above), the nature and limitations of the estimation process are disclosed and no material errors have been identified in selecting and applying the appropriate process.[4]

Understandability

Financial reports should present information that is appropriate *to the needs and knowledge base of its users.* This means that narrative information should be written in plain language and in a manner that may be readily understood by users. The technical nature of information in financial reports may make this difficult

---

4 See Appendix A.3.1 on bookkeeping for an example of a provision.

to achieve. An underlying assumption is that the user has some knowledge of the entity and of the environment in which it operates. Furthermore, information should not be excluded from GPFRs solely because it may be difficult for some users to understand.

Public sector organizations often provide different types of financial reports about the same events, but aligned to the specific needs of their users. Those citizens interested generally in the affairs of their municipality may, for instance, receive an annual report presented in a concise and user-friendly way, for example by presenting expenses allocated over policy fields in a diagram, and by illustrating the financial health of the municipality by a few key indicators, such as the reported surplus compared with budget (as explained in Chapter 4). If they wish, interested citizens can also get access to the complete and detailed version of the annual report, which probably contains hundreds of pages, and is primarily intended to be used by the members and senior officials of the city council.

Timeliness

Information should be made available to users before it loses its capacity to be useful for accountability or decision-making purposes. There is often a balance to be drawn between providing information quickly and ensuring the accuracy of such information. For example, suppose an annual music festival is sponsored by a city government in order to keep ticket prices low. The city council will have an interest in an accountability report shortly after the event has taken place, especially in order to be prepared for its involvement in the festival for the next year. It is, however, likely that shortly after the event not all obligations of the festival organization are fully known (e.g. energy costs). The city council may prefer to provide a preliminary financial report including some estimates of specific expenditures, rather than delaying a report to ensure that all income and expenses are known to be fully accurate. So, in this example the *trade-off* between timeliness and faithful representation is settled by giving priority to timeliness.

Comparability

Comparability enables users to identify similarities and differences between two sets of accounts. Comparability is aided by consistency of accounting policies and procedures from one period to another and for similar items within each period. Comparability is enhanced if statements for the same period are presented using a consistent approach (e.g. the methods of accounting in the budget statement should be consistent with the methods of accounting for the outturn for the period). Organizations may wish to compare their own financial performance and position with similar bodies (e.g. local governments, hospitals, schools) or others in the same region. This is only feasible if organizations *use consistent methods of accounting and presentation* of financial statements.

Verifiability

It will be helpful to users if information can be verified as representing events without material error or bias. In some cases an amount can be verified directly (e.g. by counting cash or by checking an invoice due to a supplier). Many financial items can be easily verified if the organization has an adequate accounting system, for example tax revenues, fee revenues, and different types of expenses (e.g. salaries and investment costs). However, some financial events cannot be easily verified, for example future revenues of an investment project (for a new football stadium or opera house) or future disinvestment costs (such as the removal of old energy installations). In these cases a search for comparable cases of other organizations can contribute to the verifiability of complex accounting items. In other cases, an item might be verified indirectly by checking available information and carrying out assessments of the process leading to the information presented in the GPFRs (e.g. assessing future legal obligations using data from professional advisers). In most cases, users of accounts are not in a position to carry out the verification, so that information in GPFRs may be included to explain the assumptions and processes which underlie the financial information. More generally, GPFRs are normally subjected to audit and the role of the auditors is partly to give assurance to users that verifiability procedures have been carried out as part of the audit process (see further in Chapter 9).

To summarize this section: accounting information is likely to be of good quality if it is relevant to the user and the decisions that they wish to make; if it represents faithfully the events and conditions that exist; if it is understandable to users; and if it is timely, verifiable, and comparable to other data.

5.4   The elements of financial statements

Items in financial statements are grouped into a number of broad categories, which are called *elements* in the IPSASB proposed conceptual framework. The broad questions that we are answering here are 'what items should be included in or excluded from public sector accounts, and why?'

The inclusion of an item in the financial statements is referred to as *recognition*. This means that the item is included at some monetary valuation in the balance sheet, the statement of financial performance and/or the cash flow statement. An item is usually included as part of a larger total although, if it is sufficiently important, it may be disclosed as a separate item or within the notes to the accounts. The recognition of an item depends upon it being controlled or attributable to the reporting organization and that it is possible to measure (or value) the item with reasonable assurance of that value.

An item which has previously been recognized in the financial statements may subsequently need to be removed. This is a process known as *derecognition* and is applied typically when an item is no longer controlled by the reporting organization or where the item has no value or is incapable of being measured (valued) accurately.

Assets

Assets are defined in a very abstract manner in order to be applicable to the many different types of item that we might find in a balance sheet.

An asset is a resource, presently controlled by the entity as a result of a past event. (par. 5.6)

In the private sector, assets are primarily used to increase cash inflows or to decrease cash outflows of a business; for example a manufacturing company may purchase machinery to produce products that it hopes to sell for profit in a market. Assets in the public sector may have wider uses. Some may contribute positively to cash flows while others may result in a financial outflow of funds but provide non-financial benefits to users or to society at large.

For example, a government body may purchase and maintain community assets such as parks and other recreational areas or heritage assets such as monuments and museum collections. These assets may cost more to provide and maintain than the direct income which they generate, but they provide a social benefit to a community and so might be recognized as assets in the financial statements of a public sector organization.

A public sector entity needs to have control over an asset if it is to recognize that asset in its financial statements. Whether an asset is controlled by the entity is an empirical matter that must be tested in each case; for example by considering whether the reporting entity has access to the resource or the ability to restrict access to the resource by others.

An event must have occurred in the past in order for an asset to be recognized in financial statements. Often this event will be the result of an *exchange transaction*, e.g. an entity buys an asset for cash or takes over an asset with an obligation to pay for it in the future. An added complication in public sector accounting is that entities may have *non-exchange transactions* in which assets are either donated or are received as a result of sovereign powers, such as the right to collect taxes.

The examples of resources below reflect some particularities of public sector assets.

Example 1 – Reputation or branding

A European City has established a reputation as a major historical and cultural centre. It attracts many thousands of tourists each year, who spend millions of euros visiting its museums, architectural sites and theatres, staying in its hotels and using its restaurants, bars and shops. So should its cultural reputation or 'branding' be included in the municipality's balance sheet?

Cultural reputation is clearly an 'asset' of a city and its surrounding locality. It is likely to contribute towards cash inflow to the locality, for example from tourist income, cultural events and general inward investment. However, it is unlikely that such an asset would be recognized in the balance sheet. Why? One reason is that for an asset to be recognized in a balance sheet, it should be controlled by the reporting entity. It would be difficult for the municipal government to prove that it has control over the city's reputation as there are so many other factors and events likely to influence it. The municipal government does not have legal ownership of the city's reputation, nor can it restrict access to other users. Finally, even if it did have such control, it would be very difficult to measure the value of reputation; it could only be measured using broad and subjective assumptions. Furthermore, even if a valuation could be obtained, it may be argued that the costs of obtaining such a valuation would outweigh the benefits of this formal accounting process. Recording reputation in financial statements may be much less important than promoting the city's image in more informal 'league table' settings (see, for example, Kornberger and Carter, 2010; Jeacle and Carter, 2011).

Example 2 – Heritage assets

A museum holds an extensive and unique collection of paintings, drawings and related artefacts which have been collected over many years, some through purchase and others by donation. Donated items normally come with a condition that the item cannot be sold or given away other than to a similar museum. The museum's own constitution requires it to maintain and use its collections to promote artistic understanding and appreciation, to provide public access to its collections and to support related educational objectives. The museum is funded by contributions from national and local governments as well by individual donations and through its museum shop. Should its collections be recognized and measured (valued) in its balance sheet?

The accounting treatment of heritage facilities, such as museum collections, draws out some of the difficulties in applying the conceptual framework to public sector activities. All items may be seen as resources of the museum as they make up the collection, but the museum does not have the freedom to sell such items on an open market. One view is that such items should be reflected as a separate type of asset, sometimes called a community asset or a trust asset, recognized separately from general asset classifications. An alternative view is that heritage assets should not be recognized in the balance sheet as they are not available to support the payments of creditors, either due to legal restrictions on sale or because the reporting entity needs to retain such assets to support its core activities. A further challenge is that, if a view is accepted that such items should be recognized in the balance sheet, it may be difficult to determine an appropriate value, particularly if the item was donated or obtained many years ago. For extended discussion of these issues see Barton (2000, 2005); Carnegie and Wolnizer (1996); Hooper et al. (2005).

There is currently no IPSASB standard on this topic. A rare national standard is the UK FRS 30 Heritage Assets which requires recognition of heritage assets, except when a cost or valuation 'is not available and cannot be obtained at a cost which is commensurate with the benefits to users of the financial statements' (ASB, 2009, par. 20). The result of this compromise regulation is that the recognition of heritage assets may be restricted to a small proportion of the full collection, typically items acquired in the years since the regulation came into effect. For example, the UK National Portrait Gallery in London has its collection valued at £13.2 million in its 2013 balance sheet, but this represents only 4% of items in its primary collection and less than 1% of its reference and photographic collections (NPG, 2013).

Example 3 – Assets from taxation

National and local governments will normally levy various types of taxes on individuals and organizations that are subject to their jurisdiction. Taxes are normally non-exchange transactions, because the taxpayer will not necessary receive benefits from the government equivalent to the tax paid. While a taxpayer might receive benefits of social and public services, these are not provided directly in exchange for taxes that are paid.

When should a government recognize the taxation that is due to be paid to it? The approach adopted in accrual based accounting (IPSASB, 2006, par. 59–75) is based upon identifying a taxable event as the point at which an event gives rise to tax becoming payable to the legislative authority. For example, in the case of a sales tax or value added tax, the event is when the taxable activity occurs, typically the date of the sales invoice. In the case of income taxes, both personal and corporate, the event is when assessable income is earned by the taxpayer. In the case of property taxes, the event is the date or period on which the tax is levied. In the case of death duties or inheritance taxes, the event is the death of the taxpayer owning taxable property.

Note that the taxable event is likely to be before the tax is actually assessed and paid by the taxpayer. In accrual accounting, this gives rise to taxation receivable in the government's balance sheet, being an estimate of those taxes at the balance sheet date which are after the taxable event but have not been paid to the government by taxpayers.

Liabilities

Liabilities are defined by IPSASB in a mirror-image form to the definition of assets.

A liability is a present obligation of the entity for an outflow of resources that results from a past event. (par 5.14)

As with assets, there is a requirement to identify a past event in order to recognize a liability. In many cases there will be documentation from an individual transaction or contract that will identify such an event; e.g. an invoice from a supplier or a contract with a provider of loan finance. In other cases, the identification of an event may be more difficult as the liability is not documented through a formal contract; e.g. a liability to a user of public health services arising from medical negligence would require the identification of inadequate healthcare treatment from hospital records and evidence that some harm has been suffered by the patient.

Liabilities may need to be included, even though they are not binding legal obligations at the balance sheet date. For example, if a government has made a firm commitment to other parties to incur expenditure and has little or no realistic alternative to avoid settling the obligation then a liability may exist for those events that have occurred and a government cannot modify its obligation. In contrast, political promises and policy announcements do not normally create liabilities because they do not represent firm obligations and are conditional upon detailed implementation agreements.

The liability may be recognised in the balance sheet as a *provision* which concerns an obligation for providing resources to an outside party in the future, without knowing the exact amount of money to be paid and the due date. For example, an organization is responsible for paying pensions to its current employees when they meet certain criteria, i.e. having reached a certain age in the future or passing away before or after that minimum age. This leads to a pension provision, which can be estimated by making use of tables of mortality probabilities. A provision for employee pensions is required because a past event has occurred; these people have worked for the organization, which gives rise to a future obligation to pay them or their relatives a future pension or death-in-service allowance.

In contrast, a provision is not included in public sector accounts for the cost of future state pensions (sometimes called old-age pensions) which are payable to citizens who have reached a certain age, irrespective of their past employment record. The state pension is treated as a non-exchange transaction where the payment of future pensions can be withdrawn unilaterally by the government and which therefore does not represent an obligation existing at the balance sheet date.

Sometimes, a public sector organization might want to voluntarily set aside resources for a specific future purpose. This will not be a liability as it is not a formal obligation arising from a past event, and so it cannot be treated as a provision; it cannot be an expense in the income statement, nor will be included as a liability in the balance sheet. Instead, the organization can represent its expected plans as a *designated reserve*, which is shown as a component of the equity in its balance sheet. For example, suppose a European city is looking forward to celebrating its 800th birthday in a few years' time. It plans to set aside a sum of €100,000 over the next two years to help towards the costs of running special events in three years' time. The city can transfer an amount of €50,000 in each of the next two years out of its '*General Reserve*' and into an '*800th Anniversary Reserve*' to show its intention of using some of its resources for this specific purpose. At the same time the city might transfer €50,000 each year into a bank deposit account to hold funds in readiness for the events.

Revenues

Revenues are increases in the net financial position of the entity other than increases arising from ownership contributions (par. 5.29). Essentially what this implies is that if external parties contribute resources (assets) to the entity for services or by way of donation, then net assets are increased and so revenue should be recognized. If the owners of the entity (e.g. the government) contribute resources as owners then this increases equity in the balance sheet and is excluded from revenue. If an external party contributes resources, but requires payment or repayment for those resources (e.g. a cash loan to be repaid in the future) then net assets are not increased so there is no revenue to record.

In practice, the revenue of public sector organizations will arise from non-exchange transactions, such as taxes or levies that are imposed by governments, or from exchange transactions where the user is charged all or part of the cost of a service, such as road tolls, fares for public transport, healthcare charges, rental charges for property and other assets.

In the case of tax revenue, as explained above, the tax will be recognized as revenue when the taxable event has occurred. If the taxpayer has not paid the amount due at the end of the year then a receivable is reported in the government's balance sheet of the amounts still expected to be collected.

Expenses

Expenses are decreases in the net financial position of the entity other than decreases arising from ownership distributions (par. 5.30). This is a mirror image definition to revenue. So if costs are incurred resulting in a past or future outflow of resources resulting in a decrease in net assets, this results in an expense having to be recognized. An exception arises when the owners (e.g. the government) take out resources by decreasing its capital contribution or by payment by the entity of dividends on public capital as this represents a direct reduction of equity in the balance sheet.

In practice, if a government uses cash-based financial reporting, expenses may include both *revenue expenses*, such as salary payments, social security payments and healthcare costs, and *capital expenses*, such as the costs of purchasing assets such as land and building, equipment and vehicles. In contrast, if a public sector organization uses accrual-based accounting its expenses will include depreciation and other losses of value of its assets, while capital expenditure on assets will be recognized in its balance sheet rather than recorded as expenses.

Net financial position, other resources and other obligations

The IPSASB gives itself flexibility to recognise other resources and obligations into public sector balance sheets that do not satisfy the definitions of assets and liabilities in its conceptual framework, referring to 'other resources and other obligations' (par. 5.27). It is unclear how these flexibilities might be used in the future. One possibility is that certain types of income or expenses might be deferred from being recognized in the income statement and, instead, carried forward in the balance sheet as deferred inflows (obligations) or deferred outflows (resources). For example, suppose that a public sector organization receives a grant of €120,000 in 2014 to provide community-based care for certain disabled citizens during 2015 and 2016. The organization will record this as a cash receipt in 2014. At the end of 2014 it may record €120,000 as a deferred inflow (similar to a liability) enabling it to transfer this amount into the statement of financial performance during 2015 and 2016 as it uses the grant to support its services. Similarly, a public body might pay a grant to promote some type of charitable or social objective over a future period and, instead of treating this as an immediate expense, it will be spread over future periods to match the objectives of the funding.

Net financial position is the difference between assets and liabilities after adding other resources and after deducting other obligations recognised in the statement of financial position (par. 5.28). The intention of the IPSASB appears to be to create a distinction between 'net assets' (assets minus liabilities) in the balance sheet which excludes these other resources and obligations and 'net financial position' which includes them if any are recognized.

Ownership contributions and ownership distributions

Ownership contributions are inflows of resources to the entity, contributed by external parties, in their capacity as its owners, which establish or increase an interest in the net financial position of the entity (par. 5.3). Example: two municipalities are the owners of a harbour authority, and each agrees to provide €500,000 to expand the facility and ensure its financial stability, increasing the amount of its equity by €1 million.

Ownership distributions are outflows of resources from the entity, distributed to external parties in their capacity as its owners which return or reduce an interest in the net financial position of the entity (par. 5.34). Example: a municipality is the owner of a commercial real estate site, which has operated very profitably in the past, and therefore can afford to reduce its equity. The municipality takes out resources which can then be used for other purposes.

Table 5.4 gives an indication of the extensive scope of assets and liabilities applicable to a large central government department and its associated activities. It is based upon extracts from the Consolidated Statement of Financial Position of the UK Department of Health at 31 March 2013. The statement is split between

Table 5.4 Extracts from the Department of Health Consolidated Statement of Financial Position as at 31 March 2013 (all figures in £000)

	Core Department	Departmental Group
Non-current assets		
Property, plant and equipment	1,168,349	47,522,789
Investment property	260	67,599
Intangible assets	1,314,345	1,796,585
Charitable non-current assets	–	158,974
Financial assets- investments	25,981,057	1,118,926
Charitable investments	–	1,611,121
Other non-current assets	125,395	548,471
Total non-current assets	**28,589,406**	**52,824,465**
Current assets		
Assets classified as held for resale	198,759	425,721
Inventories	125,904	968,911
Trade and other receivables	147,414	1,319,830
Other current assets	234,263	1,050,793
Charitable other current assets	–	161,267
Other financial assets	206,463	56,631
Cash and cash equivalents	1,206,560	7,421,705
Charitable cash	–	303,054
Total current assets	**2,119,363**	**11,707,912**
Total assets	**30,708,769**	**64,532,377**
Current liabilities		
Trade and other payables	(143,946)	(5,857,689)
Other liabilities	(2,326,519)	(8,012,700)
Charitable liabilities	–	(166,731)
Provisions	(279,274)	(2,709,816)
Total current liabilities	**(2,749,739)**	**(16,746,936)**
Non-current assets plus/less net current assets/liabilities	**27,959,030**	**47,785,441**
Non-current liabilities		
Other payables	(310,610)	(636,189)
Charitable liabilities	–	(74,531)
Provisions	(1,431,087)	(24,145,258)
Net pension asset/(liability)	–	(70,099)
Financial liabilities	(44,989)	(11,703,573)
Total non-current liabilities	**(1,786,686)**	**(36,629,650)**
Assets less liabilities	**26,172,344**	**11,155,791**
Taxpayers' equity and other reserves		
General fund	25,265,749	(531,734)
Revaluation reserve	906,595	9,512,622
Other reserves	–	181,746
Total taxpayers' equity	**26,172,344**	**9,162,634**
Charitable funds	–	1,993,157
Total reserves	**26,172,344**	**11,155,791**

Source: Adapted from Department of Health, 2013, p. 82.

the Core Department and the Departmental Group as described previously in Table 5.3.

The departmental group balance sheet is more helpful to understand the position of UK public healthcare services at this date, as it includes the assets and liabilities of all the organizations reporting through the NHS to the Department. The value of assets exceeds liabilities by around £11.1 billion. Much of this difference arises from the revaluation of fixed assets (see Section 5.5 for a discussion of measurement systems), routinely carried out in the UK public sector; in this case it has given rise to a cumulative surplus of £9.5 billion shown in the revaluation reserve. The general fund has a negative balance of £531 million, reflecting accumulated losses arising from operating activities over many years. Much of the difference between this and the positive balance shown in the core department balance sheet can be explained by the high level of provisions in the group balance sheet. A large proportion of the liability relates to the NHS clinical negligence provision. This is an estimate of the amounts that may become payable in the future as a result of claims for poor treatment. Accounting for clinical negligence claims is a good example of the difficulties in assessing the level of provisions in conditions of uncertainty. Known clinical negligence claims are valued individually based upon estimates of likely costs and probability factors that take account of the potential of a successful defence against the claim. Estimates of other claims which may have been incurred but are not yet reported are valued using actuarial models. The result of this process is that a provision for clinical negligence of over £22 billion is included in the accounts of the Departmental Group, of which over £14 billion is not expected to be paid for more than five years from the balance sheet date (Department of Health, 2013, pp. 148–151).

5.5   Measurement of assets in financial statements

The measurement of items in financial statements refers to the bases of valuation that might be used to determine the monetary values of assets and liabilities which are recognized in the balance sheet. The measurement issue has been a matter of continuing debate in financial reporting for many years. The approach taken in the conceptual frameworks of both the IASB and IPSASB has been to refer to a number of different measurement approaches and to describe the basis on which the measurement decision might be made, rather than prescribing one particular measurement system.

This section reflects the approach in the IPSASB (2014) conceptual framework. Measurement systems may be based upon entry values or exit values. Broadly, an *entry value* is represented by the cost of purchasing an asset while an *exit value* represents the value arising from the sale or disposal of an asset. Values may be *specific* to the reporting entity or may be *non-entity specific* as they are drawn from more generalised, market-based data. Table 5.5 provides a summary.

Table 5.5 Summary of measurement bases for assets

Measurement basis	Entry or exit	Entity or non-entity specific
Historical cost	Entry	Entity-specific
Market value (open, active & orderly market)	Entry and exit	Non-entity specific
Market value in an inactive market	Exit	Depends upon valuation technique
Replacement cost	Entry	Entity-specific
Net selling price	Exit	Entity-specific
Value in use	Exit	Entity-specific

Source: Adapted from IPSASB, 2014, p. 81.

Introduction to example

Suppose that a municipal authority owns an office building, which is used to enable new, small firms to start up their business at a rent which is subsidized by the municipal authority as part of its economic development plans. The office was built ten years ago at a cost of €9 million. The municipality is the only owner and it wishes to recover part of its initial investment through rental income. Currently the asset has a book value of €6 million, given that the municipality uses a depreciation rate of 3.3% per year for an expected asset lifetime of 30 years. The municipal office building was quite successful in its early years, as evidenced by a high occupation rate. However, more recently the occupation rate has declined due to the general downturn in economic activity following the financial crisis which caused some of the firms to fail. Older and cheaper office space has come onto the market as a result of the downturn in demand. The municipality believes that its own office building can attract new tenants by opening up its premises to some larger firms but that these may be less prosperous customers, resulting in increasing payment problems of its commercial tenants. These worsening prospects of the municipal office building may influence its value.

Historical cost

Historical cost is an entry value in which assets are initially reported at the cost incurred on their acquisition. The main distinguishing feature of the historical cost approach is that the measurement of an asset is not changed to reflect changes in prices (inflation or deflation). The amount of an asset may, however, be reduced systematically to recognize the consumption of the service potential of an asset – a process giving rise to depreciation expenses. The value may also be reduced by recognizing impairments to reflect a permanent loss of value of an asset due to changes in economic conditions, as distinct from its consumption. In our example, the historical cost of the municipal office building is €9 million, and based on its use over the first 10 years its historical cost book value is €6 million.

Market value

Market value is the amount for which an asset could be exchanged between knowledgeable, willing parties in an arm's length transaction (par. 7.24). It provides a current exit value in cases where there is an open, orderly market in which current market prices can be identified. There will be difficulties in applying such a measurement model in cases where active markets are not readily available (or open or orderly) to provide such value. For example, public sector bodies which use highly specialized assets may find that there is no readily appropriate market to provide such data. In our example the market value of the municipal office building will probably be lower than its current book value of €6 million, because the building is not providing a full market return as a result of lower economic activity and competing office facilities. An expert is appointed to value the building, and indicates an expected market value of €4.5 million.

Replacement cost

Replacement cost is defined as the most economic cost required for the entity to replace the service potential of an asset (including the amount that the entity will receive from its disposal at the end of its useful life) at the reporting date (par. 7.37). It differs from market value because it is an entry value and it reflects the specific costs incurred by the entity rather than being a hypothetical market price. The system has the advantage over the historical cost method of keeping asset values (and the associated depreciations expenses) up-to-date by being based on the current costs of replacement. However the process can be expensive and time consuming to implement as it requires regular assessment of the valuation of assets. In our example the replacement cost of the municipal office building could be estimated by an investigation among construction companies asking questions concerning the resources needed for building a similar office building at the current time. Inflation would be likely to make this value higher than the original historical cost price, but technological improvements during the last ten years that might have a lowering effect can be expected. We will assume that the resulting replacement cost of a modern equivalent asset is €9.6 million.

Net selling price

Net selling price is defined as the amount that the entity can obtain from sale of the asset, after deducting the costs of sale (par. 7.37). It provides an indication of the value of assets if the entity were to be closed at the balance sheet date. It may not be the same as market value as there may not be an open, orderly market for the sale of these assets. Net selling price is intended to be entity specific, rather than being based on (hypothetical) open markets. A major limitation of its use is that public sector entities are far more likely to retain assets for use in service delivery, rather than to sell them to the highest bidder. If the municipality is very pessimistic about the commercial prospects of its office building or believes that it can support economic development in more effective ways, it could try to find an interested buyer, who is likely to change the use of the building after renovation, for example by making it suitable for private housing. The resulting price is probably much lower than the current book value of €6 million, leading to a net selling price of (say) €4 million.

Value in use

Value in use is defined as the present value to the entity of the asset's remaining service potential or the ability to generate economic benefits if it continues to be used, and of the net amount that the entity will receive from its disposal at the end of its useful life (par. 7.58). It represents an estimate of the value of continuing to use the asset, rather than selling it. It is only likely to be used when the value in use is lower than replacement cost and higher than net selling price – in other words, it is not intended to replace the asset at the end of its life, but it makes economic sense to continue to use it rather than sell it. A number of practical difficulties present themselves in using this method in a public sector context. First, there is the uncertainty of the cash flows arising from the use of a public sector asset, which may not generate positive cash flows or may do so only conjointly with other assets. Second, there is the difficulty of determining the appropriate discount rate to estimate present value. The value in use of the municipal office building could be estimated by taking account of the declined rental income due to vacancy and payment problems of tenants. The resulting value will be likely to be close to the expected market value of €4.5 million; we will assume that it is €4.2 million.

Other measurement models

There are other asset measurement approaches that are not included in the IPSASB (2014) conceptual framework. The *Fair Value* model has become important as a result of its use by the IASB for accounting in the private sector. It is an exit value system based primarily on the market value of assets and liabilities. It assumes that valuations of assets and liabilities can be determined from available market prices (*mark-to-market accounting*). It is likely to be equivalent to 'market value' in the IPSASB framework when there are active, open markets for public sector assets.

The *Deprival Value* model uses a combination of replacement cost, net selling price and value in use measurement methods to reflect the loss that would occur if an entity were deprived of the use of an asset. It is used to provide some insights

Table 5.6 Valuation bases for the municipal office building

Valuation base	Value
Historical cost	€9 million (original purchase price); net book value €6 million (after depreciation of a third of its lifetime).
Market value	€4.5 million (professional valuer estimate).
Replacement cost	€9.6 million (estimated gross current replacement price); net book value €6.4 million (after depreciation of a third of its lifetime).
Net selling price	€4 million (current use of the asset is changed).
Value in use	€4.2 million (based on an estimation of lowered rental income).

of the relationship between these measurement methods in the framework (par. BC7.39).

Table 5.6 summarizes the various valuation bases for the municipal office building.

In practice, organizations are likely to measure categories of assets in a consistent manner, rather than using different valuation methods for each individual asset. The approach used may be required by a higher authority, for example a government department determines the valuation rules for its agencies. Alternatively, there may be an approach to measurement which has been adopted across a sector for many years and is only likely to change as a result of new legislation or sector reforms.

Public sector entities around the world use a variety of measurement systems and there is no single measure of valuation of those listed in table 5.5 that can be identified as always being chosen. Indeed, if pure cash-based financial reporting systems are in use then the fixed asset is not recognized at all. If accrual-based accounting systems are used these may be based on historical cost and the net book value of €6 million is recognized. If the book value is reduced to reflect the loss of value this may be based upon the professional valuation of €4.5 million (which has the advantage of being supported by an external expert) or the value in use of €4.2 million.

5.6   Measurement of liabilities in financial statements

The measurement bases for liabilities are, in many ways, similar to those applied to assets. They may be based upon entry values or exit values. Entry values relate to the amount of an obligation received or the amount that would be accepted to assume an equivalent liability. Exit values reflect the amount required to pay-off or release the entity from an equivalent obligation. They may be specific to the reporting entity or non-specific, when based upon more generalised market data. Table 5.7 provides a summary of these bases.

Table 5.7   Summary of measurement bases for liabilities

Measurement basis	Entry or exit	Entity or non-entity specific
Historical cost	Entry	Entity-specific
Market value (open, active & orderly market)	Entry and exit	Non-entity specific
Market value in an inactive market	Exit	Depends upon valuation technique
Assumption price	Entry	Entity-specific
Cost of release	Exit	Entity-specific
Cost of fulfillment	Exit	Entity-specific

Source: Adapted from IPSASB, 2014, p. 82.

Historical cost

The historical cost for a liability is the value of the consideration received at the time the liability in incurred. If there is a significant length of time before settlement of the liability is due, the amount is discounted to represent the present value of the expected future payment.[5]

Market value

Market value is the amount for which a liability could be settled between knowledgeable, willing parties in an arm's length transaction (par. 7:80). This valuation basis may be appropriate when the liability is subject to changes in rates or prices in an active market, but it is unlikely to be used for fixed, contractual liabilities or in non-exchange transactions where active markets are unlikely to exist.

Assumption price

Assumption price is the amount that the entity would rationally be willing to accept in exchange for assuming an existing liability (par. 7.87). It is the entry value equivalent of replacement cost for assets. When an exchange transaction occurs the assumption price is the amount accepted for assuming the liability, effectively its historical cost. There may be no assumption price available for non-exchange transactions. In practise, it may be unnecessary to ascertain assumption prices for routine liabilities but it may be relevant for measuring insurance obligations and financial guarantees.

---

5   See Chapter 8 for an explanation of the concept of discounting future cash flows.

Cost of release

The cost of release of a liability is the amount that a creditor will accept in settlement of its claim or that a third party would charge to accept the transfer of the liability from the entity (par. 7.82). It is the equivalent of 'net selling price' in the context of asset measurement. In practice it is unlikely to be used as routine liabilities will have a clear contractual obligation that is represented by its historical cost. In any case, the transfer of a liability is often not practically possible in the public sector. Cost of release might be used to measure a liability in the case of a cancelled contract where there is a cancellation clause in a contract and the cost is lower that fulfilling the contract terms.

Cost of fulfilment

The cost of fulfilment is the costs that the entity will incur in fulfilling the obligations represented by the liability, assuming that it does so in the least costly manner (par. 7.74). For routine contracts with a fixed price, the cost of fulfilment is the same as the historical cost. Where fulfilment requires work to be done, the cost to the entity is the cost of doing that work itself or employing a contractor to get the work done. The cost of fulfilment may be the most appropriate measurement of liabilities arising from non-exchange transactions, where there is no contractual payment agreed with the beneficiary.

Summary

The overall position for measuring liabilities is that most short term liabilities will be measured at historical cost based upon contractual terms; longer term liabilities may be discounted to allow for the time value of money. Market price may be used for financial liabilities that are traded in active markets. The cost of fulfilment is the most likely measurement system for those liabilities which have no fixed contractual obligation and those arising from non-exchange transactions.

5.7   Concluding remarks

This chapter has introduced some of the conventions that underlie financial accounting practices in the public sector. The IPSASB (2014) conceptual framework has been used to illustrate some of the key conventions. The nature of public sector activities can result in different considerations and approaches to those adopted in the private sector (IPSASB, 2011).

The *objectives* of financial statements will influence both the format and content of the financial statements; for example, public sector organizations may show comparisons of budgeted or voted expenditure with actual costs incurred. Tax funded bodies, such as central government departments and municipal authorities, may emphasize net expenditure, funded through taxation, in their accounts rather than providing an income and expenditure showing surpluses or a break-even position. A set of *qualitative characteristics* may help to ensure that accounts meet stated objectives to promote accountability and support decision-making. The IPSASB conceptual framework lists a number of *elements*, or categories of items, in financial statements, but it is still necessary to interpret these in particular contexts when accounts are being prepared. Examples were given of particular *measurement* or valuation methods that may be used in the preparation of the accounts.

We are now at the end of the financial reporting part of this book. The next three chapters will focus on related management accounting techniques of budgeting (Chapter 6), costing (Chapter 7) and investment decisions (Chapter 8).

References

Accounting Standards Board (2009), *FRS 30 – Heritage Assets*, UK ASB, London.

Barton, A. (2000), Accounting for public heritage facilities: assets or liabilities of the government?, *Accounting, Auditing and Accountability Journal*, Vol. 13, no. 2, pp. 219–235.

Barton, A. (2005), The conceptual arguments concerning accounting for public heritage assets: a note, *Accounting, Auditing and Accountability Journal*, Vol. 18, no. 23, pp. 434–40.

Carnegie, D. and P. Wolnizer (1996), Enabling accountability in museums, *Accounting, Auditing and Accountability Journal*, Vol. 9, no. 5, pp. 84–99.

Department of Health (2013), *Annual Report and Accounts 2012–13*, HC 46, 2013–14, The Stationery Office, London.

Ernst & Young (2012*), Overview and Comparison of Public Accounting and Auditing Practices in the 27 EU Member States*, Report prepared for Eurostat 19 December 2012, Ernst & Young Global Limited.

Hooper, K, K. Kearins and R. Green (2005) Knowing 'the price of everything and the value of nothing': accounting for heritage assets, *Accounting, Auditing and Accountability Journal*, Vol. 18, no, 3, pp. 410–33.

IPSASB (2006), *IPSAS 23, Revenue from Non-Exchange Transactions (Taxes and Transfers)*, International Public Sector Accounting Standards Board, IFAC, New York.

IPSASB (2011), *Exposure Draft: Key Characteristics of the Public Sector with Potential Implications for Financial Reporting*, International Public Sector Accounting Standards Board, IFAC, Toronto.

IPSASB (2014), *Conceptual Framework Exposure Draft 3: Conceptual Framework for General Purpose Financial Reporting by Public Sector Entities: Measurement of Assets and Liabilities in Financial Statements*, International Public Sector Accounting Standards Board, IFAC, New York.

Jeacle, I. and Carter, C. (2011), In Trip Adviser we trust: rankings, calculative regimes and abstract systems, *Accounting, Organizations and Society*, Vol. 36, no. 4/5, pp. 293–309.

Kornberger. M. and Carter, C. (2010), Manufacturing competition: how accounting practices shape strategy making in cities, *Accounting, Auditing and Accountability Journal*, Vol. 23, no, 3, pp. 325–49.

National Portrait Gallery (2013), *Annual Report and Accounts 2012–13*, NPG, London.

6

Budgeting: principles, functions, types and processes

Learning objectives

- ◆ Understand and illustrate the budget structure, budget principles and the functions of budgets in public sector organizations
- ◆ Being able to describe the various stages in the budgeting process
- ◆ Understand the different budget types and being able to provide illustrations of each
- ◆ Understand how the execution of the budget, including the presentation of interim reports, works in the budgeting process
- ◆ Being able to identify political aspects of budgeting in public sector organizations

6.1   Introduction

The previous chapters of this book have been dedicated to important financial documents which are used for giving account of the execution of the annual policy making: the income statement, the cash flow statement and the balance sheet. This chapter discusses the budget as the most important financial document for the planning of annual financial policy making. The budget and the interim reports about the budget execution are, together with the above financial documents, part of the planning and control cycle of a public sector organization introduced in Chapter 1 (see Figure 1.1).

Throughout this chapter the various aspects of budgeting will be illustrated by examples from the city of Oldenburg in Germany.[1] Section 6.2 provides an

---

1   The authors are indebted to Mr Markus Beier, Mr Gerd Bischoff, Mr Joachim Guttek and Mr Sebastian Kelch, senior members of the financial department of the city of Oldenburg, for their helpful contributions to the case information about their city.

introduction to this city and its public administration. Section 6.3 defines the budget and discusses the budget structure, budget principles (e.g. comprehensiveness and transparency) and budget functions (such as authorization and control). Then Section 6.4 describes the budget process, including the setting of central guidelines, preparing budget drafts for different programmes or organizational units, consultation between the central and local levels and budget decision-making. Section 6.5 deals with various types of budgets, such as activity, output and outcome budgets. Performance budgeting is discussed in more detail in this section because public sector organizations increasingly present performance information in their budgets. Section 6.6 considers the budget execution, including the presentation of interim reports as part of the planning and control cycle. Section 6.7 discusses the political context of the budgetary process, pointing to aspects of power and coalition forming in realizing political or managerial priorities. Finally, some concluding remarks are made in Section 6.8.

6.2   Introducing the city of Oldenburg's public administration

'Stadt Oldenburg' is located in the North-Western part of Germany. The city's population increased during the last thirty years from 140,000 to more than 160,000 inhabitants in 2013. Part of this population growth is influenced by Oldenburg's attractive labour market with a university and companies in the service industry, such as energy conservation and applied research. Oldenburg is located in the State of Lower Saxony ('Bundesland Niedersachsen'), which is part of the federal republic of Germany ('Bundesrepublik Deutschland'). The municipal organization of Oldenburg included about 2,300 full-time jobs in 2012. Oldenburg's budget amounted to approximately €380 million in that year. The city council has 50 members, who are elected every five years. The Executive ('Verwaltungsausschuss') includes a mayor ('Oberbürgermeister'), who is directly elected by the population every eight years, and three political officials (aldermen, in German 'Beigeordnete'; in Oldenburg called 'Stadträte' or 'Stadträtinnen'), who are appointed for eight years by the council upon proposal by the mayor (source: www.oldenburg.de).

The public administration of Oldenburg has been faced with relatively large deficits over the period 1996–2011 of about 4% of its yearly operations. However, gradually its financial situation has improved and in 2012 a surplus of about 2.5% of the yearly operations was realized. The city has been forced by the federal State of Lower Saxony to take appropriate measures to improve its financial position. Several factors contributed to the restoration of Oldenburg's financial health. The rise in tax income, especially trade tax ('Gewerbesteuer'), was important, but, additionally, several measures for cutting expenses have been taken. Certain demographic developments, particularly a rise in the proportion of elderly people, will influence the future financial needs of the city's administration, especially with regard to healthcare and social benefits.

Like most German municipalities, Oldenburg recently made the transition from the cameralistic system to the accrual system (Chapter 3 explains these terms; for general observations about reforms in the German municipal sector see Reichard, 2012). Since 2010 Oldenburg's budgeting and accounting system has been based on resource consumption rather than cash receipts and cash payments. Its first balance sheet, which is dated 1 January 2010, being the start of the new accrual accounting system, has been published only very recently, so in this respect some progress still has to be made.[2] In addition, Oldenburg started to introduce performance information in its budget in 2010, and it has gradually realized improvements in the quality of this information. Costing has been deliberately introduced in a selective way, i.e. only when fees or prices needed to be established, for instance in the case of market fees and harbour fees. Oldenburg's budgeting and accounting concept follows a general financial management framework which is mandatory for all municipalities of Lower Saxony (and in its basic features for the whole local government sector of Germany).

Oldenburg aims to avoid financial deficits in the future, because this implies that its supervisory body on finances, the State of Lower Saxony, then no longer requires plans for improving the city's financial perspectives, which contributes to the city's autonomy. Moreover, Oldenburg wants to accomplish further improvement in the quality of the information for budgeting and accountability purposes, especially with regards to the balance sheet at the year-end and the performance information in the budget.

The illustrations of Oldenburg's budgeting practice will be derived from its financial documents for 2012, such as the budget, the budget regulations and internal documents about the budgeting process and the municipal organization structure. In addition, interviews with senior members of staff of the city's financial department have informed these illustrations.

6.3   Budget: definition, structure, principles and functions

Definition

There are various definitions of a budget. In its most simple wording, a budget is a monetary representation of the planned activities of a governmental organization (Wildavsky, 1984, p. 4). In a more elaborate way a budget can be defined as an overview of the activities of a governmental organization over a certain period, at least in the form of its financial aspects, both revenue and cost items, and often supplemented by other information about these activities, such as their functions, goals or desirable impacts.

---

2   This balance sheet shows a total value of the assets of about €1 billion; tangible assets comprise the main component, amounting to 60% of the total of the assets; equity amounts to approximately 50% of the sources of finance.

Budgets are financial estimates or representations of facts. For example, a salaries budget will represent the number of employees in an organization at the expected salary level of each employee. Therefore, we would expect items in a budget to be constructed from those relevant facts. In some cases those facts can be easily determined. For example, a public sector healthcare organization may budget for annual property rental costs which are fixed by existing rental agreements. Some budget items may be more difficult to determine as they have to be estimated from incomplete information. For example, the same healthcare organization may need to estimate medical negligence costs which will depend upon factors such as the quality of healthcare provided, the risk of mistakes and the likelihood of damages being awarded after legal processes have been followed.

A budget can be identified according to various viewpoints:

- The *time span*: annual or multi-year.
- The *entity*: government as a whole (e.g. the State or a municipality) or a unit within government as a whole (such as an agency or a department).
- The *components* or the *items within the budget*: cost categories (e.g. salaries and depreciation) and revenue categories (e.g. taxes and transfers from other governments), or programmes/functions (such as economic affairs and social affairs), or products (such as kindergarten services and sewerage).
- The *level of detail of the budget items*, ranging from a global budget used primarily to inform high-level policy making to a detailed budget with hundreds of items used for direct operational decision-making.
- The *extent to which the budget items are binding on the organization*, ranging from items which are fixed in both purpose and amount to those which are able to be shifted amongst categories of items or time periods.
- The *type of information per item within the budget*: at least financial, but in addition, for example, goals and/or performance information.

In practice, budgets can combine several of these viewpoints in different ways; for a simple annual budget which only specifies revenue and cost categories, or a more advanced budget with both an annual and a multi-year budget, specifying goal-related and financial information for each programme, and within each programme, financial information on both revenues and costs.

Budget structures

These examples are an appropriate stepping stone for an explanation of the budget structure. A budget structure defines the different layers at which budgetary information (at least financial, but also non-financial) is provided. Figure 6.1 gives two examples of a budget structure, which show an increasing extent of information richness, accompanied by increasing complexity. The left-hand side of the figure indicates a budget structure with two layers, i.e. the overall body and programmes.

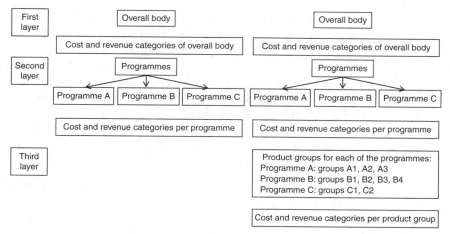

Figure 6.1 A two-layer and a three-layer budget structure

The right-hand side of Figure 6.1 is characterized by three layers, i.e. the overall body, programmes and product groups. At each layer, cost and revenue categories can be specified. Cost categories, for example, concern salaries, depreciation, interest costs, energy costs, costs for external support and material costs. Revenue categories may include taxes, fees and transfers from other governments. Programmes include, for instance, infrastructure, environment, social security, care, culture and employment. Within each of these programmes product groups can be distinguished as in the right-hand side of the figure, such as:

– Within infrastructure: maintenance of roads and maintenance of canals.
– Within culture: public library, concert house, theatre and cultural education.

At the lowest layer a budget item is, for example, the salary costs of the public library, or the energy costs of the theatre. There may be hundreds of items in an advanced budget structure.

The city of Oldenburg uses, as in other German public sector organizations, the term 'Haushaltsplan' for its budget. Literally translated, this means 'a plan of the city's household', which is an adequate indication of what the user can expect. The plan of the household of Oldenburg is an overview of its intentions including its financial aspects of costs and revenues for a certain year. The budget structure of Oldenburg is illustrated in Table 6.1. The top layer is the overall household, and the second layer includes eleven function groups (such as city planning and youth/education), which are connected to a third layer of in total 28 sub-budgets. Some function groups are related to only one sub-budget (e.g. city planning), while others contain two to five sub-budgets (e.g. governance). The sub-budgets coincide with organizational units, such as departments. The fourth layer gives for each sub-budget one or more products with a number of sub-products. There are 78 products, and each product has one to ten sub-products, for which performances are identified; so, the total number of sub-products with performance information amounts to a few hundred. At each layer of the Oldenburg budget structure the cost and revenue categories are listed. Consequently, Oldenburg uses a five-layer budget structure, from which the layers below the top of the overall household are presented in Table 6.1 (the final column includes both the layer of the products and sub-products).

In addition to the explanation of the budget structure, some more general remarks can be made about Oldenburg's budget document. First, this document encompasses three types of financial statements for each of the function groups:

– A planned income statement ('Ergebnishaushalt'), in the sense of a planning of the revenues and costs (expenses) over the year.
– A planned cash flow statement ('Finanzhaushalt'), in the sense of a planning of the cash inflows and outflows over the year.
– A planning of the investment projects to be undertaken during the year.

Second, both the planned income statement and the planned cash flow statement have a similar format. It starts with an overview of the budget as a whole, then provides figures for each of the function groups, and finally digs deeper by giving the financial details for each product and sub-product within the function groups. Third, at each layer of the budget, a multi-year presentation is provided, with the budget year in the middle, the two previous years (with preliminary realized figures) on the left, and the three years after the budget year on the right (these three future budget years only contain estimates and are not meant to authorize the relevant spendings). Finally, performance information is provided based on a pre-established format for all sub-products.

Table 6.2 gives two examples of this formatted performance information. For many sub-products performance targets are still lacking, so here the information quality is expected to be improved in the future years. Performance budgeting is further discussed in Section 6.6.

Budget rules

The budget system of a governmental organization is mostly subject to certain formal rules, which are expressed through law or regulation. These formal rules identify the steps in the budgetary process, when these steps have to be taken, and the responsibilities of the various stakeholders therein, especially of the Executive and the Legislature (Lienert, 2013). In a municipal context, the Council is the Legislature and the Cabinet of the mayor and the aldermen is the Executive. At the central level, the parliament is the Legislature and the ministries are the Executive. The Executive's main responsibilities are to prepare and submit the budget to the Legislature, and to report on its implementation to the Legislature. The main responsibilities of the Legislature are to approve the budget (including budget revisions), and to monitor the budget execution. The budget rules also

Table 6.1   Budget structure of Oldenburg

11 Function group[3]	28 Sub-budgets	78 Examples of products and sub-products (per function group)
1. Governance	01. Mayor's office 02. Press office 03. Women emancipation office 04. Audit office	Representations (related to sub-budget 01) Internal promotion of women (related to sub-budget 03)
2. Management and human resources management	10. Office for general administration and human resources management 10.1 Pension provisions	Competences improvement of employees (related to sub-budget 10)
3. Economic development and properties	11. Economic development office	Purchase of developed and undeveloped lands
4. Financial management and Law	20. Finance and control office 20.1. Properties 20.2. Funds management 20.3. Finance management 22. Law office	Budgeting and controlling (related to sub-budget 20) Giving advice and acting on behalf of the city on law affairs (related to sub-budget 22)
5. Safety and order	21. Safety and order office 21.1. Markets 23. Fire brigade 23.1. Rescue services 24. Consumer Protection and Veterinary office	Weekly market at town hall place (related to sub-budget 21.1) Fire and disaster protection (related to sub-budget 23)
6. Culture, museums, sports	30. Culture and sports office 31. Museums, collections and art houses	Music education for children (related to sub-budget 30) Organizing cultural events (related to sub-budget 31)
7. City planning	40. City planning office	Redevelopment of city districts
8. Traffic and road infrastructure	41. Traffic and road infrastructure office	Use of public parking facilities
9. Environment, building code, parks and cemeteries	43. Environment and building code office 43.1 Cemeteries/burials	Nature and landscape conservation (related to sub-budget 43) Operation of cemeteries (related to sub-budget 43.1)
10. Social and health affairs	32.Health office 50. Social services office 50.1 Jobs centre	Mentally disabled persons aid (related to sub-budget 32) Settling social service applications (related to sub-budget 50)
11. Youth and education	51. Office for youth, family and education 51.1 Youth aid centre	Support of young pregnant women and their children (related to sub-budget 51)

Source: Haushaltsplan Oldenburg 2012, p. 67 (Function groups), pp. 111–13 (Sub-budgets) and pp. 227–1496 (Products and performances).

---

3   In German, 'Teilhaushalt', literally, sub-budget, but due to its functional labelling here called 'function group'. There is also a function group of 'autonomous foundations', which is disregarded here.

Table 6.2 Examples of sub-product performance information in Oldenburg's 2012 budget

Format	Example 1: Equality of women and men	Example 2: Health protection
Responsible manager	Head of the women emancipation office	Head of the health affairs office
Brief description	Policy aimed at equalizing the professional chances for women and men	Assessment of drinking and swimming pool water quality
Controllability	Medium	Medium
Reach/Audience	Internal	Public swimming pools, schools markets, etc.
Performance target	At least 55% of new jobs to be occupied by women	Full water quality assessment of all public water facilities

Source: Haushaltsplan 2012 Oldenburg, pp. 242–3 and 1138–9. The performance description in both examples is simplified for illustrative reasons.

contain *principles of proper budgeting*, such as (Lienert, 2013, p. 71; de Renzio, 2013, p. 139; Wildavsky, 1984, Prologue):

– Comprehensiveness (all expenses and revenues are included in the budget).
– Specificity (a sufficient extent of detail in budget items in order to assure steering and monitoring opportunities for the Legislature).
– Annuality (the budget covers a year ahead in order to enable reliable predictions of financial figures).
– Transparency and accountability (giving timely and accurate information in both the budget and the reporting about the budget execution).

The budget rules also prescribe the *accounting system* to be used (e.g. cash versus accrual accounting; see Chapters 2 and 3) and the *budget decomposition* into items. There is a trend of going from a detailed to a global budget decomposition, i.e. reducing the number of items from hundreds of expense categories to, for example, 30–50 programmes or product groups. In addition, the budget rules can indicate under which restrictions non-spent resources on one item can be reallocated to other items,[4] which approach their spending limits, or whether and under what conditions non-spent resources can be transferred to the next year's budget.

Oldenburg's budget practice is based on detailed regulations and providing a summary would go beyond the scope of this chapter. Therefore, only some major elements are highlighted. The regulations prescribe that the accounting system has to be based on accrual accounting. In addition, the budget process,

----

4 This is sometimes called 'budget virement'.

both its preparation and approval, are prescribed. The State of Lower Saxony requires municipalities within its state to decompose the budget into groups of functions ('Teilhaushalte'), while these function groups need to be decomposed into sub-budgets, which have to be decomposed further into products and sub-products. The municipalities are subject to regulations regarding the function groups and sub-budgets, but they are free to choose an appropriate number of products and sub-products. So, the budget layering is mandatory but part of its content is discretionary for each municipality. As illustrated earlier, Oldenburg makes use of 11 function groups, 28 sub-budgets and 78 products (see Table 6.1).

Oldenburg's council has to decide on the total budget and the budget at the product and sub-product level. Oldenburg has some additional regulations related to shifting opportunities among budget items and the transfer of unspent resources to the next year. Shifting resources within each sub-budget is left to the deliberations between the budget holders, without a formal approval right of the Council. However, shifting resources from one to the other sub-budget requires approval from the Council, if these shifts are relatively large. The transfer of unspent money to the next budget year is restricted to those cases in which approved investments are partly delayed and to operational expenditures for which the municipality has formal commitments. The reason for this restricted policy of expense transfers over subsequent years is Oldenburg's relatively problematic financial situation, which aims to use unspent resources for lowering the municipal debt position. This policy, however, comes at a cost. Budget holders are motivated to avoid unspent resources, which could lead to what is called 'December-fever', i.e. spending all the allocated resources by the end of year in order to avoid budget cuts in the future, even if not all final spendings are rational.

Budget functions

Budgeting is seen as a main steering mechanism in organizations, both in the private and the public sector. Budgeting is distinctive because steering is focused on money. That is both an appealing feature of budgets and a feature that is symptomatic to a certain extent of their 'narrow-mindedness'. Proper steering on money is undoubtedly crucial in any organization. Money enables comparability of inherently diverging functions or tasks. Money is also scarce, in the sense that the financial requirements of all desires are often much higher than the available resources. So, it is rational to prioritize these wishes and make their implementation feasible through budgeting. However, budgeting is not the only way of steering an organization (Merchant and Van der Stede, 2007, chapters 2–4). Purely financial budgeting can be enriched by including performance information in addition to financial information (performance budgeting will be addressed in Section 6.5). Another option is 'personnel control', which includes recruiting employees whose qualifications match the demands of the organization, and training these employees to keep their competences up to date. In addition, so-called 'process control' in the form of providing action guidelines can be part of a steering repertoire. Finally, steering by means of a dialogue among members of an organization including sharing ideas about possible improvements of the organization's products/services and processes can contribute to the organization's success. This may be labelled 'interactive control' (Simons, 1995).

Basically, budgeting serves two separate but interrelated functions, i.e. *planning* and *control* (Anthony and Young, 2002, pp. 4–5; de Renzio, 2013, p. 141; see also Chapter 1, Section 1.2). In a more elaborate sense the following *budgeting functions* can be distinguished:

- *Planning*: providing an overview of the desirable activities in a future period including a possible justification, such as the expected contribution of these activities to the goals of the organization.
- *Prediction*: giving an estimation of the financial implications of certain factors on the future operations of an organization, for example about the impact of changing salary conditions or certain funding conditions, such grants from central to local government.
- *Targeting*: setting desirable levels of goal-related performances, both financial (for instance, excluding a deficit) and non-financial (for example, accomplishing a rate of client satisfaction of at least 80% in supplying services).
- *Authorization*: enabling an executive body, such as a Cabinet of mayor and aldermen in a municipality, to spend money according to constraints set by a legislative body, such as the Council in a municipal setting. This function is crucial in the public sector because it relates to different roles of the executive and the legislative body, i.e. drafting the budget and approval of the budget respectively. The approved spending levels for each of the budget items are called '*appropriations*'.
- *Co-ordination*: alignment of different functional domains within an organization. This can relate to the alignment between primary functions of the organization, for instance the extent to which different primary functions (e.g. infrastructure, care, social services) contribute to a cutback target. Alignment can also concern the relationship between primary and supporting functions in the organization (such as financial administration or IT support), particularly whether there is an appropriate balance between the resources spent on supporting functions and their benefits to the primary functions.
- *Control*: during the budget execution stage, monitoring the extent to which planned activities are executed accordingly, and considering, whenever needed, corrective actions. For example, signalling that a particular budget is likely to be exceeded and taking cutback actions in order to avoid this, or observing that desirable levels of client satisfaction will not be accomplished and changing certain processes in order to avoid this.

Some further clarifications about these budget functions are provided. Planning, prediction, targeting, authorization and coordination are all specific functions of planning in a more general sense. Moreover, planning and control are separated but mutually interconnected. A plan is, for example, often based on the experience as documented in an earlier stage, during the control phase of the activities. This is crucial, since the plan must also include views on the way and the timeframe in which the objectives pursued can be realized. Finally, as already explained in Chapter 1 (see Section 1.5), budgeting in the public sector is to some extent different from budgeting in the private sector. Two elements stand out in this respect. First, budgeting is relatively more important because public sector organizations are controlled by politicians and governments can impose taxes on citizens, so that budgets need to be detailed in terms of their elements (programmes, services), and comparisons between the budgeted and the actual realization of those elements are crucial. In addition to its function to raise resources for expenditures, taxing has a macro-economic function, for example to guarantee that the governmental deficit and debt will not be higher than a certain standard.

Oldenburg's Council has authorization rights at the level of the products and sub-products. Most of the performance of the sub-products have an informative character, in the sense that expected outcomes are presented. This relates to the planning and projection function of the budget. Some of the sub-products, however, are characterized by demanding target performances, such as in the way in which the municipality needs to issue permits for the integration of immigrants with targets concerning the proper handling of these permits. In these cases the targeting function of budgeting is seen. The coordination function of Oldenburg's budget is visible from the political priorities of the various function groups. Economic affairs (including stimulating employment) and Education can be seen as such, whereas for other function groups the share in the budget remains approximately the same over the years.

6.4 The budgeting process

The budgeting process, here taken as the process of preparing and deciding about the budget, is often quite complex and time-consuming. The main reason is that many competing demands for resources have to be aligned to a constrained amount of available resources. This requires centrally issued guidelines, de-centrally formulated plans, and consultations between certain central departments, especially the Finance department, and the decentralized operating departments. Many managers at different organizational levels are involved and elected politicians can play a decisive role in various stages of the budgeting process.

The budgeting process begins long before the start of the year for which the budget needs to be drafted; often between eight to twelve months before the budget year starts. The first step is mostly taken by the financial department, which sets out *guidelines* for the budgeting process. These guidelines are partly *technical*, for instance about the expected changes in the salary costs (wage level increases) or other production factors, such as energy and materials. Often, but not always, more *politically laden* constraints can be part of these guidelines. The type of guidelines depends on the context in which the organization operates. If, for example, the organization is faced with financial problems, such as an expected deficit, cutback targets may be part of the guidelines. These targets can be proportional – every policy field will be cut with the same proportion – but it is also possible that politicians, particularly members of the executive body, want to protect certain policy fields from cuts. Research has shown that the politically-neutral proportional cuts approach loses its significance if it has already been applied in the past and when the financial problems to be solved are larger (Raudla et al., 2013, p. 10). If an organization is financially very healthy and available resources are relatively large, politicians might point to favourite policy fields which are allocated larger resources than less favourite policy fields.

After the centrally issued guidelines are made accessible to all departments within the organizations, often these departments – called the decentralized level – will be asked to make budget proposals. These proposals may be based on what was in the budget in previous years. Only small technical adaptations are made, for price changes of production factors, and additionally for the financial consequences of certain new initiatives. This type of budget preparation is called '*incrementalism*', in the sense of budgeting through small steps. An opposite way of budget preparation is labelled as '*zero-base budgeting*', which implies that every year the financial consequences of all activities or programmes have to be thoroughly justified. So, all operations are seen as if they should start from scratch. Although zero-base budgeting is attractive for its fundamental approach to justifying budgets, it is also very time-consuming and may not be politically realistic. Public sector experiences with zero-base budgeting mostly point to failures (Wildavsky, 1984, pp. 202–1).

When the decentralized budget proposals are available, a *consultation process* between the central and de-central level follows. Departments are invited to give explanations for their proposals and after a critical assessment by the financial department they may be required to revise their proposals. This process can take several rounds, for example firstly purely managerial, and subsequently including politicians, especially from the executive body, in the consultations.

The final step in the budget preparations is to bring all the revised budgets together in the *overall budget* for the organization. There is no unambiguous way to do this. One option is to ask the Finance department to draft an overall-budget, including some alternative ways to match available and desirable resources. Another option is to ask the member of the executive with Finance as his or her domain, to prepare such a proposal, often in consultation with the Finance department. Finally, the executive body decides on the overall budget to be proposed to the legislative body.

This is the first step in the *decision-making process*. The second step concerns the debates about the overall budget in the legislative body (the Council or the parliament), including debates in committees. The overall budget has to be approved by the legislative body, possibly after amending the overall budget as proposed by the executive body.

The above description of the budgeting process in a public sector organization shows that it combines a *top-down* and *bottom-up approach*. The central guidelines and the interventions of the central financial department with the inputs coming from the de-central departments are part of a top-down approach, whereas the de-centrally developed budget proposals and the contributions to the negotiations with the financial department about these proposals are part of a bottom-up approach. In practice, both approaches are combined but the emphasis may diverge, depending on the context in which the organization operates but also on its tradition and culture. The occurrence of financial stress can, for example, be a reason for a primarily top-down approach which guarantees the accomplishment of budget cuts, while a prosperous financial situation can underlie the adoption of a mainly bottom-up approach, which aims to stimulate innovative initiatives. In addition, some public sector organizations are characterized by a strong involvement of politicians in the preparation of policy making, while politicians in other organizations hold a more detached position in this respect, which can be a reason for emphasizing a top-down or bottom-up approach respectively. Finally, large and complex organizations need some elements of a bottom-up approach, simply because the top of such an organization lacks sufficient knowledge about the capillaries of its organization.

Oldenburg's budget process is illustrated in Table 6.3, as far as budget preparation and decision-making is concerned. Budget execution is the subject of Section 6.5.

Table 6.3 shows that the budget process combines centrally provided guidelines and de-centrally prepared inputs. Possible tensions between the central and de-central level, which can be based on both conflicting interests and information asymmetry, can be solved, or at least discussed in the budgeting consultations. In addition, Oldenburg's budget process shows that politicians play a major role at the end of the process when the formal debates about the budget take place and when budget revisions can be discussed. This is also the stage at which the formal approval of the budget by the Council is settled.[5] Earlier in the process, the mayor and the political officials (i.e. a kind of aldermen) can have a say in the political aspects of the centrally issued guidelines, for example about the desirable budget cuts. Finally, the table shows that a thorough process of preparing and deciding about an annual budget is a time consuming operation: in Oldenburg it takes nine months.

---

5   In the past the Council has also been involved in establishing budgetary ceilings ('Eckwerten') for each of the function groups early in the budgeting process, but currently these budgetary ceilings are established at the managerial level within the municipality.

Table 6.3 The budgeting process in the city of Oldenburg for the 2012 budget

Time schedule	Activity	Explanation
April 2011	Accounts over 2010 are closed and pointers for the 2012 budget are provided	This is part of the cyclic process of the planning and control, for example, overspending on certain budget items in 2010 can be an input for estimations for the 2012 budget
May 2011	The various budget holders (often department heads) are invited to start drafting their budget, given a centrally provided framework for the 2012 budget	This framework can include assumptions about price changes in certain input categories (e.g. salaries, material purchases), but also more politically oriented assignments, such as necessary budget cuts in comparison with the previous year
June–August 2011	First draft of the 2012 budget based on the contributions of the budget holders on both financial figures and performance information	During this stage the de-central contributions to the budget are included in the overall budget, and the central financial department checks the de-central inputs
September–October 2011	Budget consultations between the central and de-central level, and drafting of the budget proposal by the Executive	This stage aims to clarify question marks between the central and de-central level, in which members of the Executive can also be involved
November–December 2011	Discussions and decision-making at the political level, so between the Council and the Executive	This stage starts with debates in the various council committees; in Oldenburg proposals for revisions of the budget are listed and finally the Council decides on the budget including the proposals for revisions

Source: Zeitplan Haushaltsaufstellung Oldenburg 2014 (time schedule 2014 budget preparation). The table gives a simplified version of this time schedule and explanatory notes are added based on the conducted interviews with the senior members of Oldenburg's financial staff.

6.5   Budget types

Budget types can be distinguished according to the way in which budgetary information is presented in the budget document. The presentation of budgetary information is linked with how the budget is prepared, especially with the budget structure, as explained in Section 6.3. A distinction can be made between input, activity, output and outcome budgets. Performance budgets are an umbrella term for output and outcome budgets. This section will elaborate on the different budget types.

Budget types

Budget types are often distinguished according to the stage in the transformation process of a public sector organization, which uses inputs for conducting activities

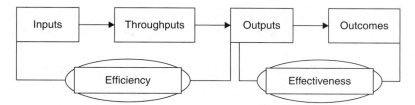

Figure 6.2 The transformation process of a public sector organization

(throughputs), which lead to the production of products or services (outputs), which in their turn bring about certain societal effects (outcomes); see Figure 6.2.

This conceptualization of a public sector organization as a transformation process also enables us to define efficiency and effectiveness. *Efficiency* relates the inputs to the outputs and establishes whether the outputs are produced at acceptable costs. *Effectiveness* links the outcomes to the outputs, enabling the organization to establish whether the outputs have led to the desired effects (see, for instance, Jackson, 2011, p. 16).

Based on the specification of a public sector organization's transformation process, a distinction can be made between four types of budgets:

1. *Input budget*: budgeted costs are presented for each of the resource categories, such as salaries, depreciation, energy costs, material costs and costs for hiring external staff. Each resource category can be sub-divided further, for example, salary costs for different employee groups or depreciation costs for different groups of fixed assets. This is also labelled as *line-item budgeting.*

2. *Programme or activity budget*: budgeted costs and revenues are presented per group of activities or a programme. A programme includes a range of inter-related activities aimed at achieving certain goals, such as an employment promotion programme, a water conservation programme or a programme aiming at involving citizens in governmental policy making.

3. *Output budget*: budgeted costs and revenues are presented per product or group of products. A product can be seen as a deliverable of the organization for specific external clients, so, for example, sports services can be seen as a product group with supporting amateur sports clubs, sport services for elderly people and swimming pool services as three separate products. It is not always easy to identify deliverables for specific clients, for instance in the case of law enforcement or city planning.

4. *Outcome budgeting*: budgeted costs and revenues are presented related to the goals to be achieved by activities/programmes or products/product groups, so their societal effects are identified rather than the product deliverables. For example, rather than the provision of sports services for elderly people the extent to which these people improve their health condition is what matters, or policing work is not measured by the number of crimes in which the police force is involved but by its contribution to an improved sense of security of

the public. However, it may be difficult to link the contribution of a particular public sector activity to these wider societal objectives.

Performance budgeting

Performance budgeting is seen as a core issue of public sector reforms. According to the OECD, many countries have adopted some form of performance budgeting, and performance budgeting is assumed to accomplish, among others, the following benefits (OECD, 2007, p. 11): it links resources to goal-related results; it contributes to the managerial planning and control of programmes; and it enhances the transparency of these programmes through better information for the public and legislative bodies.

The OECD observes a variety of performance budgeting approaches and it makes a distinction between three basic types, as summarized in Table 6.4 (OECD, 2007, pp. 20–4). Some explanations will further clarify this distinction:

1. *Direct/formula-based performance budgeting*: this type is the most ambitious because it links the volume of the production of services to the budget through a price per unit of the production (so, $p \times q = B$, where p = price per unit, q = volume of units and B = budget). Examples include funding in the higher education sector (budgeting through a price per degree programme or course) and the healthcare sector (budgeting through a price per treatment); see Groot, 1999, for illustrations in the Netherlands.

2. *Performance-informed budgeting*: now the volume of production is one of the determinants of the budget, but other factors are also important, for example, whether the existing capacity is sufficient for producing more than in the past, whether the quality of the services could be improved with a lower production volume than in the past. This budgeting type can also acknowledge the fact that the production volume only partly determines the costs of production, or

Table 6.4 Performance budgeting types

Type characteristic→ ↓	Linkage between performance information and funding	Planned or actual performance	Main purpose in the budget process
Presentational	No link	Performance targets and/or performance results	Accountability
Performance-informed budgeting	Loose/indirect link	Performance targets and/or performance results	Planning and/or accountability
Direct/formula performance budgeting	Tight/direct link	Performance results	Resource allocation and accountability

Source: OECD, 2007, p. 21.

that some governmental activities do not lead to a homogeneous production, for instance, policy making or supervision.

3. *Presentational performance budgeting*: in this case performance information is mainly used to show the content of a certain policy field, but there is no link with the budgeted amounted of money; that is why accountability is the main purpose.

Although performance budgeting is attractive for many reasons as set out earlier in this section, its application in practice is still problematic, as recent research shows (see also Wildavsky, 1978). Raudla (2012), for example, studied the use of performance information in budgetary decision-making by members of parliament (MPs) in Estonia, and especially those members that were part of the budgetary and accounting committee. Her findings indicate that these MPs are mainly interested in financial control, and pay little attention or even disregard the available performance information. The MPs argue that they do not have enough time to take notice of this performance information, which is often too detailed. They also point to a lack of connection between resources and performances. They would prefer more concise performance information, which is visualized and includes comparisons over time. A study by Ter Bogt et al. (2015) about performance budgeting in a Dutch province indicates that information overload can be avoided by focusing on a restricted number of politically relevant programmes for which concrete performance information is provided. The Council members of this province did not intensively use this information, although they appreciated its improved format.

So, even with improved performance information in the budget, there remains a gap between appreciation on paper and acting in practice. This could lead to two preliminary conclusions. First, the more ambitious type of formula-based performance budgeting will be restricted to those services which are homogeneous and can be measured easily in terms of volume. Second, for many other governmental activities or programmes, for which these conditions do not hold, performance-informed or even presentational performance budgeting is the highest achievable. It is, however, a challenge for practitioners and academics to search for better formats and conditions for effective performance budgeting, because focusing only on inputs in budgeting remains a pitiful ambition (see further, Curristine, 2005).

Table 6.5 shows Oldenburg's budget for the year ending 31.12.2012. In addition, the annual accounts have been added, including an overview of the variances between the budget and the annual accounts. As explained earlier, Oldenburg's budget can be presented at different layers, i.e. the function groups (11), the sub-budgets (28) and the products (78); see Table 6.1. Given the scope of this chapter, there is only room for presenting the budget version at the function group layer.

Some clarifications may enhance the readability of Table 6.5. Each function group shows a deficit, because the costs are higher than the specific revenues of a function group. There is one important exception: function group 'Financial

Table 6.5 Budget and annual accounts over 2012 of Oldenburg (in millions of euros)*

11 Function groups ↓	Budget		Preliminary annual accounts		Variances between budget and annual accounts	
Costs/ revenues⟶	Costs	Revenues	Costs	Revenues	Costs	Revenues
1. Governance	5.1	0.5	4.9	0.4	0.2 F	0.1 U
2. Management and human resources management	16.9	1.0	14.5	1.0	2.4 F	0.0
3. Economic development and properties	3.7	1.0	3.5	1.3	0.2 F	0.3 F
4. Financial management and Law	35.5	257.7	33.9	264.6	1.6 F	6.9 F
5. Safety and order	29.1	15.4	28.2	16.2	0.9 F	0.8 F
6. Culture, museums, sports	23.1	1.4	23.1	1.9	0.0	0.5 F
7. City planning	2.6	0.4	2.5	0.4	0.1 F	0.0
8. Traffic and road infrastructure	16.4	5.7	15.4	5.5	1.0 F	0.2 U
9. Environment, building code, parks and cemeteries	12.8	3.7	11.8	4.0	1.0 F	0.3 F
10. Social and health affairs	123.4	64.4	122.0	70.6	1.4 F	6.2 F
11. Youth and education	111.7	17.8	111.2	17.9	0.5 F	0.1 F
Income and expenses of capital investments that were externally funded	13.8	10.2	13.8	10.2	0.0	0.0
Total	394.2	379.2	384.8	394.0	9.3 F	14.9 F
Surplus (+)/Deficit (-)	−15.0		+ 9.2		+ 24.2	

Source: Derived from *Finanz- und Leistungsbericht zum 31.12.2012 (Cash flow and Income statement for 2012)*, Stadt Oldenburg, 2013, p. 5, after some simplification. In the final columns F stands for favourable (lower actual costs than budgeted or higher actual revenues than budgeted), while U stands for unfavourable (then the opposite applies).

management and Law' shows a substantial surplus of approximately €220 million, which can be explained by the fact that all general income of Oldenburg, especially general grants and tax income, are attributed to this function group. This general income is used to cover the deficits of all the other function groups. For each function group, variances are calculated between the budgeted and the actual figures, both for the costs and the revenues. This enables an assessment of the extent to which actuals are more favourable (or unfavourable) than budgeted figures. Such an assessment could inform future budgetary processes, and as such are symptomatic of the cyclic character of these processes. Moreover, the table shows an expected deficit of €15.0 million for all function groups together, while the realized surplus amounts to €9.2 million. This is equivalent to a positive variance between the actual and budgeted figures of €24.2 million (= €9.3 + €14.9), which is also equal to the sum of the favourable and unfavourable variances in the last two columns of the table. Finally, performance information is lacking in this specification of the budget. So, this points to an input budget. However, as explained earlier, Oldenburg also includes performance information in its budget at the sub-product level (see Table 6.2 for illustrations).

Oldenburg's main financial objective is to realize at least a break-even situation in the future, but accomplishing a financial surplus for funding important investment projects is seen as preferable. In addition, the information for decision-making and control in the budget has to be improved, especially regarding the quality of the performance information, i.e. more concrete performance indicators with more demanding targets. Whether the budgetary documents will get a more compact format in the future – currently this document amounts to almost 1,500 pages – is a matter of further debate. Several measures can be considered in this respect, such as lowering the number of sub-products within each of the products, and/or focusing performance information on the most important products and sub-products.

6.6   Budget execution and interim reports

Budgetary planning and budgetary control are two sides of the same coin. The overall importance of budgeting in a public sector context is assuring that resources, which are mainly raised through enforcement (i.e. taxing), are spent by political bodies according to priorities for which these bodies can be held accountable. This implies in the planning stage that the budget needs to have a sufficient extent of detail about these priorities, as reflected by different functions, programmes and/or product groups. In this way the political body clarifies its spending priorities for diverging destinations. During the execution stage of the budget there is a need to give account of the extent to which the budgeted costs and income are accomplished. This implies, in general, a *comparison between budgeted and realized figures* at the level of budget items. In addition, such a comparison can lead to a consideration by the relevant decision-maker about a *corrective action* in order to reduce the gap between what was planned and what is expected to be realized. Several issues are at stake here:

– At what level of detail does budgetary control need to take place?
– Which stakeholder, either political or managerial, is responsible for control?

– How often during an annual budget cycle is reporting about budget execution required for achieving proper control?

– What is the content of the comparison between planned and actual figures?

These questions will be considered below.

Previous sections in this chapter have shown that budget items can be defined in various ways. In a politically controlled organization, it is likely that political bodies, such as the Executive and the Council in a municipality, have authorization rights at a relatively high level of aggregation about budget items, particularly about programmes or product groups. Their control needs to match this level. Managerial budget holders can be held accountable for budget items at a lower level of aggregation, for example at revenue and cost categories for products within product groups. The reporting cycle works bottom-up, meaning that managers start to report about the execution of the budget at a detailed level, which subsequently forms the input for reporting at the more aggregate political level.

The reporting frequency is a matter of seeking a balance between being informed too often or too late about budget execution. If the reporting frequency is high, for example every month within an annual cycle, the risk of not being informed about discrepancies between expectations and realization is low. But the downside of this high frequency is that it is time-consuming and deviations by chance are difficult to separate from disorders from systematic causes. However, if the reporting frequency is too low, for example once a year, around the summer, important deviations between planned and actual figures from the first half year may come too late and those over the last half year remain invisible. In practice, reporting frequencies often range from two to four times a year. Using higher reporting frequencies for managerial, rather than for political, purposes is also an option to be considered.

In general, the reporting content should match the budgeting content. So, if budgeting combines financial and non-financial information (i.e. performances), reporting should be based on a similar format. However, pragmatic reasons may inhibit a rigid application of this principle. The first report in a year may come too early for a complete assessment of the budget execution, while later in the year more information can be gathered about both financial and non-financial data.

Just comparing budgeted and realized figures in a report is often insufficient. Major deviations require explanation; for example, to understand why the expected expenses are higher than budgeted, or why a planned project has been delayed, or why client satisfaction for a particular service is lower than targeted. In addition to explanations about such deviations, certain measures can be announced for reducing the observed gap between planning and realization, such as speeding up procedures for a delayed investment project, or improving certain processes to achieve higher client satisfaction. In practice, certain rules of thumb are developed regarding the question of what extent of deviation requires explanation and corrective action. For example, in a financial sense, deviations larger than 5% of the budget or larger than €25,000 may fall under the 'explain and correct regime'.

There can also be a wider impact of interim reports than just the annual budget execution, as explained above. An interim report can also point to more systematic failures in the planning process, for example showing that assumptions about certain cost figures were too optimistic. Then, there is also an impact on the subsequent planning cycle; if an interim report in the first quarter of 2012 gives such a signal, it can influence the budget preparation for the year 2013.

The Council of Oldenburg receives an interim report about the progress of the budget execution four times a year, i.e. at the beginning of each quarter. These progress reports include financial information and information about relevant performances of the sub-products. It is unusual that original plans, which are part of the budget, are revised in the course of the year, but the interim reports particularly inform the Council whether the original plans can be implemented as intended, and if not, what the main reasons for the observed differences are.

The interim reports' character changes in the course of the year. The first report has a mainly financial-technical character and updates certain assumptions made in the budget, for example about tax revenues or price changes of certain inputs. The reports presented in the 2nd and 3rd quarter contain more politically relevant information about differences between the original intentions and how they are executed, both financially and non-financially. The interim report presented in the 4th quarter is a first draft of the accounts over the year, in the sense of the income statement.

Oldenburg's 3rd progress report over 2012, which is dated 30 September, indicates that the reporting of variances between the budget and the expected realization will focus on financial variances of more than €100,000 at the individual product, sub-product or investment project level. This refers to a kind of 'control tolerance', in the sense that relatively small variances remain unexplained. All relatively larger variances are explained extensively, in which a variety of reasons are possible, ranging from updated assumptions on financial transfers from other governments to delayed investment projects and including excessive costs or windfall gains. Some examples may clarify this:

– The revenues from taxes and grants show an improvement from €257.7 million in the budget to €262.1 million in the budget execution, which is mainly due to a conservative estimation of these revenues.
– The available resources for road construction are €11.9 million, while the expected expenditures will be €7.6 million, which is explained by an updated overview of road construction works.
– The expenses in the domain of sports and culture will be higher than budgeted (€23.8 million in comparison with €23.2 million), mainly due to additional external funding for certain cultural events which emerged during the year, including the related expenses.

In total the financial updates in the 3rd progress report result in a reduction of the financial deficit from €13.1 according to the budget to €2.4 million after nine months of budget execution. A detailed variance analysis of performances is, in general, not provided.

The definitive version of the accounts appears in the spring of the next year. Similar to other municipalities in Germany, a draft of Oldenburg's annual accounts has to be audited. Oldenburg has an audit office with members elected by the Council, who have an independent position towards the Executive and its staff. The annual accounts have to be audited before 1 June after the year-end. The annual accounts are prepared by the Executive and its staff and require approval from the Council.

6.7   The political context of budgeting

Section 6.4 showed that many actors are involved in the decisions about drafting and approving the budget, ranging from employees of the central financial department to managers and employees of de-central departments, and from members of the executive body (the mayor or a minster) to members of the legislative body (the council or the parliament). This list can be expanded with members of pressure groups (such as labour unions and client groups) and the public at large, partly represented by the media. All actors want to have an influence in the budgeting process, and they can make use of a diversity of measures for mobilizing their interests. Influence can be exerted in an open and transparent way, for example when members of political parties fight for their competing budget proposals in official meetings of the legislative body, or when managers advocate their budget proposals in a managerial meeting about the overall budget of their organization. These influences have a mainly political character, because – in addition to the costs – difficult to compare benefits of alternative budget proposals are discussed. To put it differently, it is not easy to use a common vocabulary in propagating more money for road maintenance, food aid to less fortunate fellow citizens or events in the innovative arts.

However, political influences in the budgeting process can also be hidden behind the scenes of carefully executed tactics and tricks (see also Rubin, 2000). Which issues are raised in the debates first and which at a later stage can serve the interests of certain actors. For example: the financial department can start the discussion about next year's budget with setting some severe constraints – e.g. the budget needs to be balanced, and fees and taxes will not rise more than inflation – before the decentralized departments are asked to come up with budget proposals. This type of positioning of the financial department can be further strengthened by requiring that budget proposals which require more money than last year have to be covered within the budget of the budget holder, thus adopting the slogan 'bear your own burden'. However, managers or members of the executive body, who want to raise budget proposals, can also make use of various tactics and tricks which may strengthen their position. Examples: overemphasizing the benefits and underestimating the costs of a budget proposal, or hiding the costs of a controversial budget proposal by spreading them over various budget periods and headings. It is, of course, the task of the financial department to denounce these tricks and to require that all cards are put on the table, but game playing will be there, whatever checks and balances are built into the process.

In a broader sense, these tricks and tactics can be seen as *budget games*. Various actors in the budgeting process have diverging interests and they serve these interests through tactics which protect their position in the allocation of scarce resources. Conflicts of interest are the driver for budget games and different extents of access to certain information are enablers for budget games. Two examples can illustrate this. One actor, e.g. a local department manager, can overestimate the need for resources for his/her programme, while another actor, the financial department manager, cannot assess the soundness this claim. Another example: it can be in the interest of a certain actor to reduce his/her efforts for achieving certain goals at the year-end (not visible to other actors), in order to avoid a favourable variance in the cost budget, because he/she fears that such a variance would lead to a cost budget reduction in the future.

During the budget decision process, political arguments and interests can also be observed. Irrespective of how budget amendments are presented, it is often crucial for a proposal to be made more promising by emphasizing the advantages if it is adopted. In addition, finding coalitions for supporting certain proposals are part of the political game of budgeting.

Oldenburg's practice shows interesting examples of how political aspects are observable in the decisions about the budget. The current mayor of the city has a majority of party political support in the Council. This gives room for debates between the parties represented in the Council for finding varying majorities to support certain budget proposals. The education domain has been the arena for initiatives from Council members to spend additional money for better facilities in its primary and secondary schools. In addition, the integration of educational services for specific groups, such as disabled pupils, in the regular school system has been the subject of debates in the Council. Ultimately, decision-making resulted in proposals for spending millions of additional euros in the school system. This additional spending was often funded by higher than proposed resources coming from taxes on income. It seems that the political parties wanted to surpass each other in making proposals for better education. The proposed amendments were often the result of give and take among the collaborating parties.

6.8   Concluding remarks

This chapter has introduced the budget as the most important financial document for the planning of annual financial policy making of a public sector organization.

Throughout this chapter the various aspects of budgeting were illustrated by examples about the city of Oldenburg in Germany. The budget was defined as a monetary representation of the planned activities of a governmental organization. It was shown that a budget can have varying structures. Often three to five layers are distinguished in the budget structure, where the overall organization is the top layer, functions or programmes are at intermediate layers and products and product groups at the lowest layers. At each layer budget items are characterized by cost and revenues categories. It was argued that budgeting has to be conducted according to certain principles, such as comprehensiveness, specificity and transparency. The various functions of the budget were listed, including planning and control as well as authorization. This chapter has subsequently described the budget process, which is often a combination of central and de-central inputs, including the setting of central guidelines, the preparation of budget drafts for different programmes or organizational units, and consultations between the central and de-central levels, finally resulting in decision-making about the budget. Various types of budgets have been discussed, especially input, activity, output and outcome budgets, where performance budgeting was introduced as the umbrella term for output and outcome budgets. After a budget has been settled, it needs to be properly executed. This implies the presentation of interim reports as part of the planning and control cycle in order to establish possible corrective actions when actual and budgeted figures diverge too much. Finally, this chapter has discussed the political context of the budgetary process, pointing to aspects of power and coalition forming in realizing political or managerial priorities, among others through budget games.

Public sector organizations are part of a governmental system controlled by politicians. A major responsibility of politicians relates to their authority to establish a budget. This authority is not confined only to the total amount of resources to be spent and funded in a period; it also concerns each of the individual programmes or services. This chapter has shown the impacts of this budgetary authority: on the one hand, the budget needs to be detailed in terms of its elements or items (programmes, services), and on the other hand, comparisons between the budgeted and the actual realization of those elements are crucial.

References

Anthony, R.N. and D.W. Young (2002), *Management Control in Nonprofit Organizations*, 7th edition, McGraw-Hill, Boston.

Curristine, T. (2005), Government performance: lessons and challenges, *OECD Journal on Budgeting*, Vol. 5, no. 1, pp. 127–51.

De Renzio, P, (2013), Assessing and comparing the quality of public financial management systems; theory, history and evidence, in: Allen, R., R. Hemming and B.H. Potter (eds), *The international handbook of public financial management*, Palgrave Macmillan, Basingstoke, chapter 7.

Groot, T. (1999), Budgetary Reforms in the Non-profit Sector: A Comparative Analysis of Experiences in Health Care and Higher Education in the Netherlands, *Financial Accountability & Management*, Vol. 15, no. 3/4, pp. 353–76.

Jackson, P.M. (2011), Governance by Numbers: What Have We Learned Over the Past 30 Years?, *Public Money & Management*, Vol. 31, no. 1, pp. 13–26.

Lienert, I. (2013), The legal framework for public finances and budget systems, in: Allen, R., R. Hemming and B.H. Potter (eds), *The International Handbook of Public Financial Management*, Palgrave Macmillan, Basingstoke, chapter 3.

Merchant, K.A. and W.A. Van der Stede (2007), *Management Control Systems*, 2nd edition, Prentice Hall, Harlow.

OECD (2007), *Performance Budgeting in OECD Countries*, OECD, Paris.

Raudla, R. (2012), The use of performance information in budgetary decision-making by legislators: is Estonia different?, *Public Administration*, Vol. 90, no. 4, pp. 1000–1015.

Raudla, R., R. Savi and T. Randma-Liiv (2013), *Literature Review on Cutback Management*, COCOPS, European Commission Program on Coordinating for Cohesion in the Public Sector of the Future (www.cocops.eu).

Reichard, C. (2012), Umsetzung und Praxis des neuen kommunalen Haushalts- und Rechnungswesens; eine Auswertung vorliegender Empirie, *Verwaltung & Management*, Vol. 18, no. 3, pp. 118–121.

Rubin I.S. (2000), T*he Politics of Public Budgeting: Getting and Spending, Borrowing and Balancing*, 6th edition, Washington: CQ Press (chapter 1: The Politics of Public Budgeting).

Simons, R. (1995), *Levers of Control: How Managers Use Innovative Control Systems to Drive Strategic Renewal*, Harvard Business School Press, Boston.

Ter Bogt, H.J., G.J. van Helden and B. van der Kolk (2015), Challenging NPM Ideas about Performance Management: Selectivity and Differentiation in Outcome-oriented Performance Budgeting, *Financial Accountability & Management* (forthcoming).

Wildavsky, A. (1978), A Budget for all Seasons? Why the Traditional Budget Lasts, *Public Administration Review*, Vol. 38, pp. 501–09.

Wildavsky, A. (1984), *The Politics of the Budgetary Process*, 4th edition, Little, Brown & Company, Boston.

Documents of the city (Stadt) Oldenburg

Haushaltsplan 2012 (Budget over 2012), Oldenburg, 2011.

Haushaltsvollzug 2012 –Finanz und Leistungsbericht zum 30–09–2012 (Interim report on revenues/expenses and cash flows over the 2012 budget after three quarters of budget execution), Oldenburg, 2012.

Finanz- und Leistungsbericht zum 31.12.2012 (Cash flow and Income statement over 2012), Oldenburg, 2013.

Eröffnungsbilanz zum 1–1–2010 (First Balance sheet, 1–1–2010), Oldenburg, 2013.

Oldenburg-Flyer-Haushaltsplan-2012 (Information on Budget 2012 Oldenburg for citizens), Oldenburg, 2012.

Zeitplan Haushaltsaufstellung 2014 (Time schedule 2014 Budget), Internal document Oldenburg, 2013.

Verordnung über die Aufstellung und Ausführung des Haushaltsplan (Code about the drafting and the execution of the budget), Oldenburg, 2006.

7

Costing

Learning objectives

- ◆ To be familiar with basic cost accounting terms, such as the distinction between variable and fixed costs and between direct and indirect costs, and understand what cost allocation means in this respect
- ◆ To know the goals of cost allocation and costing in a public sector context
- ◆ To be able to apply simple and some more advanced methods of cost allocation, and to understand their outcomes
- ◆ To be able to apply cost–volume profit analysis for projects
- ◆ To understand how cost information can be used for managerial purposes, such as for cost reduction and value enhancing actions in a public sector context
- ◆ To have a basic understanding of target costing and marginal costing

---

7.1   Introduction

Cost calculation can serve various purposes. Organizations often want to be informed about the costs of their organizational units for control reasons, or they wish to know the full costs of their products and services for pricing purposes. A more specific cost calculation issue concerns the way in which the costs of internally produced supporting services, such as administration costs, can be attributed to the primary services for clients. Combining an organization's primary and supporting service costs enables the so-called 'full cost' to be calculated. Knowing the level of resources consumed by supporting services is important for the planning and control of the volume, quality and costs of those supporting services. These kinds of costing and cost allocation issues are discussed in this chapter.

The remainder of the chapter proceeds as follows. Section 7.2 introduces some important terms in the costing domain. Section 7.3 discusses the various goals of costing in a public sector context. Section 7.4 deals with the methods for allocating costs of supporting services to external services. Section 7.5 discusses a more specific costing issue, i.e. the use of cost information for the planning of projects. Section 7.6 indicates how public sector organizations can use costing information for managerial purposes, for example, for attuning internally produced supporting services to the needs of its external users. Section 7.7 introduces some cost accounting issues that cannot be comprehensively addressed within the limited scope of this chapter. Finally, Section 7.8 presents some concluding remarks.

Throughout this chapter we will use an example of an educational organization in the public sector for illustrating the various costing terms and methods. This organization is a municipal adult training institute, called 'A-LEARNING' and it offers courses for adults. It is a quite autonomous department, also called agency, within a certain municipality. This municipality requires that the costs of the services provided by A-LEARNING are mainly covered by fees, but it also provides resources to A-LEARNING in order to guarantee that certain services are accessible for lower income groups.

For simplicity only three types of courses are distinguished: IT, English and Employment Skills courses. These three types of courses are produced in different organizational units which are engaged in the so-called primary processes of the organization. There are also two departments for delivering supporting services: Product Development and Administration (financial and personnel). Figure 7.1 shows the organizational chart.[1]

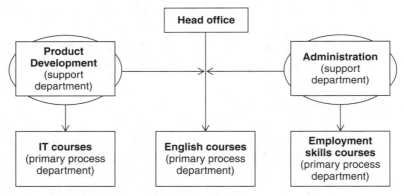

Figure 7.1 Organization chart of A-LEARNING

---

1 In this example the primary services departments only produce one type of service each. In practice, however, those departments often produce two or more services, for example IT courses with a different number of sessions and a diverging content. Then the full costs of such a primary services department have to be attributed to each of the services, which can be complicated if those services are heterogeneous in terms of the underlying activities.

7.2   Costing terms

Some costs have a direct relationship with the external services to be produced. These are called '*direct costs*'. However, for other costs that relationship is less clear or even completely absent. Those costs which have no straightforward relationship with the individual external services are called '*indirect costs*'. Indirect costs are also labelled as '*overhead costs*'. Overheads are, so to speak, located above the heads of the primary service departments, as Figure 7.1 indicates. The costs of teachers in either the IT, English or Employment Skills departments are direct costs, while the costs of the employees working in the departments of Product Development and Administration are indirect costs. These indirect costs can be attributed to the primary services departments through '*cost allocation*'. '*Costing*' is a more general term which refers to cost calculation procedures, ranging from calculating costs of different types of resources (e.g. personnel, capital), departments, services, or client groups.

It is important to understand that the distinction between direct and indirect costs is not given by nature, but it is dependent upon decisions about the way in which supporting services are organized and the way in which the costs of those services are measured in an organization. If, contrasted to the organization chart in Figure 7.1, Product Development was integrated in each of the primary process departments the underlying costs would be direct instead of indirect costs. But because Figure 7.1 indicates that Product Development is a centralized activity in A-LEARNING its costs are indirect and have to be allocated to the primary services departments. How costs of supporting services are measured also matters. Consider, for instance, the costs of heating. If those costs are measured for each of the departments separately, they will be direct costs for the primary services departments. However, if such measurement procedures are felt to be too expensive, and only the total heating costs of the organization are measured, these costs have to be attributed to each of the departments, for example related to the number of square metres used by each department; then the heating costs are indirect costs.

In addition to the distinction between direct and indirect costs, variable and fixed costs can be distinguished. *Variable costs* are those costs that change as a result of a change in the production volume, while *fixed costs* remain the same irrespective of the production volume.[2] The costs of teachers in each of the primary services departments, who have a permanent labour contract, are fixed costs. Housing costs are almost always fixed costs too, because an organization will have to pay a rent which is fixed during a certain period and will not be affected by the occupation rate of the rented buildings. Contrasted to that, the

---

2   Costs are assumed to be *fixed* only within the existing anticipated range of activity. A large expansion or reduction in activity may cause all costs to change, for example, as a result of opening a completely new production facility or closing an existing one. These are called *step* or *semi-fixed* costs.

costs of teachers for intensive individual training who are paid per hour and per trainee can be regarded as variable costs.

Often, variable costs are assumed to be the same as direct costs and fixed costs are supposed to be equal to indirect costs, but these assumptions are not true. Consider, for instance, the costs of temporary employees working in a supporting department due to peak work. These are variable but indirect costs. An opposite example regards the costs of equipment in one of the primary services departments (e.g. language computers in the department for English courses), which are direct and fixed costs.

A final distinction is that between *controllable* and *non-controllable costs*. This distinction relates to managerial responsibilities. If employees working in the departments can be recruited and dismissed by the department managers (within certain budgetary limits), these personnel costs are controllable costs for those managers. However, if the recruitment of employees is the sole responsibility of the top manager of the organization, the personnel costs are not controllable for the department managers, perhaps except the travelling costs and the costs for bonuses of their employees.

7.3   Cost allocation and costing goals

Table 7.1 gives an overview of cost allocation and costing goals. Given that the calculation of the full costs of unsold products for the balance sheet is not important in a public sector context, and regulations for cost calculation are evident, we will focus our explanations on the three remaining goals (see further: van Helden, 1997; Budding and Schoute, 2012).

Table 7.1 Goals of cost allocation and costing

Goal	Explanation
Pricing of services for external clients	Only applies to services for which a price is seen as appropriate; a price can cover either the full costs or a part of the full costs of service delivery
Policy making, budgeting and control based on the full costs of services, programmes or organizational units	Is applicable for all services and programmes, irrespective of the question of whether a price is charged; enables benchmarking of the costs of services and programmes, as well as cost control of organizational units
Valuation of the full costs of products in stock as an asset on the balance sheet	Is mostly irrelevant in the public sector because physical products are largely absent (service production is dominant in the public sector and services cannot be held in stock)
Compliance with regulations	Is dependent upon laws and regulations, which sometimes require that full costs of services or projects have to be calculated in, for example, tendering procedures
Management control of internal supporting services	Enables cost management of internal supporting services, including a consideration of outsourcing those services

a. *Costing for pricing*

If a public sector organization charges fees for certain services, those fees need to be based on well-founded cost calculations. This, for instance, applies to garbage collection, sewerage, waste-water treatment, as well as public utility services, such as water, electricity, gas and public transport. In addition, governmental bodies may ask fees for some other services that only partly cover the full costs. This could hold for library subscriptions, swimming pool tickets and all kinds of cultural services, such as theatre, concert and museum tickets. In adult training fees can cover either their full costs or part of those full costs, as will be shown below in Section 7.4.

b. *Budgeting and control*

In some public sector branches budgeting is based on the cost per unit multiplied by the volume of these units. This type of budgeting can be observed in, for instance, the healthcare and educational sectors. Both the funding of those services can be based on per unit calculations like diagnosis-related groups in hospitals and certificates in the university sector. But they can also be used internally in organizations belonging to those sectors, for example when faculties within a university receive their budget according to similar formulas as the university receives its funding from central government, i.e. through the number of certificates multiplied by the costs per certificate (see Groot, 1999 for examples in the Netherlands). In addition, cost control of various types of items – services, programmes and organizational units – is an important goal of costing; a comparison between planned and actual costs can be an input for taking corrective actions or adjusted planning for future periods.

c. *Control of supporting services*

Here the goal is to make the use of internal supporting services, such as IT, administration and housing facilities, by primary services departments transparent. Primary services departments are motivated to make efficient use of those supporting services, asking themselves how much they need (volume), at what quality and for what cost. It could lead to a kind of internal market for these supporting services, including answering the question whether certain services have to be produced in-house or outside the organization (i.e. outsourcing). We will further elaborate this in Section 7.6 on cost management.

7.4   Methods for allocating indirect costs

Definition of cost allocation terms

The objective in this section is to calculate the full costs per unit of the external services (courses) for each of the primary services departments. For a proper understanding of cost allocation methods, three terms need to be defined first:

– *Cost categories* are types of resources needed for the activities of the organization, for example salary costs, depreciation costs and material costs.
– *Cost pools* are locations in the organization, or more broadly speaking, responsibility centres where costs are caused by the execution of activities (in Figure 7.1 each of the departments can be seen as a cost pool).
– *Cost objects* are items for which the organization finds it useful to calculate costs, especially products or services, but also client groups can be cost objects.[3]

Introduction to an example

Table 7.2 shows the costs per cost category in a certain year for each of the five departments (cost pools), as introduced in Figure 7.1. Only two cost categories are distinguished: salary costs and remaining costs. These remaining costs include the costs for the building and equipment, for heating and lighting, and for materials. The costs of the head office, as introduced in Figure 7.1, are part of the costs of the administration department. Table 7.2 also shows the number of services in this year for each of the primary service departments. A-LEARNING uses a standardized definition of a service, being a course of ten three-hour sessions for a group ranging from 15 to 30 participants. The number of courses and the average number of participants per course for each of the departments are also given in Table 7.2.

Simple cost allocation methods

Given the objective is to find the full costs per unit of the external services (courses) for each of the primary services departments, the first option regards a very simple method: dividing the total costs of the organization by the total

Table 7.2 Cost information (in 1,000 euros) per department of A-LEARNING

Department⟶	IT courses	English courses	Employment Skills courses	Product-Development	Administration	Total
Salary costs	550	480	220	110	390	1,750
Remaining costs	210	190	170	100	160	830
Total costs	760	670	390	210	550	2,580
Number of courses	290	280	123	–	–	693
Average number of participants per course	28	25	19			25.2 (average)

---

3 In a more formal sense cost categories can also be regarded as cost objects, for example if the organization wants to know its total salary costs. In a similar vein, a cost pool can also be cost object if the organization needs information about the total costs of the responsibility centres.

number of courses, so: €2,580,000/693 = €3,723, which would imply that each participant has to pay €3,723/25 = €149 (more precisely, €148.9, given that the organization wants to break even, so covering its costs but not making a profit). This very simple cost calculation is called the 'peanut butter costing method', because the costs are evenly spread across the different types of external services.

Although this calculation is attractive due to its simplicity, it is also rough. It does not take account of the fact that the direct costs per course of each of the departments are not the same, nor that the average number of participants per course is unequal. If we want to account for these considerations, the following, still quite simple, calculations will do:

The indirect costs can be attributed to the primary services departments by a mark-up which is the same for all three primary services departments:

So, the total of the indirect costs is €760,000 (= 210,000 + 550,000). The total of the direct costs is €1,820,000 (= 760,000 + 670,000 + 390,000), which results in mark-up for indirect costs on direct costs of €760,000/€1,820,000 = 41.8%. Table 7.3 shows the calculations of the costs of services for each of the primary services departments. This method is called the 'mark-up method'.

Table 7.3 shows that IT courses and English courses have approximately the same full costs per participant, but Employment Skills courses have much higher costs per participant. This is mainly due to two causes. First, the Employment Skills courses are more expensive, because they may include a brief traineeship which has to be supervised individually. Second, the average number of participants is lower in comparison with the two other types of courses.

So, the mark-up method as shown in Table 7.3, leads to more accurate full costs for each of the external services than the peanut butter costing method. Nevertheless, both methods implicitly assume that indirect costs are proportionate to direct costs, irrespective of the type of service. This is, however, a contested assumption because these types of services may be using the supporting services

Table 7.3 Cost allocation results for the mark-up method (in 1,000 euros) of A-LEARNING over a year

Primary service department⟶ Cost items ↓	IT courses	English courses	Employment skills courses	Total or average
Direct costs	760	670	390	1,820
Mark-up for indirect costs (41.8%)	318	280	163	760
Full costs	1,078	950	553	2,580
Number of courses	290	280	123	693
Full costs per course	3,717	3,393	4,496	3,723
Average number of participants per course	28	25	19	25.2
Full costs per participant	0.133	0.136	0.237	0.149

Note: Numbers can show small differences due to rounding-off calculations.

Table 7.4 The use of supporting services by the departments

Department→ Supporting service ↓	IT courses	English courses	Employment Skills courses	Product Development	Administration	Total
Product Development €210,000 (number of hours used)	1,200	1,400	1,800	—	—	4,400
Administration Head office €100,000 (equal shares)	20%	20%	20%	20%	20%	100%
Administration Housing €170,000 (number of square metres)	200	150	100	50	100	600
Administration Financial-personnel €280,000 (number of hours used)	1,800	1,600	2,000	200	1,000	6,600

Product Development and Administration differently. The advanced methods of cost allocation, to be discussed next, take account of this diverging use of supporting services.

Advanced cost allocation methods

Table 7.4 gives information about the use of supporting services by the various departments. This information is needed for calculating the full costs of the external services in which their use of supporting services is taken into account. This table shows that Product Development only contributes to the primary service departments; the number of hours used by these departments is a sound allocation base. The term '*allocation base*' refers to a measure for allocating indirect costs; an equivalent term is '*cost driver*'. The activities of the Administration department are threefold: Head office (no suitable allocation base available, hence, equal shares across the departments); Housing (allocation based on the number of square metres) and Financial-personnel administration (allocation based on the number of hours used).

Table 7.5 shows the results of the cost allocation and related costs per unit of service. The information in Table 7.4 can be used for allocating the costs of all supporting services to the five departments. The outcome is the TOTAL indirect costs (1); the total of the indirect costs is €760,000, which is equal to the total of the indirect costs in Table 7.3. However, this cannot be the end-result of the cost allocation, because part of the indirect costs is allocated to the supporting departments. These costs of the departments Product Development and Administration have to be allocated to the primary services departments. This is conducted in two steps:

Table 7.5 Cost pool method: allocation of indirect costs to services and full costing of services (monetary amounts in euros)

Supporting service	IT courses	English courses	Employment Skills courses	Product Development	Administration
Product Development €210,000	$1,200/4,400*210,000$ $=57,273$	$1,400/4,400*210,000$ $=66,818$	$1,800/4,400*210,000$ $=85,909$	–	–
Administration Head office €100,000 (equal shares)	$0.2*100,00$ $=20,000$	$0.2*100,00$ $=20,000$	$0.2*100,00$ $=20,000$	$0.2*100,00$ $=20,000$	$0.2*100,00=20,000$
Administration Housing €170,000 (square metres)	$200/600*170,000$ $=56,667$	$150/600*170,000$ $=42,500$	$100/600*170,000$ $=28,333$	$50/600*170,000$ $=14,167$	$100/600*170,000$ $=28,333$
Administration Financial-personnel €280,000 (number of hours used)	$1,800/6,600*280,000$ $=76,364$	$1,600/6,600*280,000$ $=67,878$	$2,000/6,600*280,000$ $=84,848$	$200/6,600*280,000$ $=8,485$	$1,000/6,6000*280,000$ $=42,424$
TOTAL indirect costs (1)	210,304	197,196	219,090	42,652	90,757
Allocation of Administration costs €90,757 (number of hours used)	$1,800/5,600*90,757$ $=29,172$	$1,600/5,600*90,757$ $=25,931$	$2,000/5,600*90,757$ $=32,413$	$200/5,600*90,757$ $=3,241$	–
TOTAL indirect costs (2)	239,476	223,127	251,503	45,893	–
Allocation of Product Developments costs €45,893 (number of hours used)	$1,200/4,400*45,893$ $=12,516$	$1,400/4,400*45,893$ $=14,602$	$1,800/4,400*45,893$ $=18,774$	–	–
TOTAL indirect costs (3)	251,992	237,729	270,277		
Direct costs	760,000	670,000	390,000		
TOTAL full costs	1,011,992	907,729	660,277		
Number of courses	290	280	123		
Full costs per course	3,490	3,242	5,368		
Average number of participants per course	28	25	19		
Full costs per participant	125	130	283		

1. The allocated costs of Administration are further allocated to the four other departments proportionally to the number of hours of Administration used by these departments; this results in TOTAL indirect costs (2).

2. The allocated costs to Product Development, including the attributed costs under step 1, are allocated to the primary service departments proportionately to the numbers of hours these departments use for Product Development; this results TOTAL indirect costs (3).

Now we have completed the allocation of the indirect costs to the primary services departments. We can add to these indirect costs the direct costs of those departments, as given in Table 7.3, and subsequently the full costs can be calculated per course and per participant (see the final rows of Table 7.5).

The method as illustrated in Table 7.5 is called the '*cost pool method*'. This method often uses only one cost driver or allocation base for each of the supporting departments, as holds for the Product Development department. In our example, however, the other supporting department (Administration) contains three different activities, each with its specific cost driver. This resembles an even more advanced method of cost allocation, called Activity-Based Costing (ABC) as developed by Cooper and Kaplan (1991). ABC mostly makes use of a large number of cost pools each with its own specific cost driver, while the ultimate cost objects are not the primary service departments but the individual products or services.

Three variants of the cost pool method can be distinguished, which diverge depending on the assumption made about how to account for deliveries between the supporting departments (see Appendix A.7.1 for an elaboration).

Although the purpose in this section is to calculate the full costs of the various types of services, the cost pool method can also be used for other goals of costing and cost allocation, as summarized in Table 7.1. A calculation of the full costs of each of the primary services departments can also be used for *control purposes*: if the underlying data are ex-ante data (so, related to planning and targeting), a comparison between the planned full costs and the actual full costs per department can lead to the consideration of corrective actions. Moreover, full cost data about either primary services departments or external services can be compared with similar data of organizations in the same branch of the public sector (i.e. *benchmarking*), in order to find signals for improvement.

Comparison of cost allocation methods

Table 7.6 compares the full costs per unit of each of the services for the three methods of cost allocation as discussed above. The mark-up method is potentially more useful than the peanut butter costing method because it takes account of the specific direct costs and characteristics (number of participants per course) of the external services. The cost pool method is potentially more useful than the mark-up method because it takes into account the diverging uses of the external services of the internal supporting services. The cost pool method is potentially

Table 7.6 Comparison of the full cost outcomes of three different methods of cost allocation (full costs per participant in euros)

Primary service department	IT courses	English courses	Employment skills courses
Peanut butter costing	149	149	149
Mark-up method	133	136	237
Cost pool method	125	130	283

the most useful method of allocating indirect costs, and it leads to substantially higher full costs for the Employment Skills courses in comparison with the other two allocation methods, although the differences with the most simple peanut butter costing method stand out in this respect. To put it differently, if the peanut butter costing method is used, Employment Skills courses are 'under-costed' and the other two courses are 'over-costed'.

Cost allocation was illustrated in this section by using a very simple example, including three primary services departments, each with only one type of service, and additionally two supporting departments. In practice, many more primary services departments and supporting departments have to be distinguished. Complex organizations are mostly characterized by more than two layers, i.e. divisions and departments within each of the divisions. Moreover, each primary services department often produces two or more services. This makes cost allocation procedures much more complicated than shown here.

Using full costs as a basis for fees

Knowing the full costs of each of the services is not the same as pricing these services. When the example of A-LEARNING was introduced, it was indicated that certain courses had to be accessible for lower income groups, which was the reason for the municipality covering part of A-LEARNNG's costs. Table 7.3 shows that A-LEARNING's total costs are €2.580 million. Suppose further that the municipal contribution to A-LEARNING is €0.75 million. What will be the fees for each of the services, when making use of the cost pool method?

The simplest 'subsidized fee policy' is to subsidize each of the types of courses proportionally to its full costs. The municipal contribution as a percentage of the full costs is €0.75 million over €2.580 million, which is 29%. Then fees can be 71% of the full costs, so: IT courses: 0.71 * €125 = €89; English courses: 0.71* €130 = €92; Employment Skills courses: 0.71 * €283 = €201.

It is, however, questionable whether this simple fee policy complies with the municipal guideline that certain courses need to be accessible for low income groups. This requirement may apply especially for Employment Skills courses, because those courses are important to unemployed citizens, who generally have low incomes. A possible approach would be to allocate half of the municipal contribution to Employment Skills courses and the other half to IT courses and English courses. The related calculations are shown below.

- Total municipal contribution is €0.75 million, so 50% is €0.375 million.
- Total costs of Employment Skills courses are €660,277 (see Table 7.5); municipal contribution €0.375 million; this implies that the fee has to cover (€660,277 − €375.000)/€660,277 = 43%; fee = 0.43 * €283 = €122.
- Total costs of IT courses and English courses are €1,011,992 + €907,729 = €1,919,721 (Table 7.5); municipal contribution €0.375 million; this implies that the fee has to cover (€1,919,721 − €375.000)/€1,919,721 = 80%: fee = 0.80 * €125 = €100 (IT courses); fee = 0.80 * € 130 = €104 (English courses).

The consequence of this second fee policy in comparison with the first is that the most vulnerable target group is substantially subsidized, which results in fees that are close to each other for each of the three types of courses. Obviously, other fee policies could also be considered. An interesting option is to ask (almost) full cost covering fees, but to allow interested participants to ask for a fee reduction that would depend upon their income level. This option seems to be fair but its monitoring costs would be substantial.

Experiences with costing practices

In several countries public sector organizations developed costing systems during the last decades. Surveys in the public sector in Scotland, the Netherlands and Portugal showed, for instance, that respectively 50%, 33% and 48% of the organizations use full cost accounting, in which indirect costs are allocated to public sector services (Jackson and Lapsley, 2003, p. 366; Verbeeten, 2011, p. 499; Carvalho et al., 2012, p. 317). These studies also emphasize the importance of costing systems for legitimating the organization's activities towards external stakeholders (such as oversight bodies) rather than for controlling indirect costs. This is also reinforced by studies about public sector cost management practices which mainly seem to focus on costing for purposes of pricing and profitability analysis (such as Ellwood, 1996, and Jones and Mellett, 2007, about healthcare services in the UK; Arnaboldi and Lapsley, 2004, about blood transfusion services in the UK; and Groot and Budding, 2004, about municipal services in the Netherlands).

In a recent study on cost allocation methods in Dutch municipalities Budding and Schoute (2012) aim to explain the so-called cost system design, which contains three elements: the complexity of the cost allocation method (i.e. the number of cost pools and the cost drivers used), its inclusiveness (the extent to which indirect costs are allocated to cost objects, such as organizational units, activities/programmes and services), and its understandability for non-financial users, such as politicians and managers. This study comes with some intriguing findings. The complexity and inclusiveness of the cost allocation method increases as the scale of the municipality increases, but its understandability for non-financial users is reduced for these more complex systems. In addition, external information requirements for regulators and higher authorities make the cost system more complex but also less understandable to non-financial users. This study shows that the complexity of the costing system is positively related to its use for operational control, but unrelated to its use for product costing.

7.5 Cost–Volume–Profit analysis

In Cost–Volume–Profit (CVP) analysis the distinction between variable and fixed costs is core. As defined in Section 7.2, total variable costs change with a change in line with the production volume, while total fixed costs remain the same. The goal of CPV analysis is to investigate under which circumstances a project is expected to realize a surplus (profit) or a deficit (loss). We will introduce a simple example concerning a project of A-LEARNING for illustrating CVP analysis.

The municipal organization, which includes A-LEARNING, wants to organize a one-day event during which unemployed people can enhance their chances in the labour market by meeting employers and suppliers of educational services. The municipal department for labour affairs proposes to provide a fixed fee for this event of €14,000 and a fee per unemployed participant of €20; it additionally requires that each participant also pays a €10 ticket for joining this event. A-LEARNING is requested to organize this event, after consulting representatives of the municipal department for labour affairs about the features of this event. Based on a web-based survey of unemployed people in the municipality A-LEARNING provides the following estimates:

- The fixed costs, including costs of the housing, promotion activities and facilities for 'meeting points', will be €30,000.
- The variable costs per participant, including a lunch and drinks as well as a bag with learning material, will be €18.
- The number of participants will range between 900 and 1200.

During a meeting between people from the municipal department for labour affairs and A-LEARNING the feasibility of this event is discussed. First of all, it is considered important to know how many participants are needed for this event to break even. The answer requires that revenues and costs are compared with each other and the break-even point is where expected revenues equal the expected costs. Let us introduce X as the number of participants, and then we can formulate the following equation:

Revenues = Costs
$$14,000 + 20X + 10X = 30,000 + 18X$$

This can be rewritten as:
$12X = 16,000$, implying that $X = 16,000/12 = 1,333$

So, the number of participants at which this event will break even is 1,333, which lies above the expected range of participants (between 900 and 1200). This means that the event will show a deficit at a number of participants ranging from 900 to 1200. Let's take 1,050 as the middle of this range as an example, then the deficit will be: $14,000 + 30 \times 1,050$ (revenues) $- 30,000 + 18 \times 1,050$ (costs) $= 45,500 - 48,900 = -3,400$. See Figure 7.2 for a graphical presentation of this CVP analysis.

As a result of this, various options have to be discussed for making this project financially feasible, without losing its attractiveness. The municipal department for labour affairs is not willing to increase its financial contributions to the event and A-LEARNING convincingly argues that cutting on the fixed costs will make the event less attractive. So, solutions have to be found in either lowering the variable costs or increasing the fee participants have to pay. It is feared that a higher fee for participants will be a barrier for attending the event, which leads to the following question: at what variable costs per participant will the event break even and attract at least 1,200 participants?

We take Y as the unknown variable costs per participant, and then the following condition must hold:

Revenues = Costs
$14,000 + (20 \times 1,200) + (10 \times 1,200) = 30,000 + Y \times 1,200$

This can be rewritten as:
$14,000 + 24,000 + 12,000 - 30,000 = Y \times 1,200$, implying that $1,200Y = 20,000$, so $Y = 8.33$.

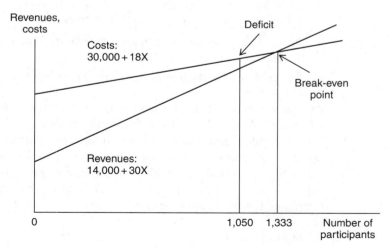

Figure 7.2 Illustration of CVP analysis

So, the variable costs have to be reduced from 20 to 8.33. This implies that drinks will be restricted to coffee and tea, lunches will only contain some rolls with cheese or ham (also called a Dutch lunch!), and the bag with relevant material has to be sponsored by organizations that want to promote themselves to the unemployed people or as part of their community support.

The CVP analysis, also denoted as *break-even analysis*, enables us to investigate the so-called what-if questions when quite simple revenue and cost functions apply (a single product or service with only fixed and variable costs and fees). Two examples of what-if questions related to the example above are:

– What combinations of fixed and variable costs will result in a feasible solution for the organizing party, given expectations about the number of participants and the fees coming in?
– What rise in price per participant must be allowed to cover a certain amount of additional fixed costs for making the event more attractive?

7.6   Cost management

Costing systems are sometimes implemented without due consideration of their usefulness. For example, organizations may imitate the costing techniques of other organizations that are perceived as successful. The risk in these instances is that costing techniques are applied, but the resulting information is not used for decision-making and control. In other words, costing information then may serve mainly symbolic purposes.

Cost calculation is important but it takes some additional efforts to make costing information useful. What has to be done in this respect depends on the goals of cost allocation and costing, as summarized in Table 7.1. Costing for pricing is, for example, an evident goal. Using cost allocation for internal control of the organization requires more to make the resulting information useful. The first step is that potential users of cost information, especially managers and their assistants, need to be informed about the opportunities for using this information in their work. This requires some training on cost allocation methods. However, this is insufficient on its own. Meetings between primary service departments and internal supporting services are needed to discuss the types of decisions that might be based on costing information. In particular, what form of control – centralized or decentralized – is the most appropriate for different types of internal services, and additionally do we need consultations between demanders and suppliers of these services in a budgeting process, or would an internal market be more suitable? (See van Helden, 2000 for a case study about the adoption of costing methods in a municipality; see also Huijben and van Helden, 2014, for a field study of public sector organizations in the Netherlands.)

Many public sector organizations struggle with the size of their indirect or overhead costs. The current economic and financial crisis has even forced many of these organizations to cut costs, often particularly in terms of overhead. But how drastic can these cuts be without losing too much value?

Huijben et al. (2014) report on an overhead benchmarking project in the Netherlands. By 2012 1,400 organizations in 26 (mainly public sector) areas of activity had participated in this study. The study indicates the following building blocks of analysis: 1) precise definitions of overhead and overhead functions, 2) a benchmarking of the overhead costs within a particular public sector area, 3) a framework for analysing the trade-off between the benefits and costs of overhead functions, and 4) pointers for obtaining a more balanced cost–benefit picture of the overhead functions. According to this approach, organizations in the same branches of the public sector can benchmark their overhead costs, both in total and for the underlying functions, such as financial administration and secretarial services. If overhead costs strongly differ from the average of the branch, this can motivate the organization to search for possible reasons and to consider revisions in the supporting functions. This can lead to various types of measures, ranging from a repositioning of the overhead functions (such as central versus local) to attuning the internal demand to the extent and type of the overhead functions supply. Furthermore, this approach can be applied to map out and justify the current supply of overhead functions.

In a more general sense, cost management also implies that a cost–benefit analysis can be carried out on the primary services of an organization, leading to make-or-buy decisions. Even if certain primary services are regarded as core to the accomplishment of the organization's strategy, the production of these services can be – either fully or partly – outsourced. A necessary condition is that the steering and control of the production and quality of those services is required (outsourcing is further discussed in Chapter 8).

7.7   Some further costing issues

This section introduces some costing issues that cannot be dealt with extensively in this chapter due its limited scope.

We only implicitly made a *distinction between planned and actual costs* of services, programmes or organizational units. In practice this distinction is important for control reasons, in order to compare the planned and actual costs for considering corrective actions. There are also relatively new tools for costing which aim to target the full costs of a service or programme related to future market conditions. This tool is called '*target costing*' (Monden and Hamada, 1991; see also Horngren et al., 2011, pp. 218–21). Target costing could be important for public services that are supplied in competitive circumstances, for instance educational programmes for executives or healthcare services which are subject to market pressure. In these instances a public sector organization could develop a partly renewed service or programme to be supplied in the future, which meets relevant client wishes. Target costing is based on the trade-off between clients' valuations of product or service attributes and the price these clients are willing to pay for them. Since the target cost is often higher than the costs of already existing products or services containing (partly) comparable attributes, cost management techniques – such as value engineering – are required to identify the appropriate combinations of the future service per unit prices, attributes and costs.

Cost–Volume Profit analysis (as discussed in Section 7.5) acknowledges the importance of the distinction between variable and fixed costs. This distinction has a broader meaning related to short-term versus long-term decisions. If, for example, an educational institute seeks to develop its programmes over a long planning period, the underlying considerations have to be based on all future costs (variable and fixed) and the related revenues. But, if such an institute is confronted with a short-term decision of whether or not to accept some additional students for a certain programme beyond its regular target group (for example, coming from abroad, while the programme is directed to domestic students), this institute could make a comparison between additional fees on the one hand and additional costs on the other hand. These additional costs are likely to be restricted to the variable costs of the programme, e.g. additional tutorials, because the fixed costs are already covered by the regular students. This approach is called 'marginal costing' or 'variable costing', i.e. including primarily variable costs in decision-making about short-term options.

7.8   Concluding remarks

This chapter has discussed costing, cost allocation and cost management in the public sector. It has firstly introduced some important terms in the costing domain, especially the distinctions between variable and fixed costs, direct and indirect costs, as well as controllable and non-controllable costs. Subsequently, the various goals of costing in a public sector context have been explained, among others, pricing of services and aligning supporting to primary services. Several methods for allocating costs of supporting services to external services were shown and illustrated, ranging from simple mark-up methods to so-called cost pools methods in which the allocation of indirect costs to primary services takes account of the extent to which these services are using supporting services. Next, this chapter has introduced Cost–Volume Profit analysis (also called Break-even analysis) as a more specific costing technique, i.e. the use of cost information for the planning of projects. Cost management was discussed by indicating how public sector organizations can use costing information for managerial purposes, for example, for attuning internally produced supporting services to the needs of its external users. Finally some specific cost accounting issues, particularly target costing and marginal costing, were briefly addressed.

Costing can be seen as a financial management tool which applies to a quite detailed level of individual services and programmes, and as such it is a necessary complement to budgetary control, which was the topic of the previous chapter.

References

Arnaboldi, M. and I. Lapsley (2004), Modern costing innovations and legitimation: a health care study, *Abacus*, Vol. 40, no. 1, pp. 1–21.

Budding, T. and M. Schoute (2012), Stakeholder information needs, cost system design and cost system effectiveness in Dutch local government, working paper Vrije Universiteit, Amsterdam.

Carvalho, J., P. Gomes and M.J. Fernandes (2012), The Main Determinants of the Use of the Cost Accounting System in Portuguese Local Government, *Financial Accountability & Management*, Vol. 28, no. 3, pp. 306–34.

Ellwood, S. (1996), Pricing Services in the UK National Health Service, *Financial Accountability & Management*, Vol. 12, no. 4, pp. 281–301.

Cooper, R. and R.S. Kaplan (1991), *The Design of Cost Management Systems: Text, Cases and Readings*, Englewood Cliffs, New Jersey: Prentice Hall.

Groot, T. (1999), Budgetary Reforms in the Non-profit Sector: A Comparative Analysis of Experiences in Health Care and Higher Education in the Netherlands, *Financial Accountability & Management*, Vol. 15, no. 3–4, pp. 353–76.

Groot, T. and T. Budding (2004), The influence of New Public Management practices on product costing and service pricing decisions in Dutch municipalities, *Financial Accountability & Management*, Vol. 20, no.4, pp. 421–44.

Helden, G.J. van (1997), Cost allocation and costing in Dutch local government, *European Accounting Review*, Vol. 6, no. 1, pp. 131–45.

Helden, G.J. van (2000), A strategy for implementing cost allocation in a Dutch municipality, in: Caperchione, E. and R. Mussari (eds), *Comparative Issues in Local Accounting*, Boston: Kluwer Academic publishers, pp. 125–41.

Horngren, C.T., G.L. Sundem, W.O. Stratton, D. Burgstahler, and J. Schatzberg (2011), *Introduction to Management Accounting*, Boston: Pearson.

Huijben, M., A. Geurtsen and G.J. van Helden (2014), Managing overhead in public sector organizations through benchmarking: lessons from the Netherlands, *Public Money and Management*, Vol. 34, no. 1, pp. 27–34.

Huijben M. and G.J. van Helden (2014), Controlling overhead in public sector organizations, *International Journal of Public Sector Management*, Vol. 27, no. 6, pp. 475–85.

Jackson, A. and I. Lapsley (2003), The diffusion of accounting practices in the new 'managerial' public sector, *International Journal of Public Sector Management*, Vol. 16, no. 5, pp. 359–79.

Jones, M.J and H.J Mellett (2007), Determinants of changes in accounting practices: accounting in the UK health service, *Critical Perspectives on Accounting*, Vol. 18, no. 1, pp. 91–112.

Monden, Y. and T. Hamada (1991), Target and kaizen costing in Japanese automobile companies, *Journal of Management Accounting Research*, Vol. 3, pp. 16–34.

Verbeeten, F.H.M. (2011), Public sector cost management practices in the Netherlands, *International Journal of Public Sector Management*, Vol. 24, no. 6, pp. 492–506.

Appendix A.7.1 Variants of the cost pool method

Three variants of the cost pool method are distinguished, which diverge depending on the assumption made about how to account for deliveries between the supporting departments.

1. The *direct method*, which ignores all deliveries between the supporting departments; in the example shown in Table 7.5, this would mean that the costs of the two supporting departments are only allocated to the primary services departments; for Administration costs this would imply that the allocation to Product Development is ignored, meaning that the primary services departments get 1,800/5,400, 1,600/5,400 and 2,000/5,400 respectively of €90,957, i.e. the Administration costs (keep in mind that the denominator has to be reduced from 5,600 to 5,400 because of the 200 hours for Product Development which are disregarded).

2. The *step-wise or step down method*, which takes into account the most important deliveries between the supporting departments ignoring the less important deliveries; this method is shown in Table 7.5 (here there are no deliveries between Product Development and Administration, but if they were to exist, they would probably be less important than the deliveries from Administration to Product Development).

3. *The reciprocal method*, which allows for mutual deliveries between the supporting departments and which is particularly relevant in circumstances where the number of supporting departments is large. See textbooks about management accounting for this method of cost allocation, such as Horngren et al. 2011.

8

Capital investment, outsourcing and partnerships

Learning objectives

◆ Understand the specific characteristics of capital investment projects, how organizations develop such projects and which financial and non-financial criteria for assessing these projects can be used

◆ Being able to apply criteria for assessing investment projects in a public sector context

◆ Understand for what reasons public sector organizations are outsourcing certain activities, including entering into public-private partnerships

◆ Being able to apply financial criteria for underpinning such outsourcing decisions

---

8.1   Introduction

The previous chapters of this book have discussed the most important financial documents that are part of the yearly planning and control cycle, such as a budget, a progress report about the execution of the budget and the reporting of financial position and performance using a balance sheet, an income statement and a cash flow statement. In addition to these regular financial statements, public sector organizations prepare financial reports for underpinning certain occasional decisions. The current chapter broadens the scope of financial management beyond the planning and control cycle and discusses two types of these occasional decisions; the first is about capital investments and the second concerns outsourcing (including public-private partnerships).

Capital investments may require relatively large amounts of resources at the start of their lifecycle which have to be recovered by revenues which are larger than the expenses throughout this lifecycle. Examples of public sector investments concern the building of an opera house, the construction of a new road connection or major information technology projects. Outsourcing requires a cost to benefit analysis of two alternatives: either doing certain activities 'in-house' or leaving it to another organization and purchasing the goods or services from that supplier. Examples of outsourcing include supporting activities such as financial administration or IT services, but also core processes can be the subject of outsourcing, such as in the case of a municipal sports facility or central government's or state's prison services.

This chapter proceeds as follows: Section 8.2 deals with the characteristics of capital investment projects, the stages in the decision-making about these projects, and the types of criteria for assessing these projects. Section 8.3 discusses a case study about a complex capital investment decision regarding either the renovation of an existing football stadium or the building of a new stadium. Section 8.4 deals with different forms of outsourcing arrangements and considers why public sector bodies might prefer outsourcing arrangements rather than providing the services themselves. Section 8.5 provides a case study in which a public sector ambulance service seeks to renew its radio communication and control system by considering outsourcing through a public-private partnership contract with a more traditionally procured in-house service. Section 8.7 provides some conclusions.

8.2   Capital investments: characteristics, decision process and assessment criteria

The main *characteristics of a capital investment project* are as follows (cf. Northcott, 1999, pp. 1–2):

- It requires a substantial amount of resources to be invested at the beginning of a certain period;
- The returns, in the sense of the differences between the yearly revenues and costs, occur over a number of years;
- Often there is some risk or uncertainty in predicting these returns, and sometimes also about the initial investments;
- Capital investments usually concern new or expanded assets for producing certain products or services, such as a swimming pool, an office building and a road connection.

A capital investment decision is illustrated here with a simple replacement decision concerning vans for collecting garbage. There are two options for replacing the three vans which the garbage collection department of a municipality currently uses:

- Option 1: three vans with a similar technology to the current ones (each van has a driver and two men for picking up the garbage).
- Option 2: three technologically more advanced vans (each van has a driver and an automatic pick-up installation).

Table 8.1   Financial numbers of two options for replacing garbage collection vans (amounts of money in thousands of euros)

Options⟶ Characteristics ↓	Option 1: Three labour-intensive vans	Option 2: Three technologically advanced vans
Initial investment	600	1,500
Annual salaries cost	310	105
Annual other costs	45	90
Annual revenues (see note below)	450	450
Number of years of operational period	5	5
Residual value after operational period	200	350

Note: Total yearly revenues are 1,125, which can be attributed to garbage collection (40% = 450), garbage recycling (40% = 450) and overhead (20% = 225).

Table 8.1 presents the financial numbers of the two options, which can handle the same workload.

What is the best option according to a *financial criterion*? We will show two financial criteria for assessing these two capital investment options, i.e. the Payback Period and the Net Present Value (see, for example Northcott, 1999, chapter 3; Helfert, 2001, chapter 7 for a further elaboration and other financial assessment tools for investments). A presentation of the cash flows of the capital investment options over time as in Table 8.2 will enhance a proper understanding of both criteria.

Payback Period

The Payback Period is the number of years it takes before the cash outflow of the investment is paid back by the net cash inflows of the revenues and costs. The costs must be calculated without the depreciation and interest costs of the investment. The payback period for the two investment options can be calculated as follows:

Option 1: After 4 years the sum of the net cash inflows = 4 × 95 = €380K, which is lower than the cash outflow of the investment of €600K; so the final year with a cash inflow of €295K is needed to pay back the investment; 380 + 295 = €675K (cash inflows) >€600K (cash outflows); with a cash surplus of €75K (= 675 − 600) remaining at the end of the operational period.

Option 2: After 4 years the sum of the net cash inflows = 4 × 255 = €1,020K, which is lower than the cash outflow of the investment of €1,500K; so the final year with a cash inflow of €605K is also needed here to pay back the investment; 1,020 + 605 = €1,625K (cash inflows) >€1,500K (cash outflows); with a cash surplus of €125K (= 1,625−1,500) remaining at the end of the operational period.

We can conclude that the investments of both options will be paid back at the end of the operational period in Year 5. Option 2 is slightly better than option 1

Table 8.2 The cash flows timeline of two investment options regarding garbage collection vans (amounts of money in thousands of euros) (cash outflows are presented with a minus sign)

	Year 0	Year 1	Year 2	Year 3	Year 4	Year 5
Option 1: Three labour-intensive vans						
Cash outflow: Investment	−600					
Cash inflow: Annual revenues		450	450	450	450	450
Cash inflow: Residual value						200
Cash outflow: Costs (310 + 45)		−355	−355	−355	−355	−355
Net cash flows	−600	95	95	95	95	295
Accumulated cash flows	−600	−505	−410	−315	−220	+75
Option 2: Three technologically advanced vans						
Cash outflow: Investment	−1500					
Cash inflow: Annual revenues		450	450	450	450	450
Cash inflow: Residual value						350
Cash outflow: Costs (105 + 90)		−195	−195	−195	−195	−195
Net cash flows	−1,500	255	255	255	255	605
Accumulated cash flows	−1,500	−1,245	−990	−735	−480	+125

because the surplus at the end of the operational period is higher (€125K versus €75K).

It is important to notice that a project might pay back its cash investment before the final year of operation; in which case, ignoring all other factors, the preferred project is that which pays back its investment in the shortest time period.

Net Present Value

A disadvantage of the Payback Period is that it does not take account of the timing of the incoming and outgoing cash flows. Some of the cash flows are expected to take place some years into the project; for example the residual value of the investment will be received five years after the initial capital investment. If cash inflows and cash outflows are to be compared properly, they should be recalculated to the moment when the initial investment has to be made. For example, the residual values will be lower than given in Table 8.2 due to the *time value of money* (Northcott, 1999, p. 35; Helfert, 2001, pp 224–230). Similar remarks can be made about the different periods in which the yearly revenues and costs occur.

Why is there a time value of money? If someone receives €1,000 at the beginning of 2013, he or she can spend it, or can postpone spending and put it in a bank deposit to earn some interest. Suppose, at the beginning of 2014, the bank balance has increased to €1,060 because of receiving interest of €60 (assume due to 6% interest rate). So, €1,000 received at the beginning of 2013 is equal in value to €1,060 received at the beginning of 2014 (assuming an interest rate of 6% per annum).

There are two main reasons for the existence of a time value for money. One is inflation, so the purchasing power of money decreases over time due to a rise in prices. The other reason is that someone postponing spending gives up spending opportunities for which he or she has to be compensated. In the given example, the time value of money over one year is 6%, which can be sub-divided approximately into, for example, a 2% inflation compensation and a 4% real time value of money. As such, a distinction can be made between a nominal interest rate (6% in this example) and a real interest rate (4% = 6% − 2% in this example).[1]

Receiving an amount of money in the future can be compared with a receipt of money immediately by making a correction for the time value of money. That is, we need to calculate the present value of future cash inflows and outflows by comparing them with the current cash outflow of the investment. A cash inflow occurring one year from now of €1,040 is equal to a current cash inflow of €1,000 due to the time value of money reflected in the real interest rate of 4%: €1000 = €1040/(1 + 0.04). The *Net Present Value (NPV) of an investment* is the present value of all future net cash inflows of an investment less the present value of the cash outflows of the investment. With a real interest rate of 4%, Table 8.3 shows the calculations of the NPV of the two garbage collection investment options. Here the present value factors are the rates at which cash flows are discounted to the current period of the investment (so-called discounted *cash flow*s are calculated). The NPV of an investment option is the sum of the present values of all cash inflows and outflows of this option.

We can conclude that the NPV of both options is negative, while the negative NPV of option 1 is slightly better than that of option 2 (−12.5 and −76.8 respectively). This conclusion is the opposite to the conclusion about the application of the Payback Period, i.e. that both options are paid back and option 2 is better than option 1. How can this be explained? Both options show quite substantial cash inflows in the future, especially in the final year of the operational period, which are valued far lower under the NPV than the Payback Period. This holds to a larger extent for option 2 than for option 1.[2]

So, should the investment be made so that one of the two options can proceed? In a private sector context the simple answer would be 'no'. This is because a negative NPV implies a loss of value to the business and its shareholders and so,

---

1 For the purposes of this example, an approximation is used that the nominal rate (NR) is equal to the real rate (RR) plus the expected inflation rate (IR). So NR (6%) = RR (4%) + IR (2%). Strictly, the relationship is that $1 + NR = (1 + RR)$ multiplied by $(1 + IR)$. In this example $1 + NR = 1.02 * 1.04 = 1.0608$. So NR = 6.08%.

2 A related criterion for assessing the financial viability of an investment project is the *internal rate of return*, which is defined as the interest rate for which the Net Present Value of a project would be zero; if the internal rate of return is higher than the actual interest rate, the project is financially viable (Northcott, 1999, pp. 41–49). In this example, the internal rate of return will be lower than the actual interest rate, which makes the project in principle not viable.

Table 8.3 The Net Present Value of two garbage collection investment options (amounts of money in thousands of euros)

	Year 0	Year 1	Year 2	Year 3	Year 4	Year 5
Option 1: Three labour-intensive vans						
Net cash flows	−600	95	95	95	95	295
Present value factors	1.0	0.962	0.925	0.889	0.855	0.822
Present value	−600	91.4	87.9	84.5	81.2	242.5
Net Present Value	**−12.5**					
Option 2: Three technologically advanced vans						
Net cash flows	−1500	255	255	255	255	605
Present value factors	1.0	0.962	0.925	0.889	0.855	0.822
Present value	−1500	245.3	235.9	226.7	218.0	497.3
Net Present Value	**−76.8**					

ignoring any non-financial implications, private businesses should only invest in projects with positive NPVs. However, this is another example of where decisions in a public sector context may be different, and arguably more complex, than in the private sector. A public sector organization may wish to proceed with a project that has a negative NPV perhaps because it is under a legal obligation to provide such services or because it believes that there are significant non-financial benefits that may outweigh the negative financial implications. The existence of a negative NPV is, however, important because it implies that additional resources, perhaps from general taxation or available budget resources, will be needed to support this project if it is authorized to proceed.

Non-financial criteria

In addition to financial criteria, *non-financial criteria* can be relevant for selecting between different options. Capital investments may extend over a long period, so the long-term strategy of the organization matters in assessing investment alternatives. In the example presented in Table 8.1, the municipality could place importance on technological innovation – the municipality wants to be seen as 'modern' – which would support the preference for option 2. In contrast, option 2 might be faced with substantial uncertainty due to limited experience with the new technology, which implies the risk of higher than expected costs. This could be a reason for preferring option 1, which is based on a well-practised technology with low uncertainty. A further reason for supporting option 1 can be that it employs more people. This can be an important issue in a municipality with unemployment problems, and it could also contribute to good relationships with the labour unions.

Some capital investments in the public sector are similar to those in the private sector because they have financial 'earning power', in the sense of their ability to raise resources through service fees. Examples might include garbage collection services (where cost covering fees are charged to businesses or households) and toll roads (where tolls are charged directly to the road users). However, other capital investments lack financial earning power and have a particular public sector character, because of their desirable societal effects, such as parks and public gardens, road connections (without a toll obligation) and possibly health services investments. These are called 'community assets' (Adam et al., 2011). Here the main challenge is to find the most appropriate capital investment given financial criteria (related to cost levels) and non-financial criteria related to societal effects.

Capital investment decisions

The *decision process regarding a capital investment project* often follows several stages (Northcott, 1999, pp. 10–22). These stages are indicated below with a brief explanation regarding the example of the replacement of garbage collection vans.

– *Stage 1: Identification of investment options*: Technical people in the department observe that the currently used vans often require maintenance, and they are familiar with different options for replacing these vans.

– *Stage 2: Project definition and screening*: Gathering data about various options via brochures and visiting relevant fairs, resulting in a qualitative assessment which gives attention to a match with what the organization wants and its feasibility.

– *Stage 3: Analysis and acceptance*: Both financial criteria and non-financial criteria as illustrated above are part of the analysis, and the most appropriate option is chosen (this type of analysis is further explained in the next section).

– *Stage 4: Implementation:* This stage includes the purchase of the selected equipment; scheduling a pilot project for testing its usefulness, including a monitoring of relevant criteria (does the investment live up to its expectations?).

– *Stage 5: Post investment audit:* This audit is conducted after some practical experience with using the asset, giving attention to critical issues, such as the achievable utilization rate of the vans and the level of remaining costs. This will help to inform future similar capital investment decisions.

8.3   Case study: Old Port's choice between a renovated old or completely new football stadium[3]

The city of Old Port struggles with a decision about its football stadium. The current stadium is outdated: it is insufficiently comfortable to the demanding

---

3   This case is inspired by discussions in Rotterdam, the Netherlands about the building of a new stadium or renovating the old stadium for football club Fyenoord (Tsjalle van de Burg, www/reddekuip.nl); this case is too complex for presentation within this book's scope; a source of inspiration is also Barton's (2005) analysis of the building of a new rugby stadium in Canberra, Australia.

football fan; it does not live up to recently established safety requirements; and it is not attractive to the business community for meeting colleagues and clients. However, there is a huge debate about the best investment option, i.e. either renovating the old one or building a completely new stadium. The directors of the football club Old Port Boys, which is the main user of the stadium, support the idea of a new stadium. Both the number of regular and business seats could be increased substantially, and there would be more room for commercial and touristic activities. The direction of the football club, which is supported by the local business association, also expects that future revenues will enhance possibilities for attracting top football players which would give opportunities for climbing the league table to the top level. Some even dream of hosting football matches of the national team. In contrast, the fans of the Old Port Boys are very much in favour of renovating the current stadium. Their arguments relate to the long history of the stadium, which goes back to the beginning of the previous century, its specific atmosphere with stands close to the playing area, and its location near to major working-class neighbourhoods within the city. Moreover, they argue: renovating is much cheaper than building new.

The city council needs to decide between the two options because it is the owner of the current stadium, but, more importantly, because both options probably require substantial financial support from Old Port's local government (bank loans are expected to require a municipal warranty). The city council attracts a consultancy firm with expertise about the football industry for advice, which results in some summarized financial figures about the two options, as presented in Table 8.4.

Although the city council places great importance on financial criteria in its decision about the two options, it also wants to include non-financial criteria in its final assessment. *Multi-criteria analysis* is used for assessing the investment options according to the different criteria, both quantitative and qualitative (the

Table 8.4 Investment options for Old Port's football stadium (money in euros)

Investment options	Renovating the old stadium		Building a new stadium	
Scenarios—→	Scenarios		Scenarios	
Characteristics of scenarios ↓	Regular case scenario	Worst case scenario	Regular case scenario	Worst case scenario
Number of seats	33,000	33,000	45,000	45,000
Occupation rate	95%	80%	90%	70%
Initial Investment	135 million	135 million	250 million	250 million
Net return per year	7.5 million	6.5 million	13 million	10.5 million
Years of operation	25	25	25	25
Residual value after years of operation	Zero	Zero	Zero	Zero

Table 8.5 Multi-criteria analysis of investment options for Old Port's football stadium

Investment options	Renovating the old stadium		Building a new stadium	
Assessment criteria (weights)	Rate	Rate × weight	Rate	Rate × weight
Financial feasibility (40%)	6	6 × 0.4 = 2.4	4	4 × 0.4 = 1.6
Support from football fans (30%)	9	9 × 0.3 = 2.7	5	5 × 0.3 = 1.5
Attractiveness to business community (15%)	6	6 × 0.15 = 0.9	9	9 × 0.15 = 1.35
Potential for climbing the league table (15%)	4	4 × 0.15 = 0.6	9	9 x 0.15 = 1.35
Total assessment	−	6.6	−	5.8

related financial calculations are included in Appendix A.8.1 to this chapter). See Table 8.5 for the results.

In order to conduct this type of analysis the municipal council first has to identify relevant criteria for making a decision. Subsequently, the council has to establish the relative importance of each criterion. The first column of Table 8.5 indicates, for example, that financial feasibility is more important than attractiveness to the business community, which get weights of 40% and 15% respectively. The sum of the weights has to be 100%. Then the two investment options are rated on each of the criteria on a scale from 1 (very bad) to 10 (excellent). The new stadium option scores, for instance, lower on financial feasibility than the renovation option (see Appendix A.8.1 for the underlying calculations), but the opposite applies to the criterion of attractiveness to the business community. As a final step the rates for each criterion are multiplied by the according weights, and then the sum of these weighted rates is calculated. Table 8.5 shows that the option of renovating the old stadium scores higher than the option of building a new stadium, with respective total rates of 6.6 and 5.8 on a scale from 1 to 10.

A multi-criteria analysis as illustrated in Table 8.5 does not replace decision-making in a political context. It has to be seen as an aid in the debate about complex investment options. Both the rating on each of the criteria for investment options and the weighting of these ratings are subjective. However, by making assessment criteria explicit, discussing their relative importance and scoring different options on each criterion, some rationality can be brought into a debate which is highly subjective and politically laden by nature.

Our case analysis is completed by presenting three reflections.

The first raises the question of how uncertainty or risk can be incorporated in a financial analysis of investment options. Investment options may differ in the extent of uncertainty about future returns: the option of building a new stadium shows, for example, larger differences between the regular and worst case scenario outcomes than the option of renovating the current stadium. The more risky option can then be assessed by using a higher present value factor than used for the less risky option. This is called a *risk premium*. In our example the risk premium could be 3%, which will result in an interest rate of 9% (= 2% inflation + 4% real time value + 3% risk premium) for the more risky option, whilst the less risky option is assessed against 6%. The consequence is that future earnings of the more risky option will lose additional value (cf. Northcott, 1999, p. 35; present value tables for a variety of interest levels can be found, for example, in Helfert, 2001, pp. 252–253).

Second, there are opportunities to take account of *flexibility* in assessing investment options. Flexibility can take various forms. One is the postponement of an investment in order to obtain more information about the possible consequences of the investment, and thus reducing the uncertainty around the investment decision. Another form of flexibility is the extent to which an investment, after some adaptations, can be made appropriate for other purposes than the original purpose: for example, if the option of building a new stadium gives more opportunities for using this facility for other purposes than professional football matches (such as concerts and other sporting events), it results in a larger flexibility than a renovated old stadium with lower 'alternative opportunities'.

Third, multi-criteria analysis as shown above is based on a popular method, which is characterized by weighting the scores on a number of criteria for the various options, although *other methods* are available (see, for instance, Hobbs et al., 1992). Two of these methods are briefly explained. The first method assesses whether option A is better than (outranks) option B, if the sum of the weights for which A is better than B is higher than a certain threshold. Suppose the threshold is 60%, then renovating the old stadium outranks building a new stadium, because the old stadium has a better score for a total of 70% of the weights than building a new stadium (see Table 8.4). A second method assesses the differences between the actual scores and target scores on each of the criteria, and subsequently weights these differences as in the method illustrated in Table 8.4. It goes beyond the scope this chapter to illustrate this more complex method, but it gives the opportunity to present some guidelines for using multi-criteria analysis (see further Hobbs et al., 1992). It is important that the users of such methods understand the underlying calculations, which gives rise to the need for some training. It further enhances the usability of the results of such an analysis if different methods are applied, including an interpretation of the possible differences in using these methods for the preferences for the various options. Finally, a multi-criteria analysis should support decision-making rather than replace the argumentation which underpins the ultimate preference for a certain option.

Cost–Benefit analysis

Cost–Benefit (CB) analysis aims to assess whether the gain to society (benefit) from a project or programme is larger than the social sacrifice (cost) to produce such a project or programme (Mikesell, 1999, p. 245). CB analysis very much resembles investment analysis or capital budgeting decisions as discussed in Section 8.2: the present value of the future net-cash inflows of an investment is compared with the resources needed for this investment. Because CB analysis is about assessing future costs and benefits of a programme or project, rather than facts, estimates about future facts underlie CB analysis. A major difference between CB analysis and regular investment analysis is that in CB analysis some of the benefits are often difficult to measure. A case will illustrate CB analysis and the difficulty of measuring benefits.

Big cities all over the world have introduced city bicycle – also called bike sharing – programmes during the last decades. Famous programmes have been initiated in London ('Boris bikes', named after London's mayor Boris Johnson), Paris and Montreal (about the latter programme see Morin, 2014). These programmes are stimulating citizens who go to work or school to use a bicycle for their transport instead of a car. Underlying goals are the reduction of congestion and pollution in the city centre and a more healthy way of living. City bicycle programmes require investments in bicycles, parking docks, and sometimes separate roads for cyclists. In addition, operating costs have to be made for the maintenance of bicycles and docks and for the transport of bicycles among different docking sites, and also for communications and administration. Benefits come from subscription and use fees, and, additionally, from more difficult to measure impacts, such as health improvement and pollution reduction. Policy makers also have to take account of unused capacity during the first years of operation. Table 8.6 gives the numbers of a city bicycle programme in a city of 200,000 inhabitants.

What is the total societal value of this city bicycle programme? Or put differently, are the expected benefits of this programme larger than the expected costs? We can answer this question by summing up the monetary values of all benefits (positive) and costs (negative) of this programme. Because some benefits and costs will occur in different future years, we need to calculate the present value of future cash inflows of these benefits and cash outflows of these costs to compare them with the current cash outflow of the investment, as explained in Section 8.2. In order to make the related calculations, we need to know the present value factor for each year at a certain interest rate; this present value factor is given in the last row of Table 8.7 at an annual interest rate of 3%. A lower interest rate is chosen than in the previous examples in Sections 8.2 and 8.3, because the city bicycle programme can be seen as a purely public good. Purely public goods can be funded based on so-called 'risk free' interest rates, which are lower than the market rate (see Mikesell, 1999, pp. 252–253).

Table 8.6 Numbers for city bicycle programme (in millions of euros)

Year	1	2	3	4	5
Investment bicycles [a]	−0.72				
Investment docks [b]	−0.40				
Cycling roads investments [c]	−1.00				
Operating costs [d]	−0.20	−0.20	−0.20	−0.20	−0.20
Remaining costs [e]	−0.15	−0.15	−0.15	−0.15	−0.15
User fees [f]	0.40	0.45	0.50	0.55	0.60
Avoided investments [g]	1.10				
Impacts on health	+?	+?	+?	+?	+?

Notes: [a] 800 bikes at 900 euros = 0.72 mil., lifetime 5 years, no residual value.
[b] 40 docks at 20,000 euros = 0.8 mil., lifetime 10 years, here for 5 years taken as 0.4 mil. euros.
[c] In total 5 mil. euros, lifetime 25 years; here taken as 1 mil. euros for 5 years.
[d] Yearly costs for maintenance and transport of bikes.
[e] Yearly costs for administration and communication.
[f] User fees: on average in year 5: 2.5 hours a day for 600 bikes and a tariff per hour of 2 euros over 200 days (2.5 × 600 × 2 × 200 days = 0.6 mil. euros); earlier years less due to unused capacity.
[g] Avoided investments for anti-pollution and congestions measures, 5.5 mil. euros with a lifetime of 25 years; here 1.1 mil. euros taken for the first 5 years.

Table 8.7 Cost–benefit analysis of city bicycle programme (in millions of euros)

Year	1	2	3	4	5
Investment bicycles	−0.72				
Investment docks	−0.40				
Cycling roads investments	−1.00				
Total investments	*−2.12*				
Operating costs	−0.20	−0.20	−0.20	−0.20	−0.20
Administration and communications costs	−0.15	−0.15	−0.15	−0.15	−0.15
Total operation costs	−0.35	−0.35	−0.35	−0.35	−0.35
Present value of total operation costs	*−0.35*	*−0.34*	*−0.33*	*−0.32*	*−0.31*
Benefits from user fees	0.40	0.45	0.50	0.55	0.60
Present value of benefits from user fees	*0.40*	*0.44*	*0.47*	*0.50*	*0.53*
Benefits from avoided investments	*1.10*				
Present value of benefits from health improvement	*+?*	*+?*	*+?*	*+?*	*+?*
Present value at annual interest of 3%	1.000	0.971	0.943	0.915	0.888

Table 8.7 presents in italics the Net Present Value of the various benefit categories and cost categories. The total societal value of the programme can now be calculated as follows (for simplicity, all costs and benefits are expected to occur at the beginning the year):

Present value of investment $= -2.12$
Present value of yearly operation costs $= -0.35 - 0.34 - 0.33 - 0.32 - 0.31$
    $= -1.65$
Total present value of costs $= -2.12 - 1.65 = -3.77$

Present value of yearly benefits: $0.40 + 0.44 + 0.47 + 0.50 + 0.53 = 2.34$
Present value of benefits from avoided investment $= 1.10$
Present value of benefits from health improvement $= ?$

Total present value of benefits $= 2.34 + 1.10 + ? = 3.44 + ?$

Societal value of programme: -3.77 (costs) $+ 3.44 + ?$ (benefits) $= -0.33 + ?$

So, the programme is expected to result in a net-cost of 330,000 euros plus unknown benefits due to health improvement. The city council thus has to decide whether the benefits from health improvement outweigh the net financial loss of 330,000 euros. The question can be raised whether the benefits from health improvement can be measured in monetary terms. If possible, this could make the decision of the city council easier. Although some impacts of governmental programmes are difficult to measure, some proxies can be considered. Regular cycling will lead to a longer and healthier life. If one additional year of healthy living is worth 20,000 euros (due to lower costs of healthcare) and the city cycling programme involves in total 12,000 regular users, each cycling for three months' additional life in a healthy condition, the benefit is huge: $12,000 \times 0.25$ year $\times$ 20,000 euros $= 60$ million euros, which is far more than the financial loss of 330,000 euros calculated above. However, these calculations are often subject to contestable assumptions: What is the monetary value of one year of additional life? What is the impact of regular cycling on living longer? A more pragmatic way is organizing a survey among citizens, in which information is given about the city bicycle programme, and which asks for the extent of support for such a programme and whether the city should invest a specified amount of money in it (see further about the valuation of saving lives in Mikesell, 1999, pp. 259–260).

In a more general sense CB analysis enables us to assess the financial impacts of different projects or programmes, in order to support decision-making about these projects or programmes by the politicians who are in charge. The example above can be taken as an illustration of this. A city bicycle programme can have different specifications, which diverge in their investments (especially the number of available bikes and docking stations, as well as the length of separate cycling roads), and fees (i.e. the types and level of fees). For each specification an analysis as presented above can be made. This analysis should take account of the fact that the value of one variable influences the value of another variable: lower numbers of bikes, for example, make the programme less attractive, and higher fees will have the same effect. Ultimately the best option, with the highest contribution to public welfare, can be chosen. A more realistic perspective may be that politicians have relevant financial information about the pros and cons of different programme specifications, which can contribute to their argumentation in the ultimate decision-making.

If a project or programme is characterized by various aspects that are difficult to measure in monetary terms – such as lifestyle and mentality (Morin, 2014) – it may be better to conduct a multi-criteria analysis, as explained in Section 8.3, instead of a CB analysis.

8.4   Outsourcing public services: objectives, limitations and assessment criteria[4]

The nature of outsourcing

Outsourcing is seen typically to represent a process in which activities, which have traditionally been done within an organization, are contracted out to be done by suppliers. The scope for outsourcing activities is considerable. It may be used to arrange only for the provision of specialist or support services which are not considered to be core to the organization; for example a government department might decide to buy in its legal services rather than to employ its own legal specialists. At the other extreme a department might, for financial or political reasons, be required to procure some of its core services externally, for example where a social services or health department outsources its residential services for elderly people to the private or not-for-profit sectors.

The type and length of outsourcing arrangements may vary from short-term contracts to long-term partnership arrangements. An example of a short-term contract might arise if a municipal authority, which has its own printing department, arranges for some printing to be done externally as a result of excess demands on its in-house facility. Examples of long-term outsourcing arise from public-private partnerships or private finance initiative contracts where a public sector body contracts for capital assets, such as hospitals or roads, to be designed, constructed, maintained and financed by the private sector and paid for over many years through some combination of charges to users and public expenditure from taxpayers.

The benefits of outsourcing

There are many reasons why outsourcing may be attractive to the public sector; some of these reflect potential economic or financial benefits, while others may

---

4 This section draws on a number of articles which contain more detailed coverage of public sector contracting and outsourcing arrangements; for example see Bandy (2011), Greve (2008) and Pollitt (2003).

reflect particular political perceptions of the role and extent of public or governmental activities. Typical arguments used to support outsourcing are described below.

First, an organization may desire to focus on its core activities with a view that other (support) activities can be outsourced safely without threatening damage to the provision of that core. For example, using one of the earlier illustrations, the government department may decide to close its printing facility and outsource of all its printing either to a single printing company or to arrange for multiple suppliers to encourage competition for future work.

Second, a public sector organization might want access to specialized knowledge, experience or modern technology that it cannot easily develop in-house. For example, it might employ consultants to improve its web-based profile and to enable more advanced e-government facilities. This might have the potential to decrease its costs and time of processing transactions.

Third, outsourcing may be seen as a way to increase the flexibility of the organization. For example, the use of multiple suppliers may enable products and services to be tailored to the individual needs of service users or it may help the organization to cope with peaks of demand at certain times of the year.

Fourth, outsourcing may be part of a process to transform fixed costs into variable costs. For example, closure of an in-house facility may avoid the need to maintain buildings and equipment and to employ staff in that facility. Instead the emphasis changes to contracting with external suppliers, perhaps on a relatively short-term basis, to meet varying levels of demand or need from users.

Finally, and more generally, outsourcing may be put forward as a means of improving innovation and operation efficiency, resulting in improved quality, faster response to service demands and reductions in risks and costs to the public sector.

The benefits described above are typical of the economic or financial justifications for outsourcing. However, in a public sector context, the decisions to outsource activities may be as much to do with political influences as economic ones.[5] The political arguments for outsourcing may be driven by a belief that the role of government is to determine public policy and to procure public services rather than to provide such services directly. So those in control of the political process, either centrally or locally, may seek to reduce direct public expenditure, reduce the 'head-count' of public sector employees, and to encourage the private financing of public services rather than the use of direct public sector borrowing.

Limitations and difficulties of outsourcing

While the potential benefits of outsourcing, such as those described above, are considerable it is not apparent that such benefits will necessarily be achieved. The

---

5 For example, the outsourcing of pre-school and primary education in Sweden is reported as being influenced by the political control of the municipality (Elinder and Jordahl, 2013).

variety of outsourcing arrangements and their varying applications in different jurisdictions means that it becomes impossible to draw generic conclusions on whether or not outsourcing will prove to be effective in any individual case. Some of the limitations and difficulties arising from outsourcing are described here.

First, any organization seeking to outsource its 'non-core' activities faces the difficulty of determining just what activities are not core to its success. Suppose an organization feels that its customer support services can be outsourced to an overseas call centre because customer or user requirements can be collected simply and securely and then transferred to be dealt with by 'core' personnel employed within the organization. There are many examples, in both the public and private sectors, of the detrimental effects that this sort of outsourcing can have, particularly if the nature of the service is complex with many non-standard inquiries. Furthermore, any communication inefficiencies between the external supplier and the public sector organization are likely to lead to service failures and to increased costs to remedy such failures.

Second, a risk in outsourcing is that the quality of service falls as a result of failure to monitor adequately the results of the outsourcing arrangements. This may be compounded by an attempt at the contracting stage to force down the cost of the outsourcing contact so that the lowest priced bid wins the contract without adequate concern for the maintenance of service quality.

Third, a related impact of the lowest price bidder winning the outsourcing contract is that it may then feel that it must work precisely to the terms of the arrangement and insist on charging additional fees for anything not expressly written into the contract. It may be difficult for the public sector organization to define exactly what is required in advance for the service to be provided. Such incomplete contracts may result in reduced quality of service, lower or unclear accountability for the services that are provided and higher unexpected or hidden costs to make good the inadequacy of the original contractual arrangements.

Fourth, there are organizational risks to public sector entities that enter into significant outsourcing arrangements. These include a potential for loss of control over significant activities or functions; an over-dependence on a single private contractor who may not deliver the service to the desired level of quality; a loss of competence or capacity within the organization which, once lost, is very difficult to reinstate; and the possibility of reputational damage if the private contractor is seen to be operating inappropriately – for example by lowering the conditions of employment; by making excessive profits or by hiding such profits from taxation by setting up overseas subsidiaries in tax havens.

So, while outsourcing may be seen as a means to transfer risk to the private sector contractor, there may be considerable limitations on the extent to which such transfer is successful. There are two particular examples to mention. First, it is most unlikely that a public sector organization can transfer out the risk of non-performance of a public service to the private sector. For example, if a private sector provider of public medical services suffers financial collapse, it is likely that the public sector will have to step in either by providing such services directly or by paying for an alternative provider. Second, obtaining significant private sector finance may be difficult without a charge on public sector assets or public sector guarantees to reduce the risks to the private sector financier.[6]

The financial assessment criteria for outsourcing arrangements

Section 8.2 of this chapter provides information on the financial assessment criteria that underpin a decision on capital expenditure or major revenue-funded projects. Similar criteria are likely to be used in assessing outsourcing arrangements. Three particular criteria should be mentioned:

- Affordability: the public sector body must have the available cash resources to cover costs when they fall due for payment. So there is a need to assess the cash flow impact of outsourcing to ensure that funds are available, either from annual revenue funding or through loans and grants to support capital expenditure.
- Value for money: there will be a need to show that outsourcing is 'better value for money' than the alternative arrangements for direct provision. For example, the NPV of the proposed outsourcing arrangements should be compared with the NPV of the alternative 'public sector comparator' of internal provision and funding. The decision criteria (ignoring all other factors) would be to choose the approach with the highest (positive) NPV or the lowest (negative) Net Present Cost (NPC).
- Risk assessment: there would be a need to relate matters of affordability and value for money to the risks attached to each alternative form of supply. For example, outsourcing the supply or the financing of projects might enable certain risks to be managed more effectively by external suppliers. On the other hand, the risks of service failure may be seen to increase without there being adequate regard to quality of service at the contracting stage and effective monitoring arrangements throughout the contract period.

8.5   Case study: the County Ambulance Service NHS Trust

The example in this section considers a form of outsourcing known as public-private partnerships (PPP)[7]. The example is based upon a UK type of PPP known

---

6 See, for example, the report of the UK National Audit Office following the collapse of Metronet (part of the London Underground PPP scheme) which reports that about 95% of the loans provided by the private sector were guaranteed by the government (NAO, 2009).

7 A more extensive analysis of PPPs is given in Vries and Yehoue (2013).

as the Private Finance Initiative (PFI).[8] The example is intended only as an illustration of broad, typical procedures and does not purport to represent the only or an optimal approach to PFI procurement.

   a. The County Ambulance Service NHS Trust (County) is seeking to replace its current radio communication and control system (CCS). A CCS Project Committee is set up and it creates a list of essential and desirable characteristics grouped under four main headings:

   b. To secure viable future communications both within the service and with other parties (e.g. local emergency services, high risk sites, hospitals).

   c. To reduce external radio interference to make speech radio communications more reliable.

   d. To improve performance standards by ensuring rapid response to calls and improving communication with and control of ambulances.

   e. To improve information systems to provide accurate statistics of the service performance.

Two different methods of financing the CCS have been identified. The first is a conventional procurement (CP) of the system, in which public sector capital funding would be used to finance its purchase. The second is the use of the private finance initiative (PFI), in which the private sector finances the installation and maintenance of the system under a long-term contract with County paying a regular service charge subject to deductions for poor performance.

Identification of options

The CCS Project Committee creates a list of options to deal with the situation.

1. Do the minimum. This option acts as a 'base-line' for other options. It would involve some capital expenditure immediately together with a replacement of the speech radio system in five years' time.

2. Replace the speech radio system.

3. Replace the speech radio and add automatic vehicle location (AVL). This would allow the control centre to register the position of all vehicles.

4. Replace the speech radio and add mobile data transmission (MDT). This would allow the control centre to automate standard messages so that the status of each ambulance is able to be continually monitored by the control centre.

5. Replace speech radio with AVL and MDT. This combines the benefits of options 3 and 4.

---

8 This is a revised and simplified version of a case based upon a mixture of three PFI schemes under development between 1995 and 2000 (Hodges, 1999).

Option scoring

The members of the CCS Project Committee carry out an option scoring exercise. This takes a form similar to the multi-criteria analysis introduced in Section 8.3 and shown in Table 8.5. This leads to the calculation of a 'benefit score' for each option. The scoring of non-financial benefits from this stage is then compared with estimates of the cost of each option based on discounted cash flow (DCF) methods, similar to the approach shown in Appendix A.8.1, to identify the net present cost of each option. A measure of 'value for money' is determined by taking the cost of each option divided by its benefit score as shown in Table 8.8. The details of these calculations are not shown here to avoid excessive length of the case. The outcome is that the CCS Project Committee recommends to the board of County that the service should procure a system based upon option 5, which replaces the existing speech radio and provides both automatic vehicle location and mobile data transmission facilities.

On this basis option 5 is identified as being best value for money[9] as its net present cost per benefit point is lower than the other options.

We might just pause a while here to reflect on this process of analysis. The decision is based upon a quantitative valuation which points towards the choice of option 5 as it has a lower cost per benefit point, at £290K, than the other four options.[10] However, it would be naive to treat the calculations as entirely objective. Recall that the non-financial options appraisal is based upon a choice of particular project objectives and a scoring mechanism that are, by their very nature, subjective. Additionally, you may recall that NPC calculations reflect the expected future cash flows of a project and not actual past results that can be verified for accuracy. The use of a particular discount rate also adds to the subjectivity of the calculations.[11] In this example the most comprehensive CCS is chosen as a result of the financial assessment criteria. The result is likely to have been influenced by the relatively high fixed costs of providing less comprehensive systems;

Table 8.8 Cost–benefit analysis for the five options

Option	NPC £000	Benefit score	Cost-benefit
1 Minimum	1,047	2.60	£403K
2 Radio only	1,405	4.55	£309K
3 Radio + AVL	1,919	5.75	£334K
4 Radio + MDT	2,116	6.10	£347K
5 Radio + AVL + MDT	2,338	8.05	£290K

9 The payback method is not used here. There is no 'payback period' as such because the project does not generate its own income. The project is financed by the NHS indirectly through taxation.

10 All cost figures are in thousands (indicated by K) of British Pounds.

11 The discount rate used was a real rate of 3.5% per annum to comply with UK Treasury requirements.

it makes operating and financial sense to add important additional benefits when installing the new CCS. Presumably, this choice of CCS is the one preferred by the management of County; they will surely want the best system that is available to them.

Descriptions of systems of project appraisal will promote a view that neutral and objective assessment leads to the best 'solution'. However, we cannot ignore the possibility, in any project appraisal situation, that a preferred 'solution' may influence the stages and data used in project appraisal. The use of numbers, particularly financial data, is always likely to be significant in project appraisal and decision-making, despite the inherent limitations of quantitative measures (for example, see Miller, 2001).

Financing this preferred option

Having chosen option 5 it is necessary to determine the preferred financing method. The two funding structures are quite different. The conventional procurement (CP) requires an initial capital payment to design and install the system followed by annual net additional costs. The PFI scheme avoids up-front capital payments, although some consultancy costs are expected. There will then be annual service charges paid each year by County to cover the provision and financing of the infrastructure together with the operation and maintenance of the CCS.

The CP scheme is estimated have a capital cost £1,340K payable at the start of the project. Net additional costs will be incurred each year, for items such as labour, repairs and maintenance and rental costs and, after deducting expected savings, the net additional costs are estimated at £120K each year. It is assumed that these costs will increase each year at the predicted 3% annual rate of inflation.

The NPC calculations for the CP scheme are shown in Table 8.9 below. The capital expenditure is incurred immediately, so its NPC is equal to the actual costs incurred. The net additional costs, incurred for years 1 to 10, are assumed to be paid at the end of each year. Each payment is discounted at the required real discount rate of 3.5% per annum. The present value factor of 8.317 is the sum of ten discount factors for years 1 to 10 at 3.5% per annum (sometimes referred to as an annuity factor). The net present cost of the capital expenditure and the net present costs of the ten years of revenue expenditure are added to give the total NPC of £2,338K.

In using PFI funding, it is expected that there will be no immediate payment for capital expenditure and this is financed by the private sector consortium.

Table 8.9 Net present cost of the CP Scheme

Year		Cost (£000)	PV Factor	NPC (£000)
0	Capital expenditure	1,340	1.000	1,340
1 to 10	Net additional costs	120 p.a.	8.317	998
	Net present cost			2,338

Table 8.10 Net present cost of the PFI Scheme

Year		Cost (£000)	PV Factor	NPC (£000)
0	Consultancy costs	55	1.000	55
1 to 10	PFI service charges	360 p.a.	7.154	2,575
	Net present cost			2,630

However it is assumed here that consultancy costs of £55K will be incurred and paid for at the start of the scheme. The PFI scheme will then be paid for by annual service charges of £360K per annum, which is fixed for the whole of the ten year period. For simplicity, it is assumed that there will be no other costs or cost saving associated with the use of PFI funding.

The NPC calculations for the PFI scheme are shown in Table 8.10 below. The consultancy fees are assumed to be paid at the start of the scheme and have an NPC equivalent to the amount paid. The PFI service charges are assumed to be paid at the end of each of years 1 to 10. The PFI service charges of £360K p.a. are fixed for the ten year period, unlike the net additional costs of the CP scheme, so it is necessary to reduce this *nominal* cash flow cost to an equivalent *real* cash flow cost by the predicted inflation rate of 3% per annum and then discount this real cash flow cost at the real discount rate of 3.5% per annum. This can be done in a single stage using the formula:

$$1 + nominal\ discount\ rate = (1 + real\ discount\ rate) * (1 + expected\ inflation\ rate)$$

In this example 1 + nominal discount rate = 1.035 * 1.03 = 1.06605. This gives a nominal discount rate of 6.605% per annum.

The present value factor of 7.154 is the sum of ten discount factors for years 1 to 10 at 6.605 % per annum.

The result of this analysis shows that the NPC of the conventional scheme is £2,338K compared with £2,630K with the PFI scheme. Intuitively it should not be a surprise that the PFI scheme has a higher NPC as private sector financing costs, for both debt and equity, are likely to be higher than the equivalent costs incurred by governments and public sector organizations.

Valuation of risk transfer

One benefit of outsourcing is the opportunity for risks to be transferred from the public sector purchaser to the private sector supplier or consortium, in cases where such risks can be better managed by the supplier/consortium. The objective of this stage of the process is to identify the risks attached to the project - by this is meant the possibility that the actual financial outcome will be different from the expected financial outcome on which the Present Value (PV) of cash flows have been calculated. There are 'upside' risks meaning that costs of the project may be lower or income from the project is higher than expected. Perhaps more significantly there are 'downside' risks meaning that costs of the project may be higher or income from the project may be lower than expected. There is no single method which can ensure that all risks are identified and valued in an appropriate way. Whatever the approach,[12] a structured analysis and valuation is likely to be needed to get the approvals necessary from higher authorities for the project to proceed to contract stage.

The objective here is to seek to identify differences between the allocations of risks under public sector conventional procurement (CP) and under a PFI contract. An outline of the approach is shown in Appendix A.8.2 at the end of the chapter. NPV methods are used here. The calculations are intended to estimate the possibilities that actual cash flows will differ from the 'best' estimates and then to state this in terms of the net present cost of these potential cash flows. The figures suggest the use of high precision in calculation, despite the highly subjective assessment of the risks involved and the measurement of each risk.

The final result of the analysis of net present costs and risks is given in Table 8.11.

The decision

The decision basis from this process is that County should choose option 5 funded through a PFI scheme. Option 5 is chosen because it has the lowest cost per unit of benefit as shown in Table 8.8. The PFI form of contract financing is chosen because the NPC of the PFI scheme, *after allowing for the estimated benefit of risks transferred to the private sector*, is lower than the NPC of the CP scheme as shown in Table 8.11.

The risk transfer calculation has switched the decision from CP to PFI as the NPC based purely on the cash flows (Tables 8.9 and 8.10) would have led to a decision to go for a conventionally financed project. The impact of the risk transfer calculations to switch the decision in favour of PFI is one that has been reported in academic studies (for example Heald, 2003; Broadbent et al., 2008). This casts some doubt on the rigour of this process, as the assumptions and estimates behind the calculations may be highly subjective.

In practical terms, the analysis should not stop here. First, it will be necessary for County to show that the scheme is affordable.[13] Someone has to pay for this

Table 8.11 Net present cost of financing options including risk transfer

	Conventional procurement	PFI scheme
Net present cost of cash flows	£2,333K	£2,630K
Net present cost of retained risk	£329K	£5K
Total net present cost	£2,662K	£2,635K

---

12 The approach shown here represents a high level of simplification to reduce the length of the case.

13 In practice, issues of affordability are likely to be considered alongside NPC and risk analysis as a continuing part of the project analysis rather than constituting a separate procedure at the end.

scheme, whether it is conventionally financed or structured as a PFI scheme. County will need to go back to those organizations in the local health sector to get promises of support in specific terms indicating how much they will each contribute towards the scheme. Second, the difference between the cost of the CP and PFI schemes, shown in Table 8.11, is very small, only about 1% of the total cost, so additional analysis will be justified to reconsider the calculations and to seek lower prices from suppliers. Third, there may be differences in the financial reporting treatment that might also influence the financing decision (Hodges and Mellett, 2012). Finally, there may be local political barriers to overcome if one particular method of financing is preferred over the other for ideological reasons.

8.6   Concluding remarks

When public sector organizations make decisions about investment in assets (sometimes called capital investment or capital expenditure) or about whether to supply services directly or through external suppliers (sometimes called outsourcing), such decisions should be based at least partly upon a financial analysis of the effects of the proposed alternative schemes.

A good financial analysis requires robust financial data. So here is the first challenge facing organizations as the analysis is largely concerned with predicting future financial outcomes rather than past financial facts. The use of carefully constructed budgets and forecasts, using recent results and supported by firm quotations from suppliers, can aid this process, but subjectivity can never be entirely removed. A number of different scenarios may be considered with estimates of probabilities of occurrence being used to aid the decision-making.

Financial decisions may be based on various criteria. We have considered two methods in this chapter. *The Payback Period* seeks to identify the period (e.g. the number of years) needed for the net income deriving from the project to recover the cost of the investment at the start of the project. The decision basis for payback is to choose the project with the shortest payback period. The *Net Present Value* method seeks to compare the present value of future income from the project with the present value of the costs expected to be incurred. This criterion aims to choose the project with the highest net present value (or, when the net present cost criterion is used, the lowest net present cost).

There are other issues that complicate these processes further in a public sector context. There will be non-financial objectives and criteria that must be considered alongside these financial issues and may be of greater importance than the financial analysis. This chapter has discussed both multi-criteria analysis and Cost–Benefit analysis to illustrate this. There may also be regulatory requirements that limit the available options, for example, by requiring Discounted Cash Flow (DCF) analysis rather than payback in the financial decision-making process.

References

Adam, B., R. Jones and R. Mussari (2011), The diversity of accrual accounting practices in local government financial reporting: an examination of infrastructure, art and heritage assets, *Financial Accountability & Management*, Vol. 27, no.2, pp. 107–33.

Bandy, G. (2011), *Financial Management and Accounting in the Public Sector*, Routledge, Abingdon.

Barton, A. (2005), Public sector accountability and commercial-in-confidence outsourcing contracts, *Accounting, Auditing and Accountability Journal*, Vol. 19, no. 2, pp. 256–71.

Broadbent, J., J. Gill and R. Laughlin (2008), Identifying and controlling risk: the problem of uncertainty in the private finance initiative in the UK's National Health Service, *Critical Perspectives on Accounting*, Vol. 19, no. 1, pp. 40–78.

Burg, T. van de (2012), *Een analyse van de plannen voor het Nieuwe Stadion* (An analysis of the plans for building a New Stadium), UTwente (www/reddekuip.nl).

Elinder, M. and Jordahl, H. (2013), Political preferences and public sector outsourcing, *European Journal of Political Economy*, Vol. 30. no. 1, pp. 43–57.

Greve, C. (2008), *Contracting for Public Services*, Routledge, Abingdon.

Heald, D. (2003), Value for money tests and accounting treatment of PFI schemes, *Accounting, Auditing and Accountability Journal*, Vol.16, no.3, pp. 342–71.

Helfert, E. (2001), *Financial Analysis Tools and Techniques: A Guide for Managers*, McGraw-Hill, New York.

Hobbs, B.F., V. Changkong, W. Hamadeh and E.Z. Stakhiv (1992), Does choice of multicriteria method matter? An experiment in water resources planning, *Water Resources Research*, Vol. 28, no. 7, pp. 1767–79.

Hodges, R (1999), *Learning to Live with the PFI: Case Studies of Three Ambulance Services*, Discussion Paper, University of Nottingham.

Hodges, R. and Mellett, H. (2012), The UK Private Finance Initiative: an accounting retrospective, *British Accounting Review*, Vol. 44, no. 4, pp. 235–47.

National Audit Office (2009), *Department for Transport: The Failure of Metronet*, HC512, Session 2008–09, The Stationery Office, London.

Mikesell, J.L. (1999), *Fiscal Administration: Analysis and Applications for the Public Sector*, 5th edition, Harcourt Brace, Philadelphia.

Miller, P. (2001), Governing by Numbers: Why Calculative Practices Matter, *Social Research*, Vol. 68, no. 2, pp. 379–96.

Morin, D. (2014), A fresh look at the performance of government enterprises, *CIGAR Newsletter, April 2014*, p. 4.

Northcott, D. (1999), *Capital Investment Decision-Making*, Thomson, London.

Pollitt, C. (2003), *The Essential Public Manager*, Open University Press, Maidenhead.

Vries, P. de and Yehoue, E. (eds) (2013), *The Routledge Companion to Public–Private Partnerships*, Routledge, Abingdon.

Appendix A.8.1 Financial calculations of the investment options for Old Port's stadium

The calculations of the net present values are based on a present value factor of 15.6, which is equivalent to an equal return per year over 25 years and which is common in all options and scenarios, given a real interest rate of 4%.

Option renovating the old stadium

Payback period: Investment/yearly returns
Regular case scenario: 135/7.5 = 18.0 years
Worst case scenario: 135/6.5 = 20.8 years
So, in both scenarios, the renovation is paid back quite a long time before the end of the operational period of 25 years.

Net present value: Yearly return × Present value factor − Investment
Regular case scenario: $(7. 5 \times 15.6) - 135 = -$ €18.0 million
Worst case scenario: $(6.5 \times 15.6) - 135 = -$ €33.6 million
So, the Net Present Value of the renovation is negative, even under the regular case scenario.

Option building a new stadium

Payback period: Investment/yearly returns
Regular case scenario: 250/13 = 19.2 years
Worst case scenario: 250/10.5 = 23.8 years
So building a new stadium is paid back quite a long time before the end of the operational period of 25 years under the regular case scenario, but very close to 25 years under the worst case scenario.

Net present value: Yearly return x Present value factor − Investment
Regular case scenario: $(13 \times 15.6) - 250 = -$ €47.2 million
Worst case scenario: $(10.5 \times 15.6) - 250 = -$ €86.2 million
So, the Net Present Value of the renovation is negative, even under the regular case scenario.

The conclusion has to be that both options are likely to require substantial financial support from the city, given the findings of the Net Present Value calculations. These calculations have to be preferred over the quite positive calculation of the Payback Period, because investments with a long lifecycle (25 years) require a financial assessment which takes account of the value of money. This conclusion also explains why banks require a municipal warranty for their loans. The option of building a new stadium scores lower on the Net Present Value criterion than the option of renovating the old stadium. It can be argued that a local government has an interest in an appropriate professional football accommodation, which deserves some financial support. Therefore, it is defendable to give the option of renovating the old stadium a rate of 6 and the option of building a new stadium a rate of 4 (on a scale from 1 to 10).

Appendix A.8.2 Net present cost of risks retained under Conventional Procurement (CP) and the Private Finance Initiative (PFI) for County Ambulance Service

The right-hand columns show the estimated net present cost (in £000) of risks retained by County under CP and under PFI.

Ref	Type of risk	Rationale	CP	PFI
1	Pre-contract risks of changes of service specification	Not evaluated as the risks are assumed to be the same under CP and PFI.		
2	Design and testing costs including technology changes	External consultancy costs and changes to design are borne by County under CP but are included in the PFI contract at a fixed price. CP cost is based on probability estimates of cost outcomes at start of the scheme.	10	0
3	Implementation delays caused by County being unprepared	CP cost based on interest charges incurred in purchasing the new system. PFI cost estimated based on estimated probability of maintaining the old system for part of the year.	7	5
	Site availability and rental costs	Rental costs are fixed under PFI. CP cost is based on estimated probabilities of rental increases.	57	0
4	Component defects	CP costs are based on estimated probability of additional costs after first year warranty expires (for 9 years discounted at 3.5%). No PFI costs as components are covered by the service charge.	27	0
5	Installation costs	CP cost based upon estimated probability of total installation costs being exceeded. Supplier has risk under PFI.	67	0
6	Service specification and standards	Not evaluated as the risks are assumed to be the same under CP and PFI.		
7	Penalty payments and commercial income	The PFI contract allows for reduced payments to the contractor and for commercial income to be generated and shared. Treated as an additional cost of the CP scheme.	16	0

8	Maintenance cost variations	CP cost is based on estimated probabilities of maintenance being different (generally higher) than those costs included in the project estimates. Annual estimated cost for ten years is discounted at 3.5% per annum. Supplier assumes this risk under PFI.	111	0
9	Loss of volume of activity	Not evaluated as the risks are assumed to be the same under CP and PFI.		
10	Inflation risk	PFI scheme of fixed service charge payments insulates County from the impact of inflation. CP costs based upon estimated probabilities of different levels of inflation on the total CP annual costs for ten years discounted at 3.5%.	34	0
	Net present costs of risks retained by County		329	5

9

Auditing

Learning objectives

◆ To have an understanding of the various meanings and types of auditing in the context of the public sector, especially external versus internal auditing, and financial versus compliance and performance auditing

◆ To appreciate the importance of auditor independence and the challenges involved in ensuring such independence

◆ To have an understanding of typical objectives, standards and procedures of audits in a public sector context and how public sector reforms are affecting the auditing environment

9.1 Introduction

This chapter considers the objectives and typical functions of auditing in a public sector context. An audit is a process leading to an evaluation of something. However, an audit may encompass a variety of objectives and activities which may vary between different legislations. This chapter will use the label 'audit' in a generic sense to refer to any type of activity that might be described in practice as 'audit', 'inquiry', 'investigation' or 'inspection' except when referring to a particular type of audit activity, when a more specific label will be used. The intention in this chapter is to provide readers with a general understanding of typical feature of these activities; we do not describe the detailed procedures that constitute audit, nor do we cover the particular legislation applying in individual countries (those seeking further information should consider the list of references and websites at the end of the chapter).

This chapter proceeds as follows. Section 9.2 provides an introduction to the significance of auditing in the public sector. It gives a classification of such audit activities. Section 9.3 considers the importance of auditor independence in a public sector context. Section 9.4 provides further discussion of the objectives, standards and procedures of the different types of public sector audits. The following two sections each provide a short case study. Section 9.5 is based upon the financial statement audit of whole of government accounts in the UK. Section 9.6 is based upon a performance audit into the criminal justice system in the Netherlands. Section 9.7 provides a concluding summary.

9.2   Significance and types of public sector audit

A public sector audit may be seen to have a key constitutional position within the public sector, at least from a Western, democratic perspective. The underlying concept is that a legislative body, such as a parliament or a local council, will collect revenues from taxation and these are then allocated to public sector organizations for particular tasks. These organizations report back to the legislative body which, in turn, scrutinizes and reports back to the taxpayers and their representatives. The data on which such reports are based are examined by auditors who may be required to express various types of opinion or judgment on the validity of the data and the appropriate use of public money.

The historical importance of audit in the public sector is evidenced by the existence of institutions set up in many counties to audit the accounts of government. These bodies are called *Supreme Audit Institutions* (SAI), a title which reflects their intended status as auditors of the activities of national governments. The *International Organization of Supreme Audit Institutions* (INTOSAI) provides a collective forum for such institutions and sets out standards of independence and practice for national public sector auditors.[1]

The significance of audit is linked to a number of contextual factors that may be seen to be increasing the prevalence of audit procedures. The importance of audit processes may increase as a result of a combination of demands of accountability and the absence of trust. Stakeholders look to governance structures, including audit, to promote effective service delivery and to restrict the potential for corrupt activities in both the public and private sectors; see, for example, Quick et al. (2008).

There are a number of ways in which 'audit' may be classified. The distinction between external and internal audits will be explained and then we compare financial audits, performance audits and compliance audits.

An *external audit* typically involves the examination of financial statements by an auditor that is perceived to be *independent* of the audited entity (sometimes called the auditee). The auditor presents an audit report, expressing an opinion on matters concerning the adequacy of the accounts in presenting fairly the financial position and performance of the organization. The objectives of an external audit are usually laid down in legal statutes or other forms of regulation. Public

---

1 The INTOSAI site includes a list of member national public sector auditing bodies at http://www.intosai.org/about-us/organisation/membership-list.html.

sector external audit may be performed by a public sector auditing body, such as an SAI, in which case the auditor is within the public sector although it is external to the audited entity. In some jurisdictions, public sector audits are contracted out to private sector audit firms. There are broadly two models: one in which a public sector body, such as the SAI, is responsible for the procurement process and regulates the appointment of private sector firms; the other in which the audited entity appoints its own auditor.

The nature and scope of an *internal audit* is normally determined by the Board of the organization rather than by legislation. There may be a Director of Finance or an Accounting Officer with responsibility to advise the Board and to ensure that an effective internal audit process is in place. The internal audit function may be provided through one or more of several models. One option is for an organization to have its own internal audit department and to employ its own internal audit staff. A second option is some sort of shared services arrangement in which several public sector bodies share an internal audit facility. A third option is to outsource the internal auditing activities to a private sector firm. Internal auditors report within the organization, typically to the Board or to an Audit Committee of the Board, or to a higher level of public sector authority; for example the auditor of a public sector agency might report to its sponsoring government department.

The second classification of audits is related to the objectives of the audit activities undertaken. The particular classification described here is that used by INTOSAI (2013a, par. 22).

Financial auditing has as its primary function, an examination of financial statements with the purpose that it will enhance the confidence of the intended users of those financial statements. The auditor provides an opinion on whether the financial statements are in accordance with an applicable financial reporting framework; in some jurisdictions this includes whether the financial statements are presented fairly or show a true and fair view. These objectives are typically the duties of the external auditor; however the external auditor may place some reliance on the work of internal auditors in assessing the systems which underlie the records of transactions needed for the production of financial statements (INTOSAI, 2010).

Compliance auditing (sometimes called regulatory auditing) is the assessment of whether a process or subject matter is in compliance with criteria laid down by applicable authorities. Compliance audits are carried out by assessing whether activities, financial transactions and information comply with the authorities governing the audited entity (INTOSAI, 2013d, p 3). Compliance audits may be carried out by independent external auditors, such as an SAI, or may be conducted on behalf of the board of the audited entity by internal auditors or a private sector auditing firm. For example, if a municipality is responsible for establishing the right to a social benefit and the payment of that benefit, a compliance audit can determine whether this municipality carries out its tasks in accordance with the national legislation in this field.

Performance auditing implies a wider scope than financial auditing; typically with both financial and non-financial matters under review. It will typically assess whether interventions, programmes or institutions are performing in accordance with the principles of economy, efficiency and effectiveness and whether there is room for improvement (INTOSAI, 2013c, p. 2). They may be called *value-for-money (VfM) audits* because such audits are likely to be concerned with relating quantity, quality and equity of service provision to the cost of resources used. They may be called *operational audits* because their scope goes beyond financial management, seeking to measure the effectiveness of non-financial operations of public sector organizations. Performance audits may be carried out internally or involve the contracting of specialist external assessors or consultants and will typically involve multi-disciplinary teams, particularly when significant non-financial assessments of activities are required.

It is useful to understand that the three types of audits described above do not represent neat and watertight compartments, so that an individual audit may involve aspects of all three of the categories described above. For example, an audit of financial statements of a government department might require an auditor's opinion about the fairness of the published financial statements (*financial audit*), an opinion on whether expenditure has been properly incurred for the purposes for which it was approved by the legislature (*compliance audit*) and whether or not the audited entity has arrangements in place to secure value for money (*performance audit*).

9.3   The critical issue of auditor independence

As was explained above, an audit is a process of investigation and assessment leading to some type of opinion, for example on the adequacy of a set of financial statements, on compliance with regulation or on matters of economy, efficiency or effectiveness of public sector activities. Whatever the specific nature of the audit assignment, it is recognized that auditors must have some independence from the audited entity if the audit opinion is to have credibility. For example, INTOSAI has long recognized the importance of independence:

> *Supreme Audit Institutions can accomplish their tasks objectively and effectively only if they are independent of the audited entity and are protected from outside influence.* (INTOSAI, 1977, par. 5.1).

Similarly, the Institute of Internal Auditors (IIA) recognizes that an internal audit function can only be effective if given freedom to conduct its work without undue interference:

> *The audit activity should have sufficient independence from those it is required to audit so that it can both conduct and be perceived to conduct its work without interference . . . Important parts of this independence are the Chief Audit*

Executive's ability to be protected from management or political interference or retaliation resulting from carrying out legitimate duties in accordance with [IIA] Standards. (IIA, 2012, p. 6).

A set of principles to promote the independence of SAIs is set down in the *Mexico Declaration on SAI Independence* (INTOSAI, 2007). These are listed below, in summary form.

1. There should be an appropriate and effective constitutional framework for SAI independence which is applied in practice.
2. SAI heads should have security of tenure and legal immunity in the normal discharge of their duties.
3. There should be a broad mandate and full discretion in the discharge of SAI functions.
4. SAIs should have unrestricted access to information to discharge their duties.
5. SAIs should have a right and obligation to report the results of their audit work.
6. SAIs should be free to decide the content, timing, publication and dissemination of their audit reports.
7. There should be effective follow-up mechanisms on SAI recommendations.
8. SAIs should have financial and administrative autonomy and appropriate human, material and financial resources.

However, it is unlikely that any auditor can be perceived to have absolute independence. In the case of an SAI, it is part of the state and will be subjected to political influences, perhaps from members of the executive government or from senior officials of audited entities. Private sector auditors of public sector bodies will wish to retain and expand their portfolio of clients. Internal auditors may find themselves reporting to senior officials who may have potential authority to restrict or even remove internal audit staff. For example, Roussy (2013) shows that internal auditors in the Canadian public sector try to cope with the tension between formal independency and a strongly felt loyalty towards top management. This study introduces the term 'grey independency', which refers to internal auditors seeking to solve role conflicts by trying to be independent, but forgiving themselves for falling short of independence in the strictest sense.

The protection of auditor independence is therefore based upon establishing structures so that an auditor is appointed by someone other than those who are the subjects of audit inquiry. For example, an SAI may be required to report to and be appointed by a parliament or a legislative body rather than the executive government. The members of an SAI, particularly the Auditor General, should be granted some independence under a national constitution to avoid a government being able to replace him or her. Audit staff should report to the SAI and not to the government or executive of audited entities. The position for internal auditors should similarly be protected. An internal auditor might be expected to have rights to report to the full board of the audited entity, or to an audit committee, whose members are largely non-executive and independent of the executive management of the audited entity. However, internal auditors will work with top management on a day-to-day basis and may perceive part of their role as assisting top management in its relationship with the audit committee (Roussy, 2013). Private sector external auditors of public sector entities might report to and be appointed by an organization that is independent of the audited body. For example, an SAI might be responsible for appointing private sector firms to some public sector audits rather than carrying out all such audits using their own staff.

The independence of an auditor might still be at risk, despite the existence of structures intended to protect them. For example, Gendron et al. (2001) examine how new public management reforms gave the Office of the Auditor General of Alberta (a federal state in Canada) extra powers to influence politicians and senior public servants, but that these measures made the Office more vulnerable to complaints about lack of independence from the government executive. Similarly, Funnell (2003) illustrates that reforms in New South Wales (Australia), which allowed the private sector providers to colonize public service provision, may create difficulties for state auditors to retain unrestricted access to information and may limit government accountability for public spending.

Another threat to independence arises when auditors face actual or potential competition for their work from other auditors. In the private sector, the threat to auditor independence from excessive competition is generally recognized, but may be subtle and difficult to measure (Houghton and Jubb, 2003). Audit competition in the public sector may be less explicit than in the private sector as some SAIs may have a monopolistic position. However, Bowerman et al. (2003) draw attention to the competition between four public sector audit bodies, the UK National Audit Office, the Audit Commission and the audit offices of Scotland and Northern Ireland[2] to suggest that there may be competition for supremacy between public sector audit bodies within jurisdictions. The UK National Audit Office (NAO) is highlighted as having a position of independence consistent with INTOSAI guidelines. The Auditor-General is protected as a parliamentary officer so that the executive government is not in a position to exert undue influence over the post-holder.[3] The Audit Commission was not an SAI; it was created as an agency of government to carry out financial audits in the local government and health sectors. Bowerman et al. (2003, p. 13), see the Audit Commission as being more exposed, in comparison with the other three bodies, as a result of powers held by the political heads of some central government departments from the legislation which had created it. What the authors could not have foreseen was that, within ten years of writing their paper, the Audit Commission was to be abolished

---

2   The Wales Audit Office (WAO) was created in 2005 and is not included in their study.

3   For example, the Auditor General can only be removed from office by the monarch after resolutions have been passed by both the House of Commons and the House of Lords.

by an incoming Conservative-Liberal Democrat coalition government. This dramatic change in the fortunes of a public sector audit body illustrates the dangers for auditors that are perceived, rightly or wrongly, to be too closely allied to one political faction, particularly if they do not have the constitutional protection of an SAI. In the UK, the Audit Commission began to be seen by some local government authorities as an enforcer of Labour central government reforms (Abu Hasan et al., 2013). Its abolition has resulted in the audits of local government and local health bodies being transferred to private sector auditors (Ellwood and Garcia-Lacalle, 2012).

9.4   Objectives, standards and processes of public sector audits

The objectives, standards and processes of public sector audits will vary according to the legislation under which the audit is mandated and, in some cases, are dependent upon contractual agreements between the auditor and the audited entity or some higher authority responsible for the conduct of that entity. However, some general observations of objectives and processes can be made. Auditing standards have been developed by the International Auditing and Assurance Standards Board (IAASB), primarily for the private sector, but they are adapted to the public sector in some jurisdictions (e.g. Auditing Practices Board, 2010). International Standards for Supreme Audit Institutions (ISSAI) have been developed by INTOSAI, and these are used in this section to provide an overview of major stages in public sector audits.

The definition of financial audit given by INTOSAI reflects that the precise objective of a financial audit will depend upon specific national or supra-national legislation:

Financial audit focuses on determining whether an entity's financial information is presented in accordance with the applicable financial reporting and regulatory framework. The scope of financial audits in the public sector may be defined by the SAI's mandate as a range of audit objectives in addition to the objectives of an audit of financial statements prepared in accordance with a financial reporting framework.

These objectives may include the auditing of: states' or entities' accounts or other financial reports, not necessarily prepared in accordance with a general-purpose financial reporting framework; budgets, budget sections, appropriations and other decisions on the allocation of resources, and the implementation thereof; policies, programmes or activities defined by their legal basis or source of financing; legally-defined areas of responsibility, such as the responsibilities of ministers; and categories of income or payments or assets or liabilities (INTOSAI, 2103b, p. 1).

International standards of auditing provide an indication of the likely processes involved in the completion of an audit, although each engagement will have specific features that may require an auditor to adapt these general procedures. INTOSAI (2013a, pp. 13–15) lists eight principles related to the audit process:

1. Ensure that the terms of the audit have been clearly established.
2. Obtain an understanding of the nature of the entity or programme to be audited.
3. Conduct a risk assessment or problem analysis and revise this as necessary in response to the audit findings.
4. Identify and assess the risks of fraud relevant to the audit objectives.
5. Plan audit work to ensure that the audit is conducted in an effective and efficient manner. Planning should include both strategic and operational issues. Strategic issues should define the scope of the audit, its objectives and the overall approach. Operational issues include setting a timetable for the audit and the extent of audit procedures, assigning the members of the audit team and required subject specialists.
6. Perform audit procedures that provide sufficient appropriate audit evidence. There are many different audit techniques that might be applied and the auditor should select methods which are relevant, valid and reliable. These might include inspection of records and documents, observation of procedures, inquiry with relevant officials or third parties, confirmation of assets and liabilities through physical inspections or confirmatory documentation, recalculation of transaction values or balances, reperformance of procedures and controls, the use of analytical procedures and research techniques such as correlation and regression.
7. Evaluate the audit evidence and draw conclusions. The auditor should take both quantitative and qualitative factors into account and should exercise professional judgement to reach a conclusion on the subject matter.
8. Auditors should prepare a report based on the conclusions reached.

The conclusion of a financial audit is a report indicating the opinions of the auditor from the work performed. An audit report may be in a *long-form*, in which the auditor describes in detail the audit scope, findings, conclusions and recommendations, or it may be a *short-form* report, which is often in a standardized format. A short-form opinion is either unmodified or modified. An *unmodified (or unqualified) opinion* is given when the auditor has obtained sufficient and appropriate evidence. A *modified opinion* may be (a) a *qualified opinion* – where the auditor has overall satisfaction with the audit findings except for certain items with which the auditor disagrees or has been unable to obtain sufficient and appropriate audit evidence; (b) an *adverse opinion* – where the auditor concludes that deviations or misstatements are pervasive; or (c) a *disclaimed opinion* – where the auditor is unable to obtain sufficient and appropriate audit evidence and, as a result, is unable to form an opinion.

Compliance auditing and performance auditing were described in Section 9.2 above, based upon INTOSAI definitions. The stages of these types of audits may be similar to financial audits in broad terms, although the specific elements will differ according to the mandate or agreement for the work. The major stages of a performance audit are summarized below (adapted from INTOSAI, 2013c).

1. Select audit topics through a strategic planning process by analysing potential topics and conducting research to identify risks and problems.
2. Plan the audit in a manner that contributes to a high-quality audit, carried out in an economical, efficient, effective and timely manner and in accordance with the principles of good project management.
3. Obtain sufficient appropriate audit evidence to establish findings, reach conclusions in response to the audit objectives and questions and issue recommendations.
4. Provide audit reports which are comprehensive, convincing, timely, reader-friendly and balanced.
5. If relevant to the mandate, seek to provide constructive recommendations that are likely to contribute significantly to addressing the weaknesses or problems identified by the audit.
6. Make audit reports widely accessible and in accordance with the mandate.
7. Follow up previous audit findings and recommendations wherever appropriate.

A recent report of the European Court of Auditors (ECA) of the operation of EU assistance to Central Asia (ECA, 2013) provides an illustration of the nature of audit work performed and the structure of the associated performance audit reports. The auditors reported that they found that EU assistance to Central Asia was planned appropriately, but that implementation of policy was slow and variable and they concluded that the European Commission should have been more rigorous in managing its budget support programme in two of the Central Asian republics. In line with stage 5 in the above list, the ECA report includes a list of recommendations for action by the Commission and European External Agency System (p. 34). The report also contains responses from the Commission (pp. 34–50) which may form the basis of a follow up by the ECA in line with stage 7 in the above list. In some jurisdictions SAI reports will be submitted for examination by a Public Accounts Committee or other form of parliamentary or judicial examination.

The maintenance of audit quality for public sector audits is problematic. In many countries there may be little competition in the public sector audit market, with an SAI often holding a monopolistic position. One of the few research studies of public sector audit quality (Clark et al., 2007) provides a survey of SAIs in Europe and concludes that audit quality is related to the achievement of independence on the types of issues discussed in Section 9.3 above. More critical perspectives of public sector auditing derive from case study based research methods. Gendron et al. (2007) illustrate, from a Canadian study, how state auditors develop their expertise in areas such as performance measurement in order to protect and extend their role in the face of public sector reforms. Radcliffe (2008), using findings from US performance auditing, suggests that auditors express their audit findings in such a careful way, within prevailing discourses, that they may be constrained from making observations that are publicly unpalatable. Skaerbaek (2009) uses a study of the role of the National Audit Office in Denmark to show that auditors need to be innovative and be prepared to develop a new professional identity to adapt to new socio-technical audit environments.

More generally, there are challenges for auditors arising from public sector reform in many parts of the world. These challenges are exacerbated by modernization programmes which create networks of commissioners and providers in place of formerly vertically integrated public sector bodies (English, 2013). A related consequence of the demands of formal accountability is the importance of 'making things auditable' (Power, 1996) by creating and recording formal processes to support decision-making. As a result, the influence of audit is felt not only when the auditors are present and conducting their audit work; it has an influence 'at a distance' on how systems are developed and maintained.

9.5   Case study: the financial audit of the UK Whole of Government Accounts (WGA)

This section provides a case study to illustrate some of the features of public sector financial auditing discussed above. It is based upon the certificate and report of the Comptroller and Auditor General (CAG), the Head of the UK National Audit Office, included within the WGA (Treasury, 2013) for the year ended 31 March 2012.[4] The publication of the annual WGA is relatively new in the UK, with the first set for 2009/10 being published as recently as 2011, although the project to develop WGA had been in progress for some years before (see Chow et al., 2007). The development of WGA involves a series of conceptual and technical issues. These include the need to determine the boundary of the 'whole of government'; in the UK the decision was made to include all those public entities that are controlled by various layers of government. So, for example, in the UK this is taken to include local government councils and agencies, but it excludes bodies that are partly funded through taxation but are taken to be independent from government control, such as public universities. The technical issues include the need to attain consistent accounting policies across the public sector and to create systems to identify those transactions taking place between those bodies within the

---

4   Extracts from the certificate or report are given in italics in this section.

'WGA boundary' that are eliminated as part of the process of consolidation to avoid the double counting of items (for more detail, see Heald and Georgiou, 2009 and 2011).

The complexity of the WGA, involving the consolidation of the accounts of over 3,000 individual entities (Treasury, 2013, p. 158) makes this one of the world's most complex public sector financial statements to construct and audit. This, together with the fairly recent development of WGA in the UK, may help to explain why the CAG produced a lengthy audit report which is *qualified* in a number of respects as described below (refer back to Section 9.4 for the meaning of a qualified audit report).

Responsibilities of the auditor and the scope of the audit

The audit report gives an overview of the responsibilities of the auditor:

> '*My responsibility is to audit, certify and report on the accounts with a view to satisfying myself that they present a true and fair view.*' (p. 149)

The report also discloses the scope of the audit, which involves obtaining evidence to give reasonable assurance that:

– the financial statements are free from material misstatement;
– appropriate accounting policies are consistently applied and disclosed;
– significant accounting estimates are reasonable; and
– the overall presentation of the financial statement is appropriate.

Boundary issues

One particular feature of WGA is the need to decide what is and what is not included in the 'whole of government'. The approach used by the Treasury is based upon those bodies which are classified as being in the public sector by the Office for National Statistics for *national accounts* purposes. The approach used in national accounts is based upon a macro-economic statistical approach and is not always consistent with consolidation principles in international accounting standards (see Chapter 5). The CAG indicated his disagreement with the method used of determining the accounting boundary, making specific reference to National Rail, a statutory corporation which owns and manages the British railway infrastructure.

> '... *HM Treasury defines the accounting boundary for the Account by reference to those bodies as being in the public sector by the Office for National Statistics. I consider that it would be more appropriate to assess the accounting boundary with reference to the accounting standards* [a footnote refers to IAS 27 of the IASB]. *By applying such accounting standards, I consider that the accounts should include Network Rail.*
>
> *I also consider that HM Treasury's accounting policy has not been applied consistently in 2011–12 as a number of significant bodies have not been included in*

the Accounts, even though they are classified by the Office for National Statistics as being in the public sector and which I consider should be included in the Accounts in line with applicable accounting standards.' (p.150)

An auditor is expected to quantify the effects of any qualification in the audit report. This can be difficult to achieve in circumstances where the auditor is uncertain as to what the figures should be because of lack of information or limitation in the scope of the audit. In this case, the CAG provides information from the accounts of those bodies which have been excluded from consolidation but which he thinks should have been included. The amounts are very large, mainly because they include the banks taken into public ownership at the height of the financial crisis around 2008.

'I cannot quantify the effect of these omissions on the Accounts with certainty as I do not have information needed to identify the transactions which would have to be eliminated to provide a consolidated view. The most significant impact could be on the Accounts Statement of Financial Position. The exclusion of the following categories of bodies could affect this Statement, illustrating the potential impact:

- *Network Rail which has gross assets of £47.8 billion and gross liabilities of £39.3 billion;*
- *Publicly-owned banks which have gross assets [of] £2,572.8 billion and gross liabilities of £2,445.5 billion; and*
- *Other bodies which have estimated gross assets of £18.9 billion and gross liabilities of £6.1 billion.'* (p. 150)

Consistency of accounting policies

One of the principles of consolidation in WGA is that the data from the individual accounts of the entities which are consolidated should be calculated using consistent accounting policies, because the figures in the individual entity accounts need to be determined on a consistent basis for their summation in the WGA to be meaningful. In a sector as large and diverse as the 'whole of government' there are likely to be a number of distinct accounting practices that are applied in different parts of the public sector. The monetary effect of many of these differences may not be significant (or 'material') in the context of the WGA. If the differences are significant, they may lead to a qualification in the audit report unless appropriate adjustments are made at the WGA level to ensure consistency. One example of this is included in this case, relating to infrastructure assets, such as roads.

'Assets held by local government bodies are valued at historic cost, whereas those held by central government are valued at depreciated replacement cost. HM Treasury's estimate of the understatement of assets due to the differences in valuation between historic cost and depreciated replacement cost for local government assets could be at least £200 billion. I do not have information to fully quantify the effect of this limitation.' (p. 151)

Disagreement on accounting policies

An auditor is expected to review the accounting policies used in the financial statements for appropriateness, as well as consistency. If the auditor believes that the accounting policy used is not appropriate and the financial effect on the accounts is material, then the audit report should be qualified by the auditor, who should identify the accounting policy of concern, disclose the preferred policy and, if possible, disclose the financial effect of switching to the preferred policy. This type of audit qualification is rare, but an example is included in this case.

'*In April 2000, the Government issued licences to access the 3G telecommunications spectrum. Each licence was awarded for 20 years and the total revenue raised was £22.5 billion. This was recognised as £22.5 billion income in 2000–01. I consider that it would be more appropriate to recognise income in the Accounts over the life of the licences as the licence holders have the right to access the spectrum for 20 years and the Government has an on-going obligation to ensure that the spectrum remains available to licence holders. The impact of this difference is that income would be £1.3 billion higher; liabilities would be £9.0 billion greater (£10.3 billion in 2010–11) and the value of the general fund would be £9.0 billion less (£10.3 billion in 2010–11).*' (p. 151)

Limitation in the scope of audit due to lack of evidence

An auditor may be unable to find sufficient evidence to be satisfied that all figures in the financial statements are correctly stated. The auditor will have to qualify the audit opinion if this limitation in evidence is severe and relates to significant items in the accounts. Two examples are given from the case. The first relates to procedures that form part of the process of consolidation. Transactions and year-end balances between entities that are part of the consolidation (in the case the whole of the UK public sector) are required to be matched against each other and eliminated on consolidation. This process becomes complicated when there are so many entities to consolidate and if individual entities use different accounting systems. The CAG, in his report, indicates that most transactions and balances have been eliminated, but gives information of the impact of the possible mismatch of other items.

'*. . . However, there remains a material value of intra-government transactions and balances which have not been eliminated. The effect of not adjusting for these could lead to a potential overstatement of up to £16 billion (£22.6 billion in 2010–11) in gross income and expenditure and up to £5.1 billion (£10.4 billion in 2010–11) in gross assets and liabilities.*' (pp. 151–2)

The second example concerns the completeness and valuation of the assets of certain types of schools. Voluntary aided and foundation schools are deemed to be within the WGA boundary, but they were not always included in the accounts of their local government authority. A new type of school, known as academies, have been transferred from direct local government control during the year and there was a mismatch between the accounting value of the assets transferred from local government and those reported as owned by the academies. The CAG reports the uncertainties as follows:

- *'local authority maintained schools' assets, which are estimated to be up to £26 billion of assets from voluntary aided and foundation schools and £8.5 billion assets from voluntary controlled schools have been omitted from these Accounts;*
- *Local authorities transferred land and buildings with book value of £6.5 billion to academies in 2011–12 with the academies reporting additions of land and building of some £12.3 billion... There is... insufficient evidence for me to establish the correct value of the assets that should be included in the Accounts;*
- *I have also been unable to obtain sufficient assurance from my audit that the data submitted by the academies is representative of the income and expenditure incurred in 2011–12.'* (p. 152)

Disagreement and limitation of audit scope relating to some of the underlying accounts

The WGA is constructed from the accounts of over 3,000 entities within the UK public sector. A risk to the adequacy of the WGA arises if any of these individual entity accounts have been qualified by their auditor. In practical terms, a disagreement or uncertainty that may be material to the accounts of an individual entity may not be significant in the context of the much larger amounts included in WGA. Nevertheless, in principle an audit qualification in the accounts of an individual entity could cause a similar qualification to the WGA accounts. In this case, the CAG refers to three such matters in his report.

First, the Ministry of Defence failed to comply with lease accounting requirements for certain contracts. The CAG reported that *'I am unable to quantify the impact on the financial statements because the Ministry has not maintained the information required to comply with the relevant accounting standards in this respect.'*

Second, the CAG was unable to obtain appropriate audit evidence from the Ministry of Defence in respect of the valuation of inventory of £3 billion and capital spares of £7 billion as a result of the failure *'to perform an adequate impairment review on a systematic basis'*.

Third, the Cabinet Office accounts were qualified in respect of the Civil Service pension scheme because *'the Cabinet Office was unable to provide me with evidence to support some service and salary records to validate the accuracy of some benefits awarded.'*

The qualified audit opinion

The notes above provide an indication of the complexity of the WGA in the UK. Nevertheless, there are many other aspects of the accounts which have been audited with a satisfactory outcome. The overall opinion of the CAG therefore provides an 'except for' type of opinion.

'In my opinion, except for the effects of the matters described in the Basis for Qualified Opinion paragraphs above:

- *The financial statements give a true and fair view of the state of affairs of the Whole of Government Accounts as at 31 March 2012 and of its net expenditure for the year then ended; and*

- *The financial statements have been properly prepared in accordance with the Government Resources and Accounts Act, 2000.'*

Emphasis of matter

Finally in this audit report there is an 'emphasis of matter' paragraph, which is used in the rare circumstances of there being a matter of uncertainty, which is of such significance to the financial statements that the auditor believes the matter should be brought to the attention of users through the audit report. So a paragraph is used to outline the nature of the uncertainties and the value of items to which it relates, but without any disagreement with the way that it has been dealt with in the accounts. In this case the CAG refers to uncertainties inherent in the estimation of the costs of decommissioning nuclear energy sites; part of his report stating:

'... *the lengthy timescales, final disposition plans for waste and spent fuel, timing of final site clearance and the confirmation of site end states means that the ultimate liability will vary as a result of subsequent information and events, and may result in significant adjustment over time to the value of the provision, which currently stands at £52.9 billion (£49.1 billion in 2010–11).'*

Summary of the case

This case has provided a complex illustration of a report deriving from a public sector financial audit of the UK WGA. It illustrates that auditors may have different reasons for qualifying their report on a set of accounts. These might include, in consolidation, the boundary decision (what is included and what is left out?); the lack of consistent application or disagreement with accounting policies; the audit being limited in scope because of the absence of appropriate audit evidence; and disagreement or uncertainty arising from inadequate accounting records. Finally, an emphasis of matter paragraph was described to draw attention to a significant, inherent uncertainty but without causing a qualification of the audit opinion.

9.6   Case study: the performance audit of the Netherlands criminal justice system

This second case deals with performance auditing of the criminal justice system in the Netherlands. It relies mainly on a report issued by the Netherlands Court of Audit, the audit office of Dutch central government (Algemene Rekenkamer, 2012).

Background to the audit

The criminal justice system consists of institutions which hold an interrelated responsibility for law enforcement, including: criminal investigation and detection (the Police); summons and indictment (the Prosecution office); trial to the execution of punishments and measures (the Courts); and implementation of these punishments and measures (such as probation services). The Ministry of Justice is in charge of the criminal justice system, which cost about 6 billion euros in 2010. The performance audit focused on violent and property crimes, which amounts to 68% of the total number of crimes, and which is regarded as a political priority in the criminal justice system.

The underlying question of the performance audit was to what extent the criminal justice system leads to undesirable flows and outflows. Undesirable flows are cases that should have been transferred to the next link in the justice chain (for example, from the Police to the Prosecution office) according to existing policy, but which were not. Similarly, outflows are fcases that would have been treated within the justice system according to existing policy, but were not. So, to put it differently: to what degree is the execution of policy making in this field ineffective?

The performance audit firstly investigates the flows and outflows of the criminal justice system in quantitative terms. Subsequently, the question of whether these flows and outflows are in accordance with existing policy making, especially with respect to criminal law, is addressed. Finally, the investigation aims at finding reasons for these undesirable flows and outflows, as well as giving recommendations for reducing them.

The main findings of the audit

Some of the main findings of this performance audit are presented below.

The total number of cases in the year of investigation – between October 2009 and September 2010 – was approximately 1 million. In 23% of these cases criminal prosecution was not necessary because criminal acts were lacking (e.g. neighbour disputes without violence). The Police report that the remaining 780,000 cases showed the following flows and outflows:

- After screening, 69.4% of the cases did not lead to prosecution, for example in cases of, in the words of the Police, 'simple assault' and bicycle theft.
- 17% of the cases would give rise to prosecution, but a defendant could not be found which leads to administrative recording.
- In 3.5% of the cases a defendant could be found but convincing evidence for the criminal act could not be provided, so that these cases are also recorded administratively.

– 2.1% of the cases were settled by the Police through a reprimand or a fine.

– The remaining 8% were transferred to the Prosecution office (this is the flow from the Police to the Prosecution office). The cases for which the Prosecution office took responsibility showed the following flows and outflows:

   ○ Dismissal: 15%.
   ○ Merging with other cases: 4%.
   ○ Fine or community service: 17%.
   ○ Proceedings for trial before a Court: 63%. These cases are attributed to the Prosecution office flows to the Courts, with the following outflows:
      ▪ Acquittal: 9%.
      ▪ Merging with other cases: 7%.
      ▪ Imposition of sentence: 83%.
      ▪ Condemnation without penalty: 1%.

So, from the original 1 million cases only a small number result in the imposition of a sentence by the Courts, i.e. approximately 50,000 cases, about 5% of the total.

The next question which the performance audit wishes to answer is whether flows and outflows in the justice system are in accordance with criminal law and related legislations. Unambiguous answers to this question could not be provided because of a lack of systematic registration of the reasons for flows and outflows. However, the Netherlands Court of Audit provides some indications.

First, capacity constraints of the Police force were the reason for a substantial proportion of undesirable inflows and outflows. On the one hand, this lack of capacity implied that selection of cases for further investigation was unavoidable, and on the other hand that old cases required more time than was available to settle them.

Second, as can be seen from the above indicated figures, the Prosecution office decided on dismissal in 15% of the cases it dealt with. Probably, this is a partly undesirable outflow, for which a lack of evidence is often the main reason.

Third, the Courts in the justice system were also faced with undesirable outflows, mainly because of long turnaround times, which were often caused by a lack of alignment with the work of the Prosecution office.

In a more general sense the audit points to major differences in the registration of flows and outflows by the various links in the criminal justice chain, i.e. the Police, the Prosecution office and the Courts. In addition, for the Ministry of Justice adequate steering to avoid undesirable flows and outflows in the criminal justice system was not an important issue. The internal steering system, which very much relies on total numbers of settled cases, was often at odds with the political priorities in crime fighting.

Recommendations derived from the audit

Finally, the audit presents recommendations for improving the performance of the criminal justice system. The main recommendations are:

– The Ministry of Justice should develop a consistent policy regarding the avoidance of undesirable flows and outflows in the justice system, which gives guidance to the work of all involved links in the criminal justice chain.

– The Ministry of Justice should align its performance measurement and funding system of the criminal justice system to its policy in this field.

– Arrange appointments between the Police force and the Prosecution office for aligning the detection of cases in the criminal justice chain, among others, in order to prevent unequal treatment of similar cases.

– Give specific attention to turnaround times of cases, for which the Police force and the Prosecution office have an interrelated responsibility.

– Develop and implement a registration system for undesirable flows and outflows in the justice system, which has to be applied by all links in the criminal justice chain.

– Regularly inform the parliament about the performance of the criminal justice system in order to contribute to fair expectations about this performance given the available resources.

Summary of the case

This case reveals various issues that underlie appropriate performance auditing. First, a specific articulation of policy goals is needed in order to assess its effectiveness. So, rather than vague formulations about effective crime fighting, it is better to indicate the types of crime that require priority given the scare resources. Second, adequate and coherently applied registration systems of relevant performance indicators are needed; otherwise, performance auditing relies too much on guesswork. Third, measuring is not sufficient; in addition interpretations of findings and recommendations have to be given. Finally, ask responsible policy makers to react to a performance audit, and arrange follow-up audits for monitoring revised policy implementation.

9.7   Concluding remarks

This chapter has outlined some of the key attributes of public sector auditing. Auditing has a place in the governance of the public sector in its role of helping to safeguard the use of public money. This may be through an examination of published financial statements (financial auditing), to ensure that their regulations are being implemented (compliance auditing) or that organizations or programmes are being implemented in ways that will provide economic, efficient and effective use of public money (performance auditing).

Auditor independence is an essential characteristic of strong audit regimes, but there are challenges to ensure that the independence of public sector audit is maintained. Guidance to promote independence and good audit practice are available to assist auditors. Public sector reforms may threaten the separation of managerial interests from those of the auditor if audit becomes too closely aligned with specific political or managerially promoted reforms. The influence of audit over the everyday work of public sector managers may be evidenced by demands to 'make things auditable' and, sometimes, by the overreliance on quantitative 'objective' data in preference to more qualitative outcomes that are more difficult to measure to support evidential demands. References to publications providing studies of the impact of reforms on public sector audit are given for those seeking to extend their understanding of this important facet of the public sector.

References

Abu Hasan, H., J. Frecknall-Hughes, D. Heald and R. Hodges (2013), Auditee Perceptions of External Evaluations of the Use of Resources by Local Authorities, *Financial Accountability & Management*, Vol. 29, no. 3, pp. 291–326.

Algemene Rekenkamer (2012), *Prestaties in de strafrechtketen (Performance of the criminal justice system)*, Den Haag.

Auditing Practices Board (2010), *Practice Note 10 (Revised): Audit of Financial Statements of Public Sector Bodies in the United Kingdom*, APB, London.

Bowerman, M., C. Humphrey and D. Owen (2003), Struggling for Supremacy: The Case of UK Public Audit Institutions, *Critical Perspectives on Accounting*, Vol. 14, no. 1 pp. 1–22.

Chow, D., C. Humphrey and J. Moll (2007), Developing Whole of Government Accounting in the UK: Grand Claims, Practical Complexities and a Suggested Future Research Agenda, *Financial Accountability & Management*, Vol. 23, no. 1, pp. 27–54.

Clark, C., M. De Martinis and M. Krambia-Kapardis (2007), Audit Quality Attributes of European Union Supreme Audit Institutions, *European Business Review*, Vol. 19, no. 1 pp. 40–70.

Ellwood, S. and J. Garcia-Lacalle (2012), New Development: Local Public Audit – the Changing Landscape, *Public Money & Management*, Vol. 32, no. 5, pp. 389–92.

English, L. (2013), The impact of an independent inspectorate on penal governance, performance and accountability: Pressure points and conflict 'in the pursuit of an ideal of perfection', *Critical Perspectives on Accounting*, Vol. 24, no. 6, pp. 532–49.

European Court of Auditors (2013), *EU Development Assistance in Central Asia*, Special Report 13//2103, European Court of Auditors, Luxembourg.

Funnell, W. (2003), Enduring fundamentals: constitutional accountability and Auditor-Generals in the reluctant state, *Critical Perspectives on Accounting*, Vol. 14, no. 1–2, pp. 107–32.

Gendron, Y., D.J. Cooper and B. Townley (2001), In the Name of Accountability: State Auditing, Independence and New Public Management, *Accounting, Auditing and Accountability Journal*, Vol. 14, no. 3, pp. 278–310.

Gendron, Y., D.J. Cooper and B. Townley (2007), The construction of auditing expertise in measuring government performance, *Accounting, Organizations & Society*, Vol. 32, no. 1–2, pp. 101–29.

Heald, D. and G. Georgiou (2009), Whole of government accounting development in the UK: conceptual, technical and timetable issues, *Public Money & Management*, Vol. 29, no. 4, pp. 219–27.

Heald, D. and G. Georgiou (2011), The macro-fiscal role of UK Whole of Government Accounts, *Abacus*, Vol. 47, no. 4, pp. 446–76.

Houghton, K. and C. Jubb (2003), The Market for Financial Report Audits: Regulation of and Competition for Auditor Independence, *Law & Policy*, Vol. 25, no. 3, pp. 299–321.

Institute of Internal Auditors (2012), *The Role of Auditing in Public Sector Governance*, 2nd edn, IIA, Altamonte Springs, FL.

International Organisation of Supreme Audit Institutions (1977), *ISSAI 1: The Lima Declaration*, INTOSAI Professional Standards Committee, Copenhagen.

International Organisation of Supreme Audit Institutions (2007), *ISSAI 10: The Mexico Declaration on SAI Independence*, INTOSAI PSC, Copenhagen.

International Organisation of Supreme Audit Institutions (2010), *ISSAI 1640: Using the Work of Internal Auditors*, INTOSAI PSC, Copenhagen.

International Organisation of Supreme Audit Institutions (2013a), *ISSAI 100: Fundamental Principles of Public-Sector Auditing*, INTOSAI PSC, Copenhagen.

International Organisation of Supreme Audit Institutions (2013b), *ISSAI 200: Fundamental Principles of Financial Auditing*, INTOSAI PSC, Copenhagen.

International Organisation of Supreme Audit Institutions (2013c), *ISSAI 300: Fundamental Principles of Performance Auditing*, INTOSAI PSC, Copenhagen.

International Organisation of Supreme Audit Institutions (2013d), *ISSAI 400: Fundamental Principles of Compliance Auditing*, INTOSAI PSC, Copenhagen.

Power, M. (1996), Making Things Auditable, *Accounting, Organizations and Society*, Vol. 21, no. 2/3, pp. 289–315.

Quick, R., S. Turley and M. Willekens (2008), *Auditing, Trust and Governance: Developing Regulation in Europe*, Routledge, Abingdon.

Radcliffe, V. (2008), Public secrecy in auditing: what government auditors cannot know, *Critical Perspectives on Accounting*, Vol. 19, no. 1–2, pp. 99–126.

Roussy, M. (2013), Internal auditors' roles: from watchdogs to helpers and protectors of the top manager, *Critical Perspectives on Accounting*, Vol. 24, no. 7–8, pp. 550–71.

Skaerbaek, P. (2009), Public sector auditor identities in making efficiency auditable: the National Audit Office of Denmark as independent auditor and modernizer, *Accounting, Organizations and Society*, Vol. 34, no. 8, pp. 971–87.

Treasury (2013), *Whole of Government Accounts year ended 31st March 2012*, HC 531, 2013/14, The Stationery Office, London.

Useful websites

European Court of Auditors (ECA) – http://eca.europa.eu.

The ECA site includes a list of EU national public sector auditing bodies at http://eca.europa.eu/portal/page/portal/contactcommittee/presentation/partici pants.

Institute of Internal Auditors (IIA) – https://na.theiia.org.

International Auditing and Assurance Standards Boards (IAASB) – http://www. ifac.org/auditing-assurance.

International Organisation of Supreme Audit Institutions (INOSAI) – http://www. intosai.org.

The INTOSAI site includes a list of member national public sector auditing bodies at http://www.intosai.org/about-us/organisation/membership-list.html.

10

Public sector financial management reforms

Learning objectives

- ◆ Be able to interpret a framework developed by Pollitt and Bouckaert for understanding public sector management reforms, in terms of reform drivers and obstacles

- ◆ Be able to interpret Lüder's framework for understanding public sector financial management reforms, in terms of reform drivers and obstacles

- ◆ Have an understanding of promising new initiatives in public sector financial management reforms

- ◆ Be able to discuss major issues in future public sector financial management reforms

---

10.1 Introduction

Public sector accounting and budgeting have been the subject of enduring reforms during the last three decades, mainly as a consequence of allegations that the public sector is performing ineffectively and inefficiently, but also due to problems of fiscal stress. Some of these reforms have evolved around purely accounting issues, such as the move from cash to accrual accounting and the introduction of performance budgeting, as discussed in Chapters 3 and 6 respectively, while other reforms relate to more managerial issues, such as decentralization of managerial responsibilities and the adoption of private sector styles, such as pay-for-performance systems. Also market-based forms of control, for example through outsourcing or arm's length steering, are seen as part of these reforms. This chapter discusses public sector financial management reforms.

There is a broad agenda for discussing public sector financial management reforms, pertaining to its content (as briefly indicated above), its process (including agenda setting, implementation, feedback and learning) as well as contextual factors that contribute to or are obstacles for such reforms. This chapter will focus on both the *reform content* and *contextual factors* for understanding reforms. This means that the reform process remains largely disregarded. As a further justification of our approach in this final chapter, we believe that it is appropriate to start with a discussion of public sector management reforms in general and subsequently address public sector financial management reforms in particular. There are two reasons for including a discussion of public sector management reforms in this chapter. First, public sector financial management is often a main component of public sector management in general. And second, an understanding of public sector financial management reforms can benefit from the way in which public management reforms are explained.

This chapter is structured as follows. Section 10.2 discusses an important framework which aims to understand differences in public sector reforms among various countries. Section 10.3 focuses on a framework for understanding public sector financial management reforms. Sections 10.4 and 10.5 present recent initiatives in public sector financial management reforms at the central government level in Austria and Australia. Section 10.6 provides a perspective on public sector financial management reforms, and Section 10.7 presents some concluding remarks. This chapter illustrates that many issues on budgeting, accounting, costing and auditing are part of the continuing process of public sector financial management reforms.

10.2   Understanding public sector management reforms

This section briefly points to diverging ways to study public management reforms, and subsequently discusses the Pollitt and Bouckaert framework for understanding public sector management reforms. Finally, some notes about the effects of NPM reforms are made.

Diverging ways for understanding public management reforms

Several authors have attempted to explain why certain public management reforms found fertile soil in some countries, while other countries kept away from such reforms. During the last decades especially, New Public Management (NPM) is seen as the major reform trend.

According to Hood (1991, 1995), NPM is based on two doctrines, i.e. a lessening or removing of the differences between the public and the private sector, and a move from process to results control and accountability. NPM increasingly substituted Old Public Administration (OPA), among other things, by replacing governmental styles and ethics by private sector styles and ethics, and rules-oriented controls by results-oriented controls (see Chapter 1, especially Section 1.7, for a complete overview of the differences between NPM and OPA). Hood observed that some countries, such as the UK and Australia, were frontrunners in NPM adoption, while others, such as Germany and Japan, were lagging behind in this respect. He found that financial stress and some degree of centralization in the governmental systems contributed to NPM adoption (Hood, 1995).

Contrasted to Hood's context-driven model for understanding NPM adoption, Barzelay (2001) takes a quite different approach. Barzelay examined 'public management policy making', which refers to fundamental ways of thinking about public management, including trajectories leading from old to new ways of thinking. In his processual approach to public management change, he distinguishes three interrelated stages of policy making, i.e. agenda setting, formulation of alternatives and decision-making. Public management change is seen as a gradual pattern of changes, in which learning plays a major role.

Pollitt and Bouckaert's public management framework

It goes beyond the scope of this book to discuss the vast amount of literature on public management reform. The above sub-section hinted at two different approaches, one for understanding differences in NPM adoption and the other for understanding more general processes of public management change. The current section discusses a seminal framework for understanding public management reform as developed by Pollitt and Bouckaert (2011). This section picks up some of their ideas and findings about these reforms in the Western world over a period of 30 years (1980–2010), while acknowledging that this section cannot do justice to the richness of their analysis. Pollitt and Bouckaert discuss three packages of public management reform, i.e. NPM, NWS (= the Neo-Weberian State) and NPG (= New Public Governance). In addition, explanations of public management reforms are based on a rich set of drivers and barriers, and findings are based on a wide spectrum of sources of evidence, not only in terms of reform components but also of reform effects. Figure 10.1 presents the framework on public management reform of Pollitt and Bouckaert (2011, p. 33).

A brief explanation of each of the main building blocks of Pollitt and Bouckaert's public management reform model will do, given the scope of our book. Socio-economic forces (block A) are an important antecedent for public management reforms. A worldwide economic crisis, for example, may give rise to the need for budget cuts of governments, which in turn might lead to public management changes, such as ideas about 'lean government' and public–private partnerships. A second building block (E) regards the political system in a country, for instance, the extent of centralization of this system, which will be influenced by internationally emerging public management ideas – such as networking with partners outside core government – and which could constrain central powers in the governmental system. Also pressures from citizens, for instance, when they require more participation in policy making, could have a similar effect. In addition, chance events, such as scandals and disasters (block I), can have an impact on public management reforms, such as in the case of substantial overspending of a budget for an important infrastructure project (e.g. a new train connection or airport) and, as a result, the rules for financial planning and reporting could become

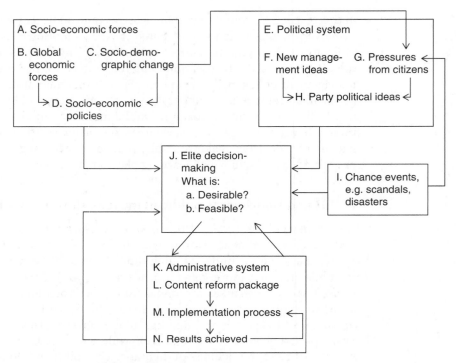

Figure 10.1 A model of public management reform

Source: Pollitt and Bouckaert, *Public Management Reform*, 3rd edition, 2011, Figure 2.1, p. 33, by permission of Oxford University Press.

tightened. These driving forces of public management reform have to be adopted by powerful people in or around the political system, such as high political or managerial officials and consultants (see elite decision-making, block J). Public management reforms will change the administrative system (block K). Whether reform ideas will lead to actual changes is also a matter of feasibility – e.g. availability of resources, or the existence of competing priorities in the governmental system – which points to the relevance of the implementation of the reform. The effects of the reform can concern the extent to which the reform goals are realized, but also include unintended, either positive or negative, side-effects, such as a loss of governmental control or more bureaucracy (red tape).

Figure 10.1 also indicates various interrelationships between the building blocks. A disaster can, for instance, mobilize citizens to put pressure on the political system for realizing certain changes (from block I to E). Another example: if the intended results of the reform are not realized, or if unforeseen negative side-effects occur, this could lead to a reconsideration of the reform package (from block K to J).

Pollitt and Bouckaert (2011, p. 117) observe two groups of countries with diverging public management reforms. The first group includes outspoken advocates of NPM, and consists of the US, the UK, Australia and New Zealand. These countries propagate an increasing role for the private sector and the adoption of private sector techniques in the public sector. The second group puts much emphasis on the state as the integrative force in society, which relates to an adherence to the Neo-Weberian State. This coincides with a relatively low extent of market principles in the public sector, whilst being prepared for a selective adoption of NPM-like tools. This second group includes Finland, France, the Netherlands, Italy and Sweden, and also Germany and Belgium below the federal level. However, these two groups are not homogeneous; for example, the US is more outspoken in its sympathy for a minimum public sector than the other countries in the first group, while Germany and France were late adopters of NPM-like innovations in the second group. Moreover, Pollitt and Bouckaert (2011, pp. 209–212) argue that basic models of public management often coexist rather than replace each other, or put differently, new forms of public management are deposited upon old ones as in sedimentation. This especially relates to the newest public management reform type, New Public Governance, which puts much weight on partnerships, trust and accountability, but which, as in the UK, coexists with the earlier adopted elements of NPM. Canada is seen as a country that combines characteristics of the first and second group.

Some elements of the framework in Figure 10.1 can be illustrated for two countries, i.e. France and New Zealand, which belong to the Neo-Weberian State and NPM groups respectively. France has been seen as resistant to NPM influences, but recently some aspects of NPM thinking gained support. Public management reform was mainly directed to regaining the loss of reputation of the state apparatus, and included decentralization within the governmental system, privatization and performance-oriented steering (Pollitt and Bouckaert, 2011, pp. 270–276). Driven by poor economic circumstances in the 1980s, New Zealand's decision-making elites, consisting of high government officials and business people, adopted radical and comprehensive NPM reforms. The reform package included the substitution of governmental trading departments by State-owned Enterprises, a strong autonomy for top level managers in the ministries, the introduction of accrual accounting and performance budgeting, as well as severe fiscal rules. The implementation process has been fast and harsh and the results in New Zealand lived up to their expectations, although recently some restoration of governmentality has been put on the agenda (Pollitt and Bouckaert, 2001, pp. 298–302).

NPM reform impacts

Although NPM reforms have lived up to their expectations to some extent, this evidence is not strong, while also adversarial effects seem to occur. Reichard (2010) reviews the evidence about NPM effects and concludes on the one hand that in many cases improvements in efficiency, service quality and response times could be observed, but, on the other hand, new forms of red tape (for instance about performance auditing) emerged, and private sector ethics in the public sector (such as high salaries for top officials) were often seen as problematic.

A recent meta-analysis by Pollitt and Dan (2013) of studies on NPM effects suggests that 44% indicate an improvement of the effects, 23% show a worsening of the effects and the remaining 33% conclude that neither positive nor negative effects occur. Put differently, although positive effects could not be demonstrated in a majority of the studies, they at least dominate negative effects. Effects or outcomes of reforms are understood as the impacts of these reforms on citizens and their representatives, civil society associations and business firms.

Pollitt and Dan's (2013, pp. 20–3) analysis points to several contextual factors that are either supportive or form an obstacle for NPM reforms. Countries with a Weberian administration (see Pollitt and Bouckaert's comparative analysis in an earlier sub-section), are faced with hindrances for an NPM-type of reform. This, for instance, may apply in the former communist countries in Eastern Europe. In addition, majoritarian political systems, such as in the UK, are more prone to realizing effective large-scale reforms than consensus-based political systems, like in the Nordic countries. A lack of administrative capacity, evidenced by the absence of suitable skills, seriously inhibits effective NPM reforms. Pollitt and Dan (2013, p. 26) argue that often many contextual factors have to be taken into account for establishing whether a certain context forms a fruitful environment for effective NPM reforms.

10.3   Understanding public sector financial management reforms

This section starts with a brief indication of the content of public sector financial management reforms. Then Lüder's framework for understanding such reforms is discussed, and subsequently studies for understanding more particular aspects of these reforms are addressed.

The content of public sector financial management reforms

In their comparative study of the adoption of NPM-related accounting tools across various countries, Guthrie et al. (1999, pp. 209–11) coined the label New Public Financial Management (NPFM) as consisting of five different categories (as introduced in Section 1.7):

- Accrual-based accounting for financial reporting, as a substitution of cash-based accounting, in combination with accounting standards developed by the accounting profession (see Chapters 2, 3, 4 and 5).

- Market-oriented management systems for contracting and pricing, both within the organization and in transactions with external parties (for which costing tools are required, see Chapter 7).

- Performance measurement, comprising financial and non-financial performance indicators, and including benchmarking and league tables (also for budgeting purposes, see Chapter 6).

- Devolvement and decentralization of budgets in combination with the linkage of budgeting and reporting information on both financial and non-financial issues (see Chapter 6).

- Auditing of efficiency and effectiveness (value-for-money auditing, in addition to more traditional financial and compliance audits, see Chapter 9).

Lüder's contingency model of public sector financial management reforms

Some 25 years ago Klaus Lüder developed a contingency model which attempts to specify the influence of the features of the political administrative environment in a country on governmental accounting reform processes. Lüder's ideas have been very influential as they have been an inspiration for many public sector accounting researchers for conducting either single country studies or comparative multi-country studies about governmental accounting reforms. Many of these studies have been discussed in the CIGAR network ('Comparative International Governmental Accounting Research; see the network's website: http://cigar-network.net). At a later stage Lüder (2002, pp. 7–15) revised his model, based on his own experiences and those of other researchers, which resulted in the so-called 'financial management reform process' model (FMR model). This sub-section sets out this model and its underlying ideas and also provides some illustrations.

A brief explanation of Lüder's model, as presented in Figure 10.2, will be provided. Stimuli for reform (A) include incidents (e.g. financial scandals) and more enduring phenomena (such as doctrines of making the public sector lean). Reform drivers (B) are institutions and professionals putting reform issues on the political agenda. Influential networks of professionals, especially from universities and consultancy firms, may be called epistemic communities (Laughlin and Pallot, 1998). Political reform promoters (C) are influential political officials, such as the Minister of Finance at the central governmental level and members of the budgeting and finance committee in the Parliament who act as advocates of the reform. Institutional arrangements (D) include contextual elements of the reform, such as the state structure (e.g. federal versus central-unitarian) and the qualifications of managers and accounting staff. Stakeholders (E) are those affected by the reform and those who can influence the reform indirectly, without being reform drivers or promoters, such as Members of Parliament in general and governmental employees.

The reform concept (F) regards the content of the reform, which in general terms will be directed towards enhancing decision-making, control and accountability. In practice, financial management reform often has a more concrete form, for instance the adoption of accrual budgeting and accounting or performance

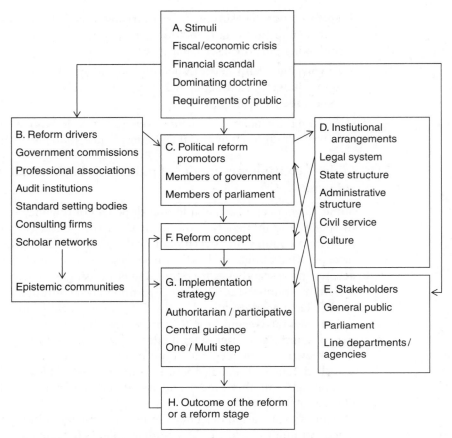

Figure 10.2 The financial management reform process model
Source: Lüder, 2002, p. 18, after some simplification about indirect influences of antecedents.

budgeting. The implementation strategy (G) includes the pace of the reform, how it is guided (for example, by a Ministry of Finance) and how people on the shop floor are involved in the reform process. Reform outcomes (H) relate to the goals of the reform, such as enhanced accountability or more efficiency in the provision of services.

There are several feedback loops in the model, of which the most important ones are shown in Figure 10.2. When reform outcomes are, for example, below expectations, the implementation process can be revised, or even the content of reform can be reconsidered (from H, to G or F). There are also influences between the reform outcomes and various antecedents of the reform, for example, on the reform stakeholders and reform promoters (from H to E and C, not shown in Figure 10.2). Lüder's model is assumed to contain three clusters of variables, i.e. contextual (such as stimuli and institutional arrangements), behavioural (such as reform implementation) and instrumental (e.g. the reform content).

Lüder's contingency model shows many similarities with the earlier discussed Pollitt and Bouckaert framework. Evidently, Lüder's model is more accounting oriented. This relates to the reform content, but also to various aspects of the reform context, such as auditing institutions, standard setters and statistical offices. We will now give an example of the application of Lüder's model, for the Portuguese central government (see further Lüder and Jones, 2003, for a multi-country application).

Portugal conducted a reform of its central government accounting system in the years 1997–2002. Major elements were the introduction of accrual financial accounting and cost accounting for functions (groups of activities), departments and services; budgetary accounting remained cash-based. The underlying goals were enhancing budgetary and accounting information not only for accountability purposes but also for management, financial control and analysis, contributing to a more efficient operating governmental sector. Jorge (2005) analysed this reform based on documentary evidence and in the light of Lüder's model. Her main findings are that financial pressure (related to EU requirements), the superiority of a businesslike accounting doctrine and international public sector reform examples were stimuli for the Portuguese reform. In addition, the hierarchical structure of central government and increasing accounting skills in ministries, departments and public sector entities in general, were elements of the institutional arrangements, which contributed to the reform. A crucial promoter of the reform was the Ministry of Finance. Jorge's analysis also points to building blocks of Lüder's model which were unimportant in the Portuguese reform, particularly financial scandals, consulting firms and epistemic communities.

A comparative study about budgeting and accounting reforms

One of the most recent studies on financial management reforms regards a comparative analysis of the status of the budgeting and accounting reforms around the year 2010 in the central governments of Germany, France, the UK and the US (Jones et al., 2013). All four countries belong to the group of rich countries in the world, and their starting position some twenty to thirty years ago was the same, i.e. budgeting and accounting were cash-based. The analysis of Jones et al. (2013) shows that the budgeting system in France, Germany and the US remained cash-based, more specifically cash-commitment based. Although the UK was the only one of the four countries that included accrual accounting information in its budgets, it also retained cash-based budgets. All four countries developed accrual-based accounting for financial reporting (although in Germany it was later postponed or abandoned). The countries differed in their choice for the reporting entities, i.e. in Germany and France for the government as a whole, and in the UK and the US for the individual departments. In all four countries performance information has been included in the budgetary or reporting documents.

The most striking outcome of this international comparative study is that the accounting system for reporting can differ from the accounting system for budgeting. Budgeting is seen as the expression of the intended priorities of a legislative body, including holding the executive body accountable for a proper execution of this expression. This seems to be best achievable through budgeting of cash expenditures and commitments and comparing cash expenditures against cash budgets. Accrual information is seen as preferable for financial reporting purposes, perhaps because this information better expresses the actual resource consumption arising from the policies undertaken.

Valuation of infrastructure and heritage assets

We now turn to a public sector specific accounting theme, i.e. the valuation of infrastructure and heritage assets. As was explained in Chapter 5, there are various principles for valuing tangible fixed assets, such as buildings and machinery. In some cases these assets are used for earning money, as in the case of the vans and buildings of a municipal department for garbage collection, if there are user fees which have to cover all the costs of services. Such assets are often valued at their purchase costs less the cumulative depreciation over the lifetime to date, while the yearly depreciation is recorded as a cost in the income statement. This all resembles what private sector companies would do. However, infrastructure and heritage assets often deserve a different approach, more aligned to their function in the operations of a public sector organization, whilst revenue generation is absent or at least relatively unimportant.

Infrastructure assets – such as roads, canals and parks – have to contribute to the well-being of the citizens, and often using these assets does not lead to payments for their users.[1] These assets are purchased by means of resources coming from taxes, and there is no direct relationship between taxing and using. The same holds in an even stronger sense for heritage assets, such as arts collections of governmental museums and monuments of governments. How are these types of assets to be valued and is depreciation of these assets appropriate? Adam et al. (2011) provide a comparative study between local governments in three countries, i.e. Germany, Italy and the UK; the accounting system in all cities is based on accrual accounting. Their investigations show that in the German and UK cities infrastructure assets were valued at their purchase price less depreciation and depreciation was a cost on the income statement. The Italian cities made use of outstanding loans as a valuation base, and repayment of loans was seen as a kind of depreciation. Although the norm was quite similar for heritage assets, these assets were mostly either valued at a symbolic price of one euro or left out of the balance sheet. In accordance with this practice, depreciation of heritage assets did not take place. So, obviously, in the case of heritage assets, the underlying goal is their preservation for the long-term future, which seems to have inspired the cities in this examination to treat those assets off-balance sheet, either formally or practically (by an almost zero book value). Adam et al. (2011) conclude

---

1 Various reasons are pertinent here, mainly that these investments are collective goods.

that practices differ from norms and comparability of valuation and depreciation procedures across countries is not achieved.

10.4   Performance budgeting at the Austrian federal state level

The Austrian federal government started a budgetary reform process around 2004. This reform process deliberately searched for support from many stake-holders, such as Members of Parliament, the Audit office, the various ministries and the public at large, among others through media coverage. Moreover, much effort was put into organizing central guidance and support from the Ministry of Finance as the key player in the reform process (Steger, 2010). The reform was divided into two stages. During the first stage (2006–2009) fundamentally new budget principles were settled by a revision of the constitution and related laws. These principles evolved around outcome-orientation, efficiency, transparency and 'true and fair view' (the latter is an auditing principle as discussed in Chapter 9). The main elements of the reform were a Medium-Term Expenditure Frame-work (MTEF) and larger spending flexibility for ministries. During the second stage of the reform (2010–2012), an elaboration of the various reform principles and elements took place. Performance budgeting was key in this stage, as will be discussed further below (Steger, 2010).[2]

The Austrian federal government is managed according to the principles of *outcome-orientation*, started in 2013. This reform orientation is part of a *holistic financial management framework*, which includes the following elements: a legally binding medium-term expenditure framework; a flexible budgeting system based on global budgets with large possibilities for shifting among budget items and for transferring resources to the next year; accrual budgeting and accounting; and performance information in the budgets structured according to programmes.

The outcome-orientation of this reform is based on the premise that politicians identify objectives and hold themselves, as well as the administration, account-able for achieving them. After some experimentation with the introduction of performance indicators and cost accounting, the organic budget law approved in 2009 and implemented in 2013 launched an integrated mandatory performance budgeting framework. The aims of this framework were twofold: firstly to ensure that all ministries present outcome and output information in their budget docu-ments; and secondly that this performance information is systematically cascaded down from the higher layer of the programmes presented to the parliament to lower layers of departments and agencies within the ministries. Performance information has to meet high standards, that is, being concretely formulated by showing benefits for citizens and guiding actions. Moreover, the programme

---

2   The remainder of this section is based on Seiwald and Geppl (2013).

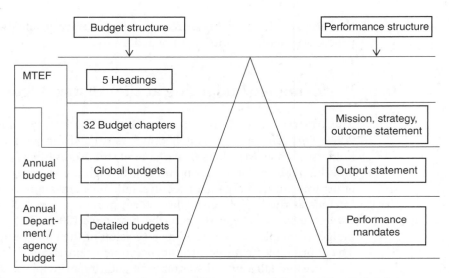

Figure 10.3 Performance budgeting framework of the Austrian federal government
Source: Seiwald and Geppl, 2013, p. 23.

structure of the budget has to guarantee that actions of different ministries are aligned to each other, for example, a programme of aid to particular youngsters requires coherent contributions from the Ministry of Welfare and the Ministry of Education. Figure 10.3 presents the performance budgeting framework as a pyramid.

This figure shows a layered structure of the budget; from headings, via budget chapters, and global budgets to departmental/agency budgets; the lower in the pyramid, the more budgetary items, so the more detailed the budget. The figure also indicates the link between the budgetary layer and the type of performance information, from mission-oriented (the political goals and outcomes) in the budget chapters, via output statements in the global budgets, to performance mandates at the departmental/agency level. Figure 10.3 further reveals that there is a multi-year and an annual perspective: the MTEF (= Medium-Term Expenditure Framework) sets budget ceilings at an aggregate level for four years; subsequently the annual budget can be specified at a more detailed level. The first three layers are part of the political decision-making, while the lowest layer is a matter of internal management within the ministries. During the annual budget cycle interim reports are presented, both about resource consumption (which is crucial to accrual accounting) and related performance information; whenever, desirable corrective actions can be announced.

Outcome orientation is an ambitious goal of public sector financial management reforms, because outcomes are often difficult to measure during a budgetary cycle and also because other than the controllable factors may be influential. Table 10.1 gives an illustration of an outcome statement in the Austrian federal budget.

Table 10.1   Example of outcome statement

Outcome objective	Increase of objective road safety
Why this objective?	In key words: too many accidents on the roads, increasing number of bicycle accidents; main causes are high speed of motor cars and cyclists wearing no helmet, especially children
Actions	Fully automated speed control at certain highway segments and mandatory use of helmets by young cyclists
What is success?	Deviation of maximum speed level has to be reduced by 50% Share of head injuries by young cyclists has to be reduced by 30%

Source: Seiwald and Geppl, 2013, p. 24, after some simplification.

The Austrian case forms an interesting illustration of many of the concepts introduced in previous chapters of this book. It is an example of a fully developed planning and control cycle, even with a multi-year perspective in addition to an annual perspective (see Chapter 1, Section 1.2). It is also an illustration of an advanced form of performance budgeting, with different types of performance indicators aligned to the various budgetary layers. In terms of the OECD classification of performance budgeting types, the Austrian case points to performance-informed budgeting, which links performance information to resources but in a loose way, i.e. also giving room for other than performance related arguments (OECD, 2007; see Chapter 6, Section 6.6). It further illustrates budget layering in which budgeting at the political level is linked to internal budgeting in the ministries (see Chapter 6, Section 6.3). The Austrian reform is also characterized by coherence and centrally organized guidance and support for developing these ambitious planning and control documents. The reform has just been implemented, so, we need to wait for experience before a full assessment can be made. However, the reform stands out in terms of its ambitions and coherence. That is why it promises to be a 'good practice' example of public sector financial management reform.

10.5   Old and new reforms at the federal government level in Australia

Whilst Austria can be seen as an ambitious but late adopter of NPM-like reforms in the public sector, Australia is widely regarded as a NPM frontrunner (see the analysis by Pollitt and Bouckaert as discussed in Section 10.2). Given these diverging positions of Austria and Australia, a brief overview of past and recent reforms in Australian government is interesting. We will focus, as in the case of Austria, on central, i.e. the federal or commonwealth government.

Federal government in Australia started with performance budgeting as well as accrual-based budgeting and accounting in the 1980s and 1990s (MacKay, 2011). Currently performance budgets are drafted for programmes. Performance information is outcome-oriented, e.g. about effectiveness, quality and timeliness, although also input indicators have remained part of the budgetary documents. Performance indicators are shown for the last year's revised budget, this year's budget and as estimates for the next three years. Also contextual information is added, particularly about strategies and actions (Marti, 2013, p. 43). In addition, budgeting is based on accrual principles, which implies that budgeted financial statements coincide with the formats of financial statements at the year-end, including an income statement, a cash flow statement and a balance sheet. These documents are prepared for the federal state as a whole and for departments within the federal state (Marti, 2013, p. 43). Interim reports have a similar format to the budgetary documents, which also regard the format of the presented performance information.

MacKay (2011) shows that federal departments in Australia were also required to evaluate their programmes, and that new priorities and saving proposals were influenced by these programme evaluations. This implies that policy making is positioned in a kind of control cycle. MacKay, however, indicates that the impact of policy evaluations varied over time, dependent upon the priorities of the ruling party and the extent to which the Ministry of Finance was given a position in coordinating the programme evaluations and making them suitable for decision-making at the political level, i.e. the Cabinet.

Barret (2014) argues that public sector reform in Australia has lost its momentum during the last decade, but new initiatives still appear. According to Barret (2014), further financial management reforms are to be expected, which revolve around the following key words: good governance, stressing performance and accountability, in addition to risk management, the reduction of 'red tape' and 'earned autonomy'. Performance auditing (see Chapter 9) is seen as a main prerogative for enhanced public sector accountability. Reduction of red tape ('less bureaucracy') is stimulated by financial targets, and it wishes to give more emphasis to certain principles for governmental officials as a replacement of detailed rules. Risk management has not been very successful until now, so new initiatives especially about strategic risk management were required. The reform also aims at a refreshment of performance-oriented budgeting, as introduced above, in the sense that in many programmes relevant impact indicators about the programme goals are still lacking. The notion of earned autonomy relates to gaining more independence in decision-making as a consequence of good performance. As in the Austrian case (Section 10.4), we need to wait for experience with these new initiatives in Australian federal government before a full assessment can be made.

10.6   Perspectives on public sector financial management reforms

It is not easy to sketch perspectives on public sector financial management reforms. Although some extent of speculation cannot be ruled out, we nevertheless observe some recent trends which may suggest promising changes with a longer life. This final section will address the following perspectives on public sector financial management reforms:

- the simplification in budgeting and accounting documents as a response to the desire to put emphasis on the usefulness of those documents;
- benefiting from IT tools in getting access to budgeting and accounting documents;
- the impact on budgeting and accounting documents of public sector organizations being part of broader networks;
- finding a balance between trusting professionals and holding them accountable for their performances;
- attempts to make accounting practices more comparable across countries;
- and finally a plea for continuing innovations in performance management.

Keep it simple

The layering of budgeting and accounting documents (with two to four aggregation levels), the transition from cash to accrual-based accounting information and particularly the inclusion of performance information have made budgeting and accounting documents often lengthy and sometimes difficult to understand, especially for laymen-politicians and non-accounting managers. We need to be aware that innovations in budgeting and accounting are not primarily meant to meet high standards on paper, nor because consultants and academics advocate those innovations, but because the resulting documents are useful for politicians and managers. More precisely, users need to value these documents more than the traditional documents they have used in the past (see, for instance, Moynihan and Panday, 2010; Ter Bogt et al., 2015). Moreover, preparing advanced budgeting and accounting documents takes a lot of resources, which need to be 'paid back' by the presumed benefits for their users.

We envisage a trend to simplify the planning and control cycle. First, by focusing budgetary documents for decision-making by politicians on key issues, for example, those issues that concern resources for new policy initiatives and cutbacks, or for policy issues with a major political impact (for illustrations, see Ter Bogt et al., 2015). Second, by reducing the frequency of interim reports, for instance by issuing only one or two interim reports instead of three or four as in the past. In addition, interim reports could be concentrated on major deviations from the budget. In order to avoid any misunderstanding about these types of simplifications, it has to be emphasized that an all-inclusive budget document remains important and mostly mandatory, but it could focus on financials rather than aiming at providing a comprehensive overview of performance indicators. Further, more detailed information, both financial and non-financial, could be made available for managerial levels in the governmental organization. What is crucial in the endeavours to simplify budgeting and accounting documents is that it could contribute to a more intensive use by politicians and managers, although we have a long way to go to reach this target.

Digging deeper with IT tools

Many governmental organizations make their planning and control documents available on their websites for various user groups, such as the members of the legislative body (the parliament or council), interested pressure groups, the media and the citizens. Some of these governmental organizations make use of different formats which are aligned to the diverging user needs of the groups mentioned above. So, there may be a brochure of a few pages with general information on the budget and the annual accounts for citizens, while documents for the legislative body require a greater extent of detail (see, for instance, the city of Oldenburg in Germany, which provided the budgeting illustrations in Chapter 6).

IT applications also enable a flexible use of budgeting and accounting documents. Councillors of a municipality read or take notice of the budgetary document which is drafted for the council, but if they want to know more on specific issues, they can find detailed information. Put differently, by clicking on certain underlying documents they can dig deeper, not in a general sense but to answer problem-driven inquiries.

In a more general sense, there is potential for improvements in accountability through the internet, which is part of the broader concept of e-government that also includes, for example, interactive internet services for citizens. Pina et al. (2007) conducted a comparative study of accountability through the internet of central governments in 15 European countries and the US, Canada, Australia and New Zealand. This study shows that the internet has made all kinds of documents, including budgetary and accounting documents, more easily assessable for citizens. In a study of 75 European local government websites, Pina et al. (2010) conclude that the internet has made it easier for citizens to locate official information and to conduct transactions with governments, but that this has not promoted financial accountability beyond legal requirements. They found that the internet had not substantially contributed to a greater participation by citizens in the policy making processes of governments and had not achieved its potential to transform the relationships between citizens and public administrations.

Government's changing boundaries

The organizational domain of a public sector organization is not always clearly identifiable (see Broadbent and Guthrie, 2008). One reason relates to the emphasis NPM puts on decentralization within the governmental sector and within governmental organizations. Autonomous bodies were separated from core government and, within governmental organizations, semi-independent units were formed, often called agencies. These changes in organizational boundaries are raising important accounting issues for both managers and researchers (Hodges, 2012). For example, do we need accounting documents for groups of related organizations, such as big cities including their autonomous bodies and public enterprises, and central governments including their related local governmental layers? Another reason for the changing organizational boundaries is that public sector organizations might operate in a more effective way when they see themselves as a part of a network, for example in public transport (regulators and public transport companies) and in care for elderly citizens (hospitals, care and nursing homes). Although the various types of organizations in a network remain independent in a formal way, their effectiveness is mainly determined by the ways in which they connect their activities. In accounting terms, there may be a need for accountability reports for the networks as a whole and for individual organizations, and the former will include different issues from the latter.

Provan and Milward (2001) have elaborated this and propose a framework for public sector network performance at three levels: the community, the network and the service provider level. At the community level networks have to be valued based on criteria such as client access to the various services, the extent of service integration, responsiveness to client needs and the costs of the services. These criteria are mostly measured at an aggregate level, i.e. for the network as a whole. Provan and Milward (2001, p. 421) emphasize that the identification of criteria at the community level may be complicated by the absence of powerful stakeholders with clearly articulated ambitions. At the network level the criteria are related to the mix of services and the extent to which these services are coordinated (e.g. little overlap and according to the links in the service provision value chain). At the service provider level client satisfaction, responsiveness to client needs, and the cost of the services for the specific client groups are major criteria. Service providers may also show the added value of forming part of the network by demonstrating, for example, that their services have a larger impact through the availability of related services provided by other network participants. The challenges of developing such networks or collaborations should not be underestimated. Financial management structures can easily become barriers to change rather than promoters of innovation. For example, in examining the working between health and social care organizations in the UK, Kurunmäki and Miller (2011) found that professional groups took different perspectives on the nature of appropriate performance measures and that there was limited use of management accounting techniques such as the pooling of budgets from different government departments.

A more specific accounting implication is the desire for 'whole of government accounting' (WGA). The aim of WGA is to produce a single financial report that encompasses all government activities within its area of authority, i.e. a city or central government or government in a country (Grossi and Newberry, 2009, p. 209). WGA requires that the multiplicity of organizations belonging to 'the whole' are using the same accounting systems, for example, accrual accounting or, perhaps more specifically, accrual accounting according to IPSAS standards. Grossi and Newberry (2007, p. 210) observe that the UK, Australia and New Zealand are frontrunners in adopting WGA based on businesslike accounting procedures, although not being based upon IPSAS. However, there are also differences. Whilst the UK wants to produce WGA for the whole public sector in the country, Australia adopted WGA only for its federal government and the states.

Balancing trusting professionals and holding them accountable for their performances

As was set out in Chapter 9, making things measurable and accountable has become a main trend in the public sector. Organizations in the educational and healthcare sectors are often seen as examples 'suffering' from this trend. These organizations and their employees have to account for what they are doing and achieving to various stakeholders, such as oversight bodies, funding bodies, inspectorate offices, auditing offices and media with an interest in benchmarking and league tables. Several types of concerns are raised against this trend (see also Lapsley, 2009). The most important one relates to the negative side-effect of overemphasizing things that have to be measured at the expense of other, sometimes more important, issues. Another concern is that registration and reporting are time-consuming and drive out the available time for core processes. An underlying argument is that professionals are no longer trusted for what they do and accomplish due to their expertise, but constantly have to give evidence.

It is a challenge for academics and practitioners in the field of public sector accounting and management to find a balance between professional autonomy and accountability requirements. It seems too simple to move back to the past when professional autonomy dominated accountability. However, some suggestions can be put forward. First, different stakeholders, who share an interest in a public sector organization, could coordinate their accountability requirements or wishes, in order to avoid the production of different but comparable performance information. Second, whenever possible, the reporting frequency could be reduced. Third, proven 'good performance' could lead to lowering the accountability requirements. Fourth, requiring and maintaining high levels of expertise, including a work process and client-oriented culture, could also induce a relaxing of accountability requirements.

International comparability in governmental accounting

The global financial crisis of 2007/8 and its resulting detrimental impact on public expenditure in many countries has emphasized the variability in quality of financial reporting by governments. A recent report from the International Monetary Fund (IMF) has highlighted the need to strengthen fiscal transparency standards and practices. A 2011 survey shows that a majority of national governments follow the cash basis of financial reporting and do not publish a balance sheet. Many of those governments that use some form of accrual accounting do so in a limited form so that less than 10% of nation states provide a comprehensive balance sheet that includes both financial and non-financial assets (Cottarelli, 2012, p. 21).

There continues to be variability in both the basis of accounting (accruals or cash or some modified form between them) and of the standards used in their construction (IASB, IPSASB or national regulations). One challenge to international comparability is the desire of nation states or supra-national bodies to retain sovereignty over their own systems of public sector accounting. A recent example (European Commission, 2013) of this is the proposal in the European Union to develop European Public Sector Accounting Standards (EPSAS). It is unclear how similar EPSAS might be to international standards (IPSAS) but the proposals indicate just how important the European Commission considers accounting standards to be. A future outcome of this proposal might be greater comparability between governmental accounting of member states in the EU, following EPSAS, but increasing divergence from international standards under IPSAS.

Performance management remains a key issue

In all public sector reforms and innovations, performance management (for decision-making and control) is and will remain crucial. This also holds for related innovations in performance budgeting and performance auditing. The main reason is that stakeholders challenge public sector organizations to show what they deliver, i.e. 'value for money'. It is simply not sufficient to use resources according to priorities and formal guidelines. However, performance management is an area in which it is difficult to realize the benefits from innovation. Technical reasons are at stake, for example about the identification and measurement of decision-relevant performance indicators, but also contextual factors are important. The latter relates to the driving forces or hindrances for effective performance management. A recent literature review by Kroll (2014) indicates that the maturity of the performance measurement system and effective stakeholder involvement are the most important drivers. Mature performance measurement systems link a variety of performance indicators to different user needs and strategic goals, and relate the resulting information to actions. Stakeholder involvement means that managers are encouraged to take performance information seriously, that is, to use it for decision-making and control in order to improve performance.

10.7   Concluding remarks

This final chapter dealt with public sector financial management reforms, both in terms of their content and drivers or hindrances. The content of financial management reforms especially regards the transition from cash to accrual accounting and from input to output or outcome budgeting, although also other reform issues can be at stake, such as multi-annual budgeting, costing for pricing and performance auditing. The chapter first introduced and illustrated important frameworks for understanding differences among countries in public sector reforms in general (as developed by Pollitt and Bouckaert) and public sector financial management reforms in particular (as developed by Lüder). Drivers for reforms can, for instance, come from poor performance, financial scandals or certain international trends and fashions, while hindrances for reform may, for example, be attributed to the governmental system (such as its degree of centralization) or implementation barriers related to available resources. Subsequently, this chapter has presented recent initiatives of public sector financial management reforms at the federal government level in Austria (among others, global budget ceilings in combination with increased spending flexibility) and Australia (including relaxing accountability conditions and reduction of red tape). Finally, several perspectives on future public sector financial management reforms were sketched, including the simplification of budgeting and accounting documents, and finding a suitable balance between trust and accountability of professionals in public sector organizations.

This chapter has illustrated a variety of intriguing aspects of public sector financial management reforms. It has shown that we have already achieved a lot in revising issues on budgeting, accounting, costing and auditing. However, developing user-relevant and user-friendly budgeting and accounting documents remains a challenging task for practitioners and academics active in the public sector. The same holds for finding contextual conditions that potentially contribute to successful public sector financial management reforms.

References

Adam, B., R. Mussari and R. Jones (2011), The diversity of accrual policies in local government financial reporting: an examination of infrastructure, art and heritage assets in Germany, Italy and the UK, *Financial Accountability & Management*, Vol. 27, no. 2, pp. 107–33.

Barret, P. (2014), New development: financial reform and good governance, *Public Money & Management*, Vol. 34, no. 1, pp. 59–66.

Barzelay, M. (2001), *The New Public Management: Improving Research and Policy Dialogue*, University of California Press, Berkeley.

Broadbent, J. and J. Guthrie (2008), Public sector to public services: 20 years of 'contextual' accounting research, *Accounting, Auditing & Accountability Journal*, Vol. 21, no. 2, pp. 129–69.

Cottarelli, C. (2012), *Fiscal Transparency, Accountability and Risk*, IMF Policy Paper, on-line at http://www.imf.org/external/np/pp/eng/2012/080712.pdf (accessed 23 January 2014), International Monetary Fund, Washington.

European Commission (2013), *Towards Implementing Harmonised Public Sector Accounting Standards in Member States: The Suitability of IPSAS for Member States, Report from the Commission to the Council and the European Parliament, COM (2013) 114*, March, European Commission, Brussels.

Grossi, G. and S. Newberry (2009), Theme: whole of government accounting; international trends, *Public Money & Management*, Vol. 29, no. 4, pp. 209–13.

Guthrie, J., O. Olson and C. Humphrey (1999), Debating Developments in New Public Financial Management: The Limits of Global Theorizing and Some New Ways Forward, *Financial Accountability & Management*, Vol. 15, no. 2–3, pp. 209–28.

Hodges, R. (2012), Joined-up Government and the Challenges to Accounting and Accountability Researchers, *Financial Accountability & Management*, Vol. 28, no. 1, pp. 26–51.

Hood, C. (1991), A Public Management for all Seasons, *Public Administration*, Vol. 69, no. 1, pp. 3–19.

Hood, C. (1995), The 'New Public Management' in the 1980s: Variations on a Theme, *Accounting, Organizations and Society*, Vol. 20, no. 1–2, pp. 93–109.

Jones, R., E. Lande, K. Lüder and M. Portal (2013), A comparison of budgeting and accounting reforms in the central governments of France, Germany, the UK and the US, *Financial Accountability & Management*, Vol. 29, no. 4, pp. 419–41.

Jorge, S. (2005), The Reform of Governmental Accounting in Portugal: An Application of Lüder's Contingency Model, in: A. Bourmistrov. and F. Mellemvik (eds) (2005), *International Trends and Experiences in Government Accounting*, Capellen Akademisk Forlag, pp. 28–48.

Kroll, A. (2014), Drivers for Performance Information Use: Systematic Literature Review and Directions for Future Research, *Public Performance & Management Review*, Vol. 38, forthcoming.

Kurunmäki, L. and P. Miller (2011), Regulatory Hybrids: Partnerships, Budgeting and Modernising Government, *Management Accounting Research*, Vol. 22, no. 4, pp. 220–41.

Lapsley, I. (2009), New Public Management: the cruellest invention of the human spirit?, *Abacus*, Vol. 45, no. 1, pp. 1–21.

Laughlin, R. and J. Pallot (1998), Trends, patterns and influencing factors: some reflections, in: O. Olson, et al. (eds), *Global warming! Debating international developments in new public financial managements*, Oslo, Cappelen, pp. 376–99.

Lüder, K. (2002), Research in comparative governmental accounting over the last decade: achievements and problems, in: V. Montesinos and J. M. Vela (eds), *Innovations in governmental accounting*, Kluwer, Dordrecht, pp. 1–21.

Lüder, K. and R. Jones (eds) (2003), *Reforming Governmental Accounting and Budgeting in Europe*, Fachverlag Moderne Wirtschaft, Frankfurt, Germany.

Mackay, K. (2011), The performance framework of the Australian government, 1987 to 2011, *OECD Journal on Budgeting*, Vol. 2011, no. 3, pp. 1–55.

Marti, C. (2013), Performance budgeting and accrual budgeting: a study of the United Kingdom, Australia and New Zealand, *Public Performance & Management Review*, Vol. 37, no. 1, pp. 33–58.

Moynihan, D.P. and S.K. Pandey (2010), The big question for performance management: why do managers use performance information?, *Journal of Public Administration Research and Theory*, Vol. 20, no. 4, pp. 849–66.

OECD (2007), *Performance Budgeting in OECD Countries*, OECD, Paris.

Pina, V., L. Torres and B. Acerete (2007), Are ICTs promoting government accountability? A comparative analysis of e-governance developments in 19 OECD countries, *Critical Perspectives on Accounting*, Vol. 18, no. 6, pp. 583–602.

Pina, V., L. Torres and S. Royo (2010), Is e-government leading to more accountable and transparent local governments? An overall view, *Financial Accountability & Management*, Vol. 26, no. 1, pp. 3–20.

Pollitt, C. and G. Bouckaert (2011), *Public Management Reform: A Comparative Analysis*, 3rd edition, Oxford University Press, Oxford.

Pollitt, C. and S. Dan (2013), Searching for impacts in performance-oriented management reforms, *Public Performance & Management Review*, Vol. 37, no. 1, pp. 7–32.

Provan, K.G. and H.B. Milward (2001), Do networks really work? A framework for evaluating public-sector organizational networks, *Public Administration Review*, Vol. 61, no. 4, pp. 414–23.

Reichard, C. (2010), New Public Management, in: H.K. Anheier and S. Toepler (eds), *International Encyclopaedia of Civil Society*, Springer, Berlin, pp. 1030–34.

Seiwald, J. and M. Geppl (2013), Performance framework in Austria: opportunities and challenges, *Tékhne: Review of Applied Management Studies*, Vol. 11, no. 1, pp. 21–7.

Steger, G. (2010), Austria's budget reform: how to create consensus for a decisive change of fiscal rules?, *OECD Journal of Budgeting*, Vol. 10, no. 1, pp. 7–20.

Ter Bogt, H.J., G.J. van Helden and B. van der Kolk (2015), Challenging NPM Ideas about Performance Management: Selectivity and Differentiation in Outcome-oriented Performance Budgeting, *Financial Accountability & Management*, forthcoming.

Index